AMERICAN OUTLAWS

WANTED

JOHN HERBERT
DILLINGER

On June 23, 1934, HOMER S. CUMMINGS, Attorney General of the United States, under the
authority vested in him by an Act of Congress approved June 6, 1934, offered a reward of

$10,000.00
for the capture of John Herbert Dillinger or a reward of
$5,000.00
for information leading to the arrest of John Herbert Dillinger

DESCRIPTION

Age, 32 years;
Weight

◆ Visual History Collection ◆

AMERICAN OUTLAWS

True Stories of the Most Wanted: Wild West Outlaws, Bank Robbers, Mobsters, Mafia, and More

Robert Stahl

FOX CHAPEL
PUBLISHING

©2023 by Future Publishing Limited

Articles in this issue are translated or reproduced from *American Outlaws* and are the copyright of or licensed to Future Publishing Limited, a Future plc group company, UK 2022.

FUTURE

Used under license. All rights reserved. This version published by
Fox Chapel Publishing Company, Inc., 903 Square Street, Mount Joy, PA 17552.

ISBN 978-1-4971-0375-7

Library of Congress Cataloging-in-Publication Data

To learn more about the other great books from Fox Chapel Publishing, or to find a retailer near you, call toll-free 800-457-9112 or visit us at *www.FoxChapelPublishing.com*.

We are always looking for talented authors. To submit an idea, please send a brief inquiry to acquisitions@foxchapelpublishing.com.

Printed in China
First printing

WELCOME TO THE BOOK OF
AMERICAN OUTLAWS

Have you ever wondered how Bonnie met Clyde? How the Mob came to rule the east coast? Or how some of the most notorious criminals escaped Alcatraz? *American Outlaws* has the answers.

Explore the tumultuous Wild West, the seedy underbelly of New York, and the conmen who made their living across the United States as we take you on a tour of America's most wanted outlaws. We reveal the true stories behind gunslingers like Jesse James, the gangs who made their money in astonishing bank heists, the Prohibition Era's greatest gangsters – and the men who tried to take them down. Discover what really happened at the OK Corral and meet the man who created the first pyramid scheme. Find out who bought Machine Gun Kelly the weapon that gave him his name, and discover the farmer who created a safe house for fugitives on the run.

Filled with incredible stories, turn the page to enter the world of America's greatest outlaws and see why they live on in infamy today.

CONTENTS

WILD WEST

GANGSTERS & THE MOB

64

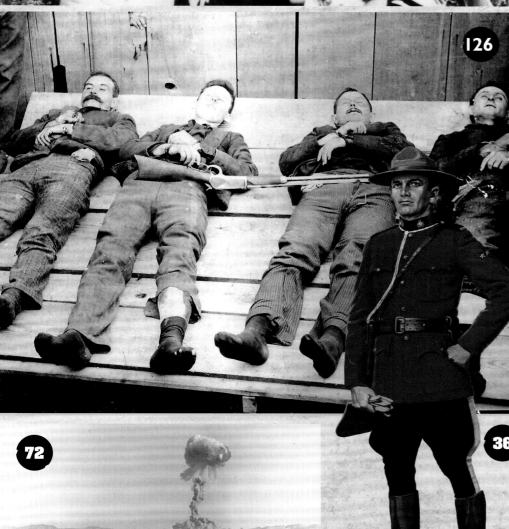

126

72

36

CONMEN & COMMON CRIMINALS

WILD WEST

BUTCH CASSIDY

His exploits with the Wild Bunch captured the imagination of the public and even his death became the stuff of legends. Is Butch Cassidy the most infamous figure of the Wild West?

Say the name Butch Cassidy and it's hard to not immediately think of the Sundance Kid and the 1969 film. Its story of two wise-cracking buddies is so ingrained in culture, some could take it as fact. But it isn't. For a start, Cassidy and Sundance were not best friends. They did flee to Argentina together, but that was more opportunity than choice. But even if the film didn't nail it in terms of accuracy, that is not to say that Butch Cassidy's life wasn't full of thrills, adventure, and intrigue.

Born Robert Leroy Parker on April 13, 1866, in Utah, Cassidy's parents were staunch Mormons. His dad, Maximillian Parker, was 12 when he arrived with his family in Salt Lake City in 1856, and they became Mormon pioneers. Cassidy's childhood was spent on his family's ranch but perhaps sensing that the Mormon life was not for him, he left home during his early teens. He supported himself by working on various ranches, and it was while at a dairy farm that he started to get drawn into the criminal world.

Mike Cassidy, whose real name was John Tolliver McClammy, was a cowboy and rustler and soon-to-be mentor and friend of the young Parker. In fact, it's said that Robert dropped his last name, changing it to Cassidy in honor of his friend, adding it to his nickname of Butch. It is also said that the name change was due to a desire to not disrespect his family, as at the time he had a feeling his path would take a significant diversion from the Mormon lifestyle he had been brought up to believe in.

For a while, Butch continued to move between ranches, living the life of a cowboy in Wyoming and Montana until he gravitated to Telluride, Colorado, in 1887. After striking up a friendship with racehorse owner Matt Warner some time earlier, Cassidy robbed his first bank.

It was June 24, 1889 and Cassidy, Warner, and the two McCarty brothers helped themselves to about $21,000 from the San Miguel Valley Bank. The crew didn't hang around for long, making their way to the Robbers Roost, an area of rough terrain in southeast Utah. The natural crags and canyons made this a popular hideout for outlaws, and in fact it was while Cassidy and his best friend Elzy Lay were lying low there that they formed the Wild Bunch.

When the heat had died down, Cassidy made his way to Wyoming, where he bought a ranch on the outskirts of Dubois. Although it's possible he did this in an attempt to earn an honest living, the fact he never actually made any money from it and that the location was just over from another outlaw hangout – the Hole in the Wall – suggests the ranch was a front for nefarious activities. There's also the fact he was arrested in 1894 for stealing horses and possibly running a protection racket among ranchers.

Cassidy served 18 months of a two-year sentence at the Wyoming State Prison, where upon his release in 1896 he was pardoned by Governor William Alford Richards. While some may have taken the pardon as an opportunity to turn their life around and walk the straight and narrow, it did absolutely nothing to quash Cassidy's criminal tendencies. After his release from

The Pinkerton Detective Agency became the main adversaries of Cassidy and his Wild Bunch

Butch Cassidy took great pride in the fact that he never had to take a life in his criminal career

jail, he instead went on to form the Wild Bunch and forever seal his place in the Wild West's notorious hall of fame.

Perhaps fittingly for a bunch of thieves, the gang's name was literally taken from the Doolin-Dalton Gang (also known as the Wild Bunch) and consisted of a rag-tag crew of criminals. In addition to Cassidy and his best friend, William Ellsworth "Elzy" Lay, the core gang consisted of Harvey "Kid Curry" Logan, Ben Kilpatrick, Harry Tracy, Will "News" Carver, Laura Bullion, and George "Flat Nose" Curry.

Other members would come and go, including Harry Alonzo Longabaugh, perhaps better known as the "Sundance Kid," who Cassidy recruited not long after leaving jail. But it was this core group who went on to perform the longest stretch of successful train and bank robberies in American history.

They wasted no time. Cassidy, Lay, Logan, and Bob Meeks targeted the bank in Montpelier, Idaho, on August 13, 1896, just a few months after his release from prison. This first robbery set off a chain of others, taking the gang across South Dakota, Wyoming, Nevada, and New Mexico. Their hauls would range from just a few thousand to $70,000 from a train outside Folsom, New Mexico.

Rather than encourage the ire of law-abiding citizens, the public were enamored with their adventures, almost rooting for them to do well. Some of the reason for that could be because Cassidy had a bit of a Robin Hood persona, often sharing his loot with local people who were struggling to get by.

Although seen as the leader of the gang, Cassidy was always a little bit removed from his criminal colleagues. For a start, he took great pride in the fact he had never killed anyone in his criminal career. If being chased, his preferred defence was to shoot the horse carrying the person chasing him. However, this refusal to shed human blood did not extend to his criminal comrades, many of whom had no qualms about killing people – usually officers of the law – during close pursuits.

Wilcox, Wyoming, became the location of the most famous and most destructive Wild Bunch robbery. On June 2, 1899, the gang robbed a Union Pacific Overland Flyer passenger train. There was a shootout with the law following the robbery, which saw Kid Curry and George Curry kill Sheriff Joe Hazen. The gang got away with $30,000.

For Cassidy, the robbery had serious ramifications. The train was carrying gold to pay troops in the Spanish-American War, and by robbing it he was deemed to have committed an act of terrorism. From that robbery onwards, Cassidy and the Wild Bunch were targeted as national terrorists with a reward of $18,000 if they were caught dead or alive.

Even though it's doubtful Cassidy actually robbed the train – one of the terms of his 1896 pardon was to not commit a crime in Wyoming, and Cassidy was a man of his word – it put the gang firmly in the sights of local law enforcement and the infamous Pinkerton Detective Agency. Yet, still they robbed. In fact, just a few weeks later on July 11, the Bunch robbed a Colorado and Southern Railroad train near Folsom, New Mexico. Another shootout with law enforcement ensued, and this time Cassidy's best friend, Elzy Lay, killed sheriffs Edward Far and Henry Love. Lay was eventually caught and convicted for his crimes, sentenced to life imprisonment for the double murders.

Things then went from bad to worse. During 1900 and 1901, various members of the Wild Bunch were either shot or captured. It was too much for Cassidy. He had gone from being seen as a cowboy Robin Hood to feeling suffocated by the law, so he fled to New York City with Sundance and his girlfriend, Etta Place, and then on to Buenos Aires, Argentina, in February 1901. They bought a ranch and settled down for a few years. But the peace was not to last.

The Pinkerton Detective Agency had been hired by Union Pacific after the Wilcox robbery to hunt down Cassidy, and its agents were very good at their jobs. Agent Frank Dimaio had learned of Cassidy's location, and everything

was in place to make an arrest. However, a local sheriff who had become friends with Cassidy tipped the trio off, so in May 1905 they made their escape north, ending up in Chile. Then for some reason they returned to Argentina, and not only did they return, but they also robbed a bank. Now being pursued for certain, they returned to Chile once again.

But it was too much for Etta Place. Sundance took her back to San Francisco while Cassidy took an alias of James "Santiago" Maxwell and worked at the Concordia Tin Mine. Sundance eventually joined him there. In 1907, the pair moved to Santa Cruz, apparently to lead the life of ranchers. But somehow it all went wrong.

The Wicox train robbery is the most infamous crime of the Wild Bunch but Cassidy might not have even been there

When did Cassidy Actually Die?

One of the most memorable scenes from *Butch Cassidy and the Sundance Kid* is the great shootout at the end, with both of the outlaws going down in a blaze of glory. But there have been many theories that Cassidy did not die in Bolivia, that he instead returned to America to live out the rest of his days in peace.

One of the most interesting theories came from a 1978 TV series called *In Search Of. . .* It focused on an argument made by Wild West historian Charles Kelly in his 1938 book *The Outlaw Trail: A History of Butch Cassidy and his Wild Bunch*. In it, Kelly states that if Cassidy was alive he would have visited his

father, and because he didn't do so he must have been dead.

In the episode, residents of Baggs, Wyoming, all state that Cassidy visited during 1924. There was also an interview with Cassidy's sister, Lula Parker Betenson, who says that not only did he visit his father, but he went on to live out his life in Washington. Betenson's 1975 book *Butch Cassidy, My Brother* also states that Cassidy told her he had got a friend to say one of the bodies in Bolivia was his so he could live a life free of pursuit. Although these theories are vastly different, it's important to remember that there is no actual evidence one way or another.

A still from *Butch Cassidy and the Sundance Kid*. Did the infamous shootout actually happen?

The famous Fort Worth Five photo of Cassidy, Sundance, Logan, Carver, and Ben Kilpatrick

On November 3, 1908 in Bolivia, a courier for the Aramavo Franke and Cia Silver Mine was transporting his company's payroll, worth around 15,000 Bolivian pesos. Two masked Americans attacked and robbed him, before lodging in a small boarding house nearby. But the boarding house owner was suspicious.

After alerting a nearby telegraph officer, on the night of November 6, soldiers, the police chief, the local mayor, and his officials all surrounded the boarding house, waiting to arrest the robbers. Things didn't quite go to plan. The robbers started to shoot, killing one soldier and wounding another. The gunfire was returned and before long an all-out gunfight erupted. Then there was a scream, a shot, and then another shot. Silence followed.

The authorities entered the boarding house the next morning and found two dead bodies. One had a bullet wound in the forehead, while the other had one in the temple, in addition to various bullet wounds in the arms and legs. The police report assumed that one robber had shot his partner to spare him further agony before then killing himself.

The report also concluded that the two bodies were the men who had robbed the courier, but there were no other forms of identification, although it was assumed that the bodies belonged to Cassidy and Sundance. They were buried in a small cemetery in unmarked graves. It was an inauspicious end to an action-packed era of looting and shooting, and perhaps not one that suited the legend of Butch Cassidy and the Sundance Kid.

However, death was by no means the end for this notorious duo. While the eponymous 1969 film is the most widely recognized tribute to them, its sequel, *Butch and Sundance: The Early Days*, released in 1979, is just one more example of many media portrayals of their famous escapades.

The Sundance Kid and girlfriend Etta Place, taken while in New York before heading to Argentina

BILLY THE KID

It's the iconic Wild West story and thus, in the 150 years since its making, it has become fraught with embellishment and myth. What was the real history of the hunt that made the legendary lawman Pat Garrett?

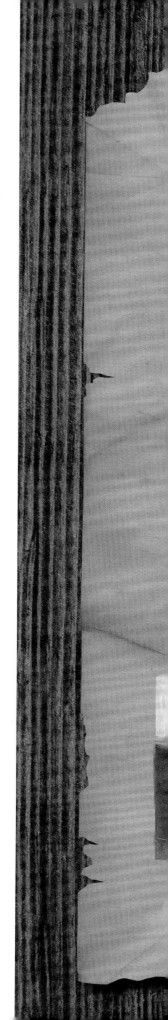

By the late nineteenth century, cartographers had mapped much of the world and the globe, almost as we know it today was a well-established fact. To the east, the Victorian Empire had peaked despite being ousted from its interests in the New World colonies a century earlier, and the decades that followed Independence Day had seen a fledgling United States simmer with civil war and lawlessness.

In the wake of the British, the new American government had made vast territorial gains, picking up the entire Louisiana region – a huge swathe of grasslands over 600,000 square miles– from France's Napolean Bonaparte for a bargain, at just $15 million. Border disputes and infighting followed, but that did not halt the USA's progress from the Great Plains to the coastline of the Golden State.

The boundary of this new nation had spilled westward too rapidly for any population to fill, let alone for the lawmakers of the White House to effectively control it. The West was true frontier territory, its people as feral and intense as its unrelenting climate – it was no place for the timid or fragile. This crucible forged two characters, the outlaw Billy the Kid and sheriff Patrick Floyd Garrett. Their independent life stories alone have resonated through generations, but it is perhaps Pat's pursuit and the ultimate death of the Kid that has defined them both.

Hollywood has traditionally presented an extremely romanticized notion of this era, so while the stereotypes of sherriff, outlaw, saloon owner, settler, Mexican, cowboy, and their ilk can usually be taken with a mere pinch of salt, the black and white morality of the Silver Screen is laughably far from the truth. There was often little to separate lawman from lawless but a small steel star, so we're going to rub away the sepia and journey to New Mexico in late 1880, where Pat Garrett has just been appointed the sheriff of Lincoln County.

Garrett was an imposing 6 foot, 5 inches of lean gunman and a known deadeye shot. Coupled with his imposing figure and reputation, he made a first-class choice for a visiting detective in the employ of the Treasury Department, Azariah Wild, to help track down the source of $30,000 worth of counterfeit bills that were circulating the county. Garrett himself employed another man – Barney Mason – to bait the two suspected of distributing this currency: ranch owner Dan Dedrick and another, W.H. West, who had made himself and their intentions clear in a letter that Mason had intercepted. Those intentions were that they would launder the money by buying cattle in Mexico as fast as they could with an assistant, who would unwittingly take the hit in the event that their ruse was discovered. Mason was to be the fall guy. Now that they had the advantage, Garrett instructed Mason to travel to the White Oaks ranch and play along with their nefarious plans.

In the brisk New Mexico winter, Mason rode out to Dedrick's. There, he ran into three gunslingers on the run from the authorities:

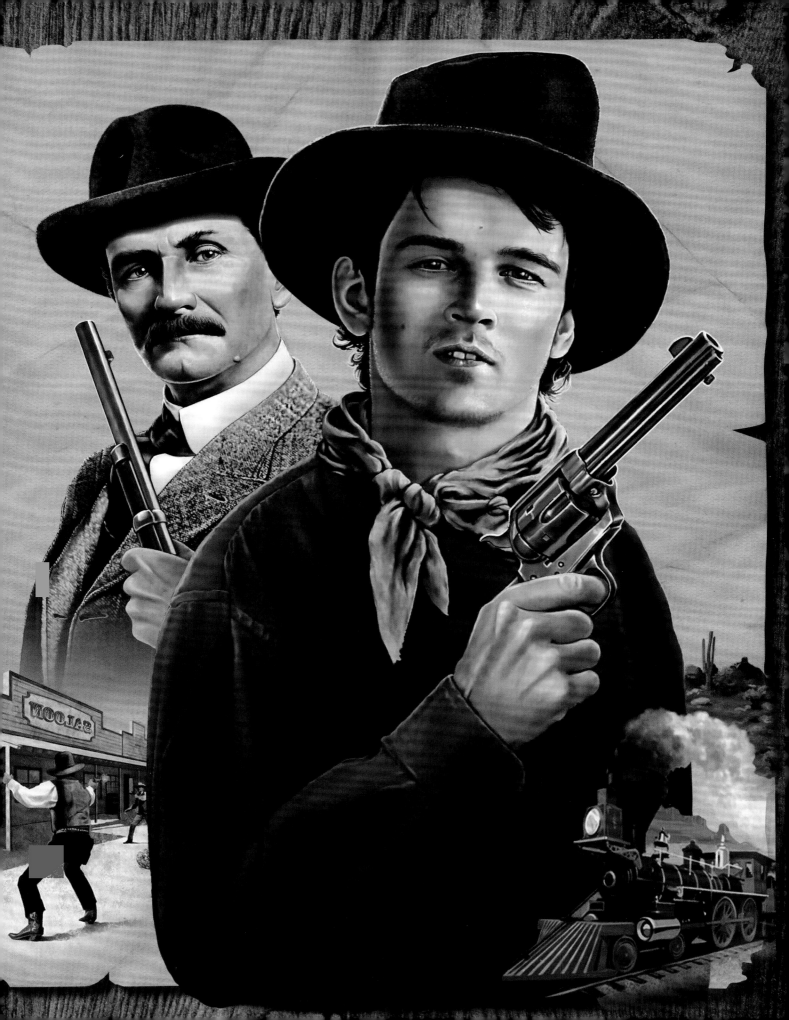

The shooting of Billy the Kid solidified Garrett's fame as a lawman and gunman

Dave Rudabaugh, who had killed a Las Vegas jailer during a break-out; Billy Wilson, another murderer yet to be caught; and the last was none other than Billy the Kid – the unlawful killer who had busted himself out of jail once already, made a living by cattle rustling and gambling, surrounded himself with like-minded outlaws, and whose reputation was on the cusp of snowballing towards near-mythological status.

The attitude of the era was such that a lawman and a wanted man could be trading campfire stories one day, then bullets the next. The Kid and Garrett were once thought to have gambled together, and Mason was also known to be on friendly terms with these three. Thus, both parties made their pleasantries then entered a game of high-stakes mind games, whereby the Kid attempted to ferret out the true nature of Mason's visit (suspecting he had come to ascertain his location and then report to the sheriff), while Mason threw the Kid a red herring, stating that he was there to take in some horses. The Kid didn't buy it. Smelling a rat, he met with Dedrick and his fellow outlaws with the intention of killing Mason, but Dedrick feared the repercussions would ruin his illicit plans, so the Kid relaxed his proverbial itchy trigger finger.

> Born in New York City, Billy the Kid moved to New Mexico after brief periods in Kansas and Indiana

A local posse on the hunt for Billy had been raized and the town of White Oaks was agitated with the news that the outlaw was in the area. The heat was too much for Mason to follow through with his orders without raising suspicion, so he lay low for a few days before returning to report at Garrett's place in Roswell. Shortly after, Garrett received a letter from Roswell Prison's Captain Lea, detailing the criminal activities of the Kid and his companions in the area. Garrett was commissioned as a United States marshal and given a warrant for the arrest of Henry McCarty, a.k.a. William H. Bonney, a.k.a. Billy the Kid, on the charge of murder. The hunt was on. The Kid's days were numbered and on November 27, 1880, the curtain was lifted on one of history's most famous Wild West dramas.

The new marshal already had a reputation and might have put the fear of God into the common criminal, but he was no fool. The Kid was by now a true desperado, one who had cut his teeth in the revenge killings of the Lincoln County War, and he was more likely to go out in a blaze of glory than he was to lay down his arms and come quietly. Garrett had raized a posse of about a dozen men from the

The Kid rode for a time with the gang of cattle rustlers known as the Jesse Evans Gang

citizens of Roswell and made his way to Fort Sumner to pick up the outlaws' trail, which would lead them to his suspected hideout at Los Portales. The many miles of desert scrub and overgrown track were neither an easy nor uneventful ride, and saw a Kid associate named Tom Foliard flee the posse in a hail of bullets. When the "hideout" at Los Portales – a hole in a cliff face with a fresh water spring – turned up nothing more than a few head of cattle, the posse fed and watered themselves before returning to Fort Sumner, where Garrett dismissed them. It was not the showdown he had hoped for, but Garrett wasn't the quitting kind.

Over the next few days, Garrett, accompanied by Mason, encountered Sheriff Romero leading a posse of swaggering Mexicans to Puerto de Luna, shot and wounded a felon named Mariano Leiva, talked his way out of Romero and his posse's attempts to arrest him for this shooting, and then learned of another party – led by an agent for the Panhandle stockmen the Kid had rustled cattle from – who was also on the trail of the Kid. Steel nerves, a steady hand, sharp wit, and some luck had eventually seen Garrett true once again.

Billy the Kid's date of birth is unknown, but it's thought that he was just twenty-one years old at the time of his death

The Kid is thought to have killed his first victim a few months before his eighteenth birthday

The Wild West in Numbers

The times were hard, but surprisingly, the crimes were nowhere near as bad as they are in the western United States today

3 murders

The highest annual body count for Tombstone, Arizona, happened in 1881, the same year as Wyatt Earp's famous gunfight at the OK Corral

$5-10 million

The biggest value stagecoach shipments in today's equivalent – usually gold bullion

6

The number of bank robberies across 15 states from 1859 to 1900. There weren't many banks and no cars, so it was a lot harder to get away with it back then

45

The number of murders from 1870-85 in five Kansas towns, a lower per capita than today

May 13, 1881

Billy the Kid's hanging date set by Lincoln County courts

28

The number of times the outlaw Black Bart robbed stagecoaches in California, making thousands of dollars a year

FIREARM SHOWDOWN

For shootouts, showdowns, soldiers, and civilians, these were the guns that won the West. The Kid and Garrett made darned sure their tools of the trade were the best

Pat Garrett's Sharps rifle
USA 1850-81
- »DESIGNERS: CHRISTIAN SHARPS
- »MANUFACTURER: SHARPS RIFLE MANUFACTURING COMPANY
- »NUMBER PRODUCED: 120,000+
- »EFFECTIVE RANGE: 500 YARDS
- »WEIGHT: 9.5 LBS
- »CALIBER: .52
- »FEED SYSTEM: 1 ROUND
- »ACTION: FALLING BLOCK, BREECH LOADING
- »ADVANTAGES: VERSATILE
- »DISADVANTAGES: WASTEFUL, EXPENSIVE
- »POPULAR USES: MILITARY, HUNTING, SPORT

Pat Garrett's Frontier Colt
USA 1878-1907
- »DESIGNERS: WILLIAM MASON
- »MANUFACTURER: COLT'S PATENT FIREARMS MANUFACTURING COMPANY
- »NUMBER PRODUCED: 51,210
- »MUZZLE VELOCITY: TWENTY-FIVE3 M/S
- »WEIGHT: 2.3 LBS
- »CALIBER: .44-40 WINCHESTER
- »FEED SYSTEM: CYLINDER MAGAZINE
- »ACTION: DOUBLE-ACTION REVOLVER
- »ADVANTAGES: INTERCHANGEABLE AMMUNITION WITH RIFLE, GOOD STOPPING POWER
- »DISADVANTAGES: NONE
- »POPULAR USES: CIVILIAN, SHERIFF

"The jig was up for Garrett, but the Kid's gang was now down to four"

Garrett met with Panhandle agent Frank Stewart at Las Vegas, the former Spanish colonial town of New Mexico and not the bright-light city-to-be more than 600 miles to the west. They left on December 14 to catch up with Stewart's party and broke the news to them: some baulked at the idea of an encounter with the Kid and his gang, but Stewart did not reproach any man who had reservations. "Do as you please boys, but there is no time to talk," he told them. "Those who are going with me, get ready at once. I want no man who hesitates." In the end, they added a further six men to their cause.

Ahead of the party, Garrett had sent a spy, a trustworthy man named Jose Roibal, who rode tirelessly to Fort Sumner to sniff the Kid out. Roibal performed his duty in a suitably subtle

fashion and returned to meet Garrett with the news that the outlaw he sought was certainly at Fort Sumner, that he was on the lookout for Garrett and Mason, and that he was prepared to ambush them. The Kid had no idea that Garrett had company with him.

Following this, the posse made their way to an old hospital building on the eastern side of the town to await the return of the outlaws. The Kid arrived sooner than expected. A light snow carpeted the ground so that, despite the low light of the evening, it was still bright outside. Nevertheless, Garrett and company were able to position themselves around the building to their advantage. Outlaws Foliard and Pickett rode up front and were first to feel the sting of the posse's six-shooters, though whose bullets

killed Foliard that day remains unknown. Garrett himself missed Pickett, who wheeled around and made for their ranch retreat along with the Kid, Bowdre, Wilson, and Rudabaugh—the stagecoach robber and a particularly unsavory character who the Kid admitted to being the only man he feared.

The marshal's posse regrouped and made preparations for the chase. There were just five men to track now. Garrett had learned from another reliable local that they had holed up in an abandoned house near Stinking Springs, a piece of no-man's land where murky water bubbled up into a pool in a depression. It was a few hours before dawn that they made this short ride, which proved their new information true: horses were tied to the rafters outside the building. The Kid was cornered and furthermore, Garrett's approach had not been detected, so they still had the advantage of surprise. The posse split and spread out along the perimeter to play the waiting game in the darkness.

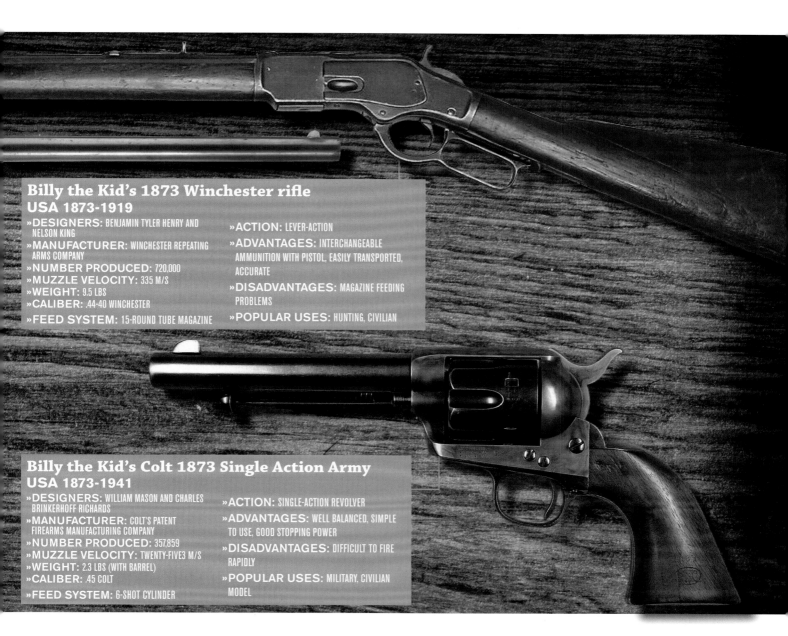

Billy the Kid's 1873 Winchester rifle
USA 1873-1919

- »DESIGNERS: BENJAMIN TYLER HENRY AND NELSON KING
- »MANUFACTURER: WINCHESTER REPEATING ARMS COMPANY
- »NUMBER PRODUCED: 720,000
- »MUZZLE VELOCITY: 335 M/S
- »WEIGHT: 9.5 LBS
- »CALIBER: .44-40 WINCHESTER
- »FEED SYSTEM: 15-ROUND TUBE MAGAZINE
- »ACTION: LEVER-ACTION
- »ADVANTAGES: INTERCHANGEABLE AMMUNITION WITH PISTOL, EASILY TRANSPORTED, ACCURATE
- »DISADVANTAGES: MAGAZINE FEEDING PROBLEMS
- »POPULAR USES: HUNTING, CIVILIAN

Billy the Kid's Colt 1873 Single Action Army
USA 1873-1941

- »DESIGNERS: WILLIAM MASON AND CHARLES BRINKERHOFF RICHARDS
- »MANUFACTURER: COLT'S PATENT FIREARMS MANUFACTURING COMPANY
- »NUMBER PRODUCED: 357,859
- »MUZZLE VELOCITY: TWENTY-FIVE3 M/S
- »WEIGHT: 2.3 LBS (WITH BARREL)
- »CALIBER: .45 COLT
- »FEED SYSTEM: 6-SHOT CYLINDER
- »ACTION: SINGLE-ACTION REVOLVER
- »ADVANTAGES: WELL BALANCED, SIMPLE TO USE, GOOD STOPPING POWER
- »DISADVANTAGES: DIFFICULT TO FIRE RAPIDLY
- »POPULAR USES: MILITARY, CIVILIAN MODEL

As day broke, one of the gang left the building via its only exit. In the half-light, he appeared to have the height, build and, most importantly, was wearing the characteristic Stetson of Billy the Kid. Knowing the Kid would not give up easily, Garrett signaled to the posse, who peppered the figure with bullets. Mortally wounded, Charley Bowdre stumbled back into the house but the Kid pushed him back out with the words: "They have murdered you Charley, but you can still get revenge. Kill some of the sons of bitches before you die." But if the blood hadn't all leaked out of him by then, the fight certainly had, because Bowdre lurched towards the posse and collapsed in a heap on the floor before he could even get his hand to his pistol.

The jig was up for Garrett, but the Kid's gang was now down to four and their only exit was covered. Just to tip the scales further in his favor, Garrett shot one of the three horses dead to partially cover the exit and then shot the ropes on the other two, both of which promptly cantered away. The marshal felt he was in a position now, to parley: "How you fixed in there, Kid?"

"Pretty well," came the reply, "but we have no wood to get breakfast."

"Come out and get some. Be a little sociable."

"Can't do it, Pat. Business is too confining. No time to run around."

An idea struck Garrett. Having rode through the pre-dawn and played the waiting game in the bitter cold, his men were likewise famished, so he sent for some provisions from Wilcox's ranch; a few hours later, a fire had been built. The sweet scent of roasting meat further weakened the outlaws' resolve until Rudabaugh dangled a filthy handkerchief out of a window in surrender. An eager foursome exited the house to collect the meal that had just cost them their freedom.

Garrett now had his man, but the Kid was as slippery as an eel. They survived a lynch mob at Las Vegas before the Kid was tried at Mesilla for the murder of Andrew "Buckshot" Roberts. He was acquitted in March 1881, but was then found guilty of the murder of Sheriff William Brady and sentenced to be hung five weeks later on May 13. Because there was no jail in Lincoln county, he was held in a two-story repurposed warehouse watched by Deputy Sheriff Bell and Deputy Marshal Olinger, where the Kid made the most of a window of opportunity to steal a gun, kill his guards, and make a spectacular escape from his prison.

Garrett was smarting when he realized his inadequate provision for the incarceration of the Kid and returned to Fort Sumner, where the Kid was believed to have fled, but the trail had once again gone cold. For the next two and a half months, Garrett would be kicking over stones well into the sweltering New Mexico summer before his final encounter with the fugitive.

In early July and in the company of Frank Stewart's replacement, John W. Poe, and Thomas K. Mckinney, who had been deputized, Garrett could be found a few miles north of Fort Sumner, adjusting his course according to hearsay and

Some believe Billy the Kid wasn't killed in 1881 and that he faked his own death – or Pat Garrett got the wrong man

Pat Garrett (left) with fellow Lincoln County sheriffs James Brent and John W. Poe

EXPERT Q&A

Robert Stahl

Robert was a historian, professor emeritus at Arizona State University, and member of the Billy The Kid Outlaw Gang (BTKOG) – a nonprofit organization with the aim of preserving the truth and promoting education in the history of Billy the Kid.

Several theories counter the reports of the Kid's death with tales of his survival. Why do you think these tales persist today?

Number one is that a great many people who accept the "survival" tale have not read the histories of the Kid's death by serious historians, so they are susceptible to entertaining stories about the Kid not being killed. Number two is the fact that many people cannot accept that it was mere coincidence that Garrett and the Kid were in Pete Maxwell's bedroom at the same time while believing the Kid was too smart or too fast on the draw to allow himself to be killed in the dark as he was. Number three is the fact that many documentaries – even those that include professional historians – bring up the rumors that the Kid was not killed as though these rumors have a touch of credibility.

Is it possible that Garrett could have shot the wrong man in that darkened room?

The whole hamlet of more than fifty people saw the Kid's body once or more during the morning of his death, as his body was washed and clothed by local women and was on display in the saloon for part of the morning. It was also taken back to Pete Maxwell's bedroom and placed at or near the spot where the Kid fell. Not one of the individuals who were there ever said it was not the Kid. Indeed all went to their graves, some over fifty years after the Kid's death, insisting they saw the Kid dead. Furthermore, six men who knew the Kid well both in person and on sight served on the coroner's jury, and all swore it was the Kid. So there is ample eyewitness support by numerous credible persons that Garrett did not kill the wrong man in that darkened room.

You've been pursuing a death certificate from the New Mexico Supreme Court for the man known as "Billy the Kid," for July 15, 1881. Why wasn't that originally issued? What would the reason be for the court not to create the certificate today?

My colleagues, Dr. Nancy N. Stahl and Marilyn Stahl Fischer, and I pursued a death certificate for the Kid because one was never created – and as part of that certificate we have been adamant about the fact that it should include the Kid's actual death date of July 15, 1881 as opposed to the traditional date of July 14.

William Henry Roberts claimed to be Billy the Kid after his death

The coroner's jury report never stated a time or date of death, which was typical of the era in rural areas of the Old West. Furthermore, I have yet to find a violent death in New Mexico in the 1800s that was followed by a death certificate being created. The Supreme Court cannot "create" a death certificate, but can order the state office that can to do its duty and create one. We went to the Supreme Court after months of trying to get the Office of the Medical Investigator to act. They refused to do their statutory duties and then refused to get back to us. We had no other legal recourse in New Mexico other than to go to the Supreme Court. We supplied credible and substantial documentary evidence to the Supreme Court for them to act in our favor, but they have not issued the court order to the New Mexico Office of the Medical Investigator for them to act. We believe that the Supreme Court and the New Mexico Office of the Medical Investigator consider our efforts to be publicity stunts rather than a good faith request by three historians to correct the historical record.

The BTKOG seeks to preserve and promote the truth about the Kid. Is there much in the way of rumor surrounding the legend you'd like to quash?

I do believe that important events in the current accepted stories of his escape from the Lincoln County Jail on April 28 need to be "squashed," such as the notion that he picked up a gun in the bathroom when he went to relieve himself and that he intended all along to kill Bob Olinger. Another that needs to end immediately is the rumor that there was widespread belief that Garrett did not kill the "real" Billy the Kid. Quite the contrary, for more than three decades after 1881 there were no stories – not even a hint of a rumor – printed in even one New Mexico newspaper that suggested the Kid was still alive. Indeed, at the time of his death in 1908, Garrett was well recognized throughout New Mexico and the nation as the man who killed Billy the Kid. Had there been any doubt, he would not have been acclaimed by everyone as the killer of the Kid.

How the Kid Met his Maker

A blow-by-blow account of how Pat Garrett sent Billy the Kid to his grave

11:55 p.m., July 14, 1881
The Kid is in one of the run-down houses on Peter Maxwell's property when he decides he's hungry, grabs a knife and makes his way over to Maxwell's house to cut himself some beef.

Midnight, July 15, 1881
Garrett has already entered the house himself and goes to the bedroom to speak to Maxwell to glean information on the whereabouts of the Kid. He sits on a chair near his pillow.

12:04 a.m.
Garrett's companions are outside when the Kid passes them, but they have no idea what he looks like and this person speaks fluent Spanish to some nearby Mexicans, so they don't identify him.

12:05 a.m.
The Kid enters the house. He is barefoot and not wearing his trademark hat. It's dark, so Garrett doesn't recognize him. Garrett stiffens as Maxwell whispers the identity of the man.

12:05 a.m.
As the Kid approaches Maxwell, he makes out a second figure in the chair. Garrett pulls his gun and, almost simultaneously, the Kid goes for his own revolver, asking, "Quien es? Quien es?"

12:05 a.m.
A heartbeat later, Garrett has pulled the trigger and thrown himself to the floor for another shot, but his aim was true. The Kid falls to the floor and barely has time to exhale before he is dead.

instinct. This took them to the home of Peter Maxwell where, near a row of dilapidated buildings, a slim man in a broad-rimmed hat could be heard talking in Spanish to some Mexicans. They had found their man – but none of the trio recognized him from a distance. As it turned out, the Kid hadn't recognized them either. He slipped off the wall he was perched on and walked casually away to Maxwell's house.

After the stand-off at Stinking Springs and the Kid's dramatic escape from jail, his death seems somewhat anticlimactic. Just after midnight on July 15, Billy the Kid entered Peter Maxwell's house to pick up some beef for his supper. Garrett was in Pete's darkened bedroom, quizzing him on the whereabouts of the Kid, when the very man he was hunting stepped through the door. Pete whispered to Garrett his identity and, leaving

> The Kid was most famous for cattle rustling and, unlike most Wild West outlaws, never robbed a bank or a train

nothing to chance, Garrett took two shots, struck the Kid in his left breast, and killed him.

In the memoirs he wrote shortly after the inquest that had discharged the marshal of his duty and deemed the homicide justifiable, Garrett dedicates no more than a short paragraph to the unfolding scene in the dark room. There was no classic showdown – the men weren't even aware of each other's presence until those final mortal seconds – and with his last words, it seems the Kid didn't even know who had sent him to meet his maker.

In as much that the Kid's infamy began to spread during the long nothing periods of Garrett's hunt, when rumor of this rebellious young gunslinger and his long-legged lawman nemesis gestated into legend, his ignominious demise has, perhaps fittingly, been made much of by countless authors and Hollywood film makers since.

This is one of the only images of Billy the Kid that exists

JESSE JAMES

Was this daring outlaw the Robin Hood of Missouri or a self-mythologizing murderer and thief?

Jesse James was a celebrity in his lifetime, and he remains an icon of the Wild West and a hero of the Confederate South. Born in Clay County, Missouri, in 1847, James was the middle of three children. His mother, Zerelda, had attended Catholic school in Kentucky, and his father, Robert, was a prosperous, slave-holding farmer and evangelical preacher. When Jesse was three, his father, having gone West to save souls in the Gold Rush, died. Zerelda married twice in the next five years, giving Jesse four half-siblings.

Through the 1850s, the USA slid towards civil war. Missouri was on the border between the North and the South, and the front line cut across its society. Clay County, with more slaveholders and more slaves than average, was known as "Little Dixie." When the Civil War began in 1861, Jesse's elder brother Frank joined the Confederate Army.

Missouri became a battleground for militias – the "Bushwhackers" for the Confederacy the "Jayhawkers" for the Union. Both groups committed atrocities. The Bushwhackers murdered Unionist sympathizers and executed Unionist prisoners, sometimes scalping the corpses. The Jayhawkers burned farms, executed Confederate sympathizers, and even expelled them from Missouri. In 1863, after Frank James had joined the Bushwhackers, a Jayhawker militia raided his family's farm. The Unionists tortured Jesse's stepfather, and may have flogged fifteen-year-old Jesse too. Frank escaped and joined Quantrill's Raiders, a notorious guerrilla cavalry unit led by William C. Quantrill. Frank probably took part in the massacre by Quantrill's Raiders of more than 200 men and boys at the Jayhawker stronghold of Lawrence, Kansas, in August 1863.

Frank returned home in the summer of 1864, and recruited his younger brother. Soon, they were riding with another notorious Bushwhacker leader, William "Bloody Bill" Anderson. Jesse was shot in the chest within weeks but he recovered in time to take part in the Centralia Massacre. In September 1864, Anderson's men, drunk on whiskey, raided Centralia, Missouri, and captured a train. They ordered the twenty-three Union soldiers on the train to strip, then shot, maimed, and scalped them all. Pursued by a Jayhawker militia, the next day Anderson's men ambushed and slaughtered more than 100 men.

When the Union authorities expelled Jesse and Frank's family from Clay County, and after Anderson's death a few weeks later, the brothers split up. Frank went to Kentucky with Quantrill, and Jesse to Texas with Anderson's lieutenant, Archie Clement. In a fight with a Union patrol near Lexington, Jesse survived a second chest wound. Recovering at his uncle's house in nearby Harlem, he fell in love with his first cousin, Zerelda Mimms.

The war ended in 1865 but Jesse, like many Confederate veterans, failed to adjust to the peace. The society he'd known was in ruins and the Republican government was set upon Reconstruction, the rebuilding of Southern society. The Bushwhackers carried on their war. In 1866, Clement's gang conducted America's first armed bank robbery against a bank owned by Republican ex-Jayhawkers. A government militia killed Clement soon afterwards, but his gang carried on robbing, usually killing civilians in the process.

In 1869, raiding a bank in Gallatin, Missouri, Jesse murdered a cashier – he had mistaken him for the killer of "Bloody Bill" Anderson. The

Jesse (left) and Frank James in 1872

Bob, Jim, and Cole Younger, sitting left to right with their sister Henrietta

killing, and the brothers' daring escape from the posse that chased them out of town, made Jesse the most famous of the ex-guerrilla "outlaws."

Jesse liked his fame. He formed an alliance with another ex-Confederate cavalryman, John Edwards, the editor of the *Kansas City Times*, who published letters in which James claimed his innocence, defended the Confederacy, and denounced the Republicans. Edwards, who campaigned to undo Reconstruction by bringing ex-Confederates to office in Missouri, praized James for remaining true to old Dixie. The legend of Jesse James was born.

Meanwhile, the James brothers teamed up with the Younger brothers, four ex-Bushwhackers from Missouri. For the next six years, the gang ranged across Iowa, Kentucky, Missouri, and Louisiana, robbing banks, trains, and stagecoaches as they went. Numerous civilians were killed along the way, but the gang also acquired a reputation for chivalry. Not all of this was the work of John Edwards of the *Kansas City Times*.

In 1872, after a young girl had been shot in the crossfire during a bank robbery at Columbia, Kentucky, Jesse wrote to the *Kansas City Times* denying that his men had shot her, even though by clearing his name so publicly he incriminated the Younger Brothers in the robbery. In January

1874, during a stagecoach robbery in Arkansas, the gang returned a watch to its owner when they discovered that he was a Confederate veteran. They told him that the North had driven them to crime. Two weeks later, when the gang robbed a train at Gads Hill, Missouri, they checked the passengers' hands so as to not steal from any manual laborers.

By now, the Pinkerton Detective Agency was on their trail. In January 1875, following the murder of several Pinkerton agents, a group of Pinkerton detectives firebombed the James family farm. Jesse's mother lost her right arm and his nine-year-old half-brother Archie was killed.

The gang's luck ran out on September 7, 1876, when it raided the First National Bank at Northfield, Minnesota. While Frank James, Bob Younger, and an accomplice named Charlie Pitts held up the bank, Jesse James and four other men rode up and down the street, firing their guns in the air to keep people indoors. But the residents broke out their own weapons. Two of the gang were killed. Cole Younger was hit in the leg, Bob Younger in the arm, and Jim Younger in the face. The survivors escaped with only a few bags of

nickels, and all had been wounded – Jesse in the leg – as they fled.

Chased by hundreds of militiamen, the gang split up. Two weeks later, the Youngers and Charlie Pitts were captured after a gunfight near La Salle, Minnesota. Tried, they received life sentences. Frank and Jesse escaped to a farm in Nashville, Tennessee. They lived quietly for the next three years. In early 1879, Jesse recruited a new gang and returned to crime. After a spree of train robberies, Missouri's new governor Thomas T. Crittenden persuaded his officials and the railroad executives to offer a large reward for Jesse's capture but no one turned the gang in: sympathy ran high among ex-Confederates.

Instead, Jesse was murdered in his own home by one of his own men, a new recruit named Robert Ford. With his brother Charley, Robert Ford approached Governor Crittenden and agreed to solve the problem of Jesse James in return for a reward of $5,000. Just after breakfast on April 3, 1882, as an unarmed Jesse climbed onto a chair in his living room to wipe dust from a picture, Robert Ford shot him in the back of the head at point-blank range.

The gun that shot Jesse James was a Smith & Wesson Model 3

A young Jesse James photographed c.1864

Robert Ford, the man who shot Jesse James

"When the gang robbed a train at Gads Hill, Missouri, they checked the passengers" hands so as to not steal from any manual laborers"

In a single day, the Ford brothers surrendered, were indicted for murder, sentenced to death, and then pardoned. The cowardly nature of Jesse's killing and the impression that Missouri's governor had conspired his assassination further burnished Jesse's legend. Charley Ford, a morphine addict, committed suicide the following year.

In June 1892, a man named Edward O'Kelley served the verdict of the court of public opinion on Robert Ford – with both barrels of a shotgun. After murdering Jesse, Ford had opened a saloon in Creede, Colorado. O'Kelley was sentenced to life in prison but was pardoned in 1902 after a petition was signed by thousands.

Surprisingly, several of the key members of the James-Younger gang survived – and played a part in maintaining the legend of Jesse James. Frank James surrendered in October 1882 in Missouri, apparently on the condition that he would not be extradited to Northfield, Minnesota. Frank was tried for two robberies in Missouri but convicted of neither.

The Younger brothers served time in a Minnesota prison but they never assisted the prosecution of Frank James. Bob Younger died of tuberculosis in jail, but in 1901, Cole and Jim were paroled on the condition that they remained in Minnesota. Jim Younger shot himself in 1902 and a year later, Cole was finally pardoned on condition that he never return to the state.

This was a different time: the Gilded Age of fantastic fortunes and populist politicians. Jesse was remembered as a Robin Hood, an ordinary man who had stood up against powerful corporations, rather than the killer who had donned a Ku Klux Klan hood – and not just as a disguise. Jesse James robbed the rich from their banks and railroads but without feeding the poor. If he was loyal to his family and friends, he was also a habitual thief and killer.

How to ROB A TRAIN

Need cash but a bank heist is a little too risky?

Often lightly defended and on a set track, the world's railway carriages have regularly been targets for criminals. A popular endeavor of the outlaws of the American Wild West, this sort of crime lingered right through to the twentieth century.

In recent years, trains have stopped being a favored source of travel for the rich and famous, so the sums of money aboard are smaller. This, combined with a tightening of security and faster trains, has resulted in a decline in train robberies. However, perhaps the most famous of all time actually took place in 1963, when a train was hijacked in the heist that would become known as the Great Train Robbery.

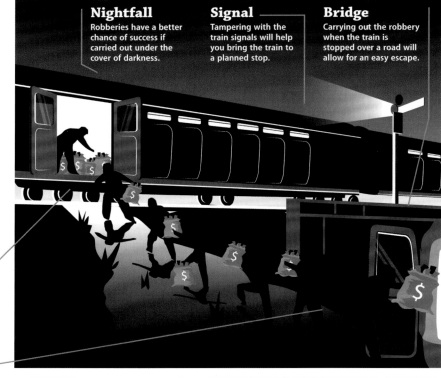

Nightfall
Robberies have a better chance of success if carried out under the cover of darkness.

Signal
Tampering with the train signals will help you bring the train to a planned stop.

Bridge
Carrying out the robbery when the train is stopped over a road will allow for an easy escape.

Supplies

BALACLAVA

GLOVES

PISTOL

CUTTERS

TRAIN TIMETABLE

TIMETABLE

WESTERN RAILWAYS

Gang of robbers
There were fifteen crooks working on the Great Train Robbery – make sure you trust them all.

Getaway vehicle
You could always run, but it's good to have a vehicle on hand to whisk you and your buddies away.

01 Preparation is key
Trains are fast, so the location of the holdup has to be planned carefully. A low bridge is usually a good area to attempt a heist, as being close to a road increases the chance of making a quick and clean getaway. Additionally, it may be a good idea to undertake the robbery in a rural area and ideally at night – that way, there are fewer witnesses.

02 Tamper with the signals
The world of rail is controlled by signals, so if you master these, the whole process will become much simpler. A train driver and the guards on board won't be suspicious of a red stoplight, so rewiring the signal system is a must. Now you have a small window when the train is stationary, it's the perfect opportunity to climb aboard.

How Not to. . .Loot a Locomotive

One of the most meticulously planned train heists of all time, the Great Train Robbery is now a story of legend. Holding up a train traveling from Glasgow to Euston, the gang of fifteen thieves boarded the postal train in rural Buckinghamshire at about three in the morning. Stopping the locomotive at a red signal, the robbers climbed aboard and stole 120 sacks of bank notes containing £2.6 million.

Thanks to a tip-off, the police got their men after a five-day search. How were they found? Some of the gang already had criminal records and their fingerprints were found in their deserted hideout. The biggest clue, however, came when one of the gang ordered the train staff to wait thirty minutes before calling the police. This revealed a vital clue; the hideout would be a half-hour radius from the scene.

03 Don't raise the alarm!

If someone suspects a heist is happening, it won't be long until the mission is compromised. To maintain secrecy, move covertly and wear an outfit that will help you blend into the dark of the night. In the planning stage, ensure that the layout of the train has been noted so all of the conspirators know their role.

04 Take what you need

The classic Hollywood villain mistake is to take too much, so stick to the task at hand. If you came with a set amount in mind, do your job and then leave as planned. Any waiting around could affect the robbery and leave you exposed to the security services, who will undoubtedly soon discover what's going on.

05 Escape

With the robbery complete, now's the time for the getaway. One member of the crew should be the designated driver, and make sure the vehicle has enough space for both the loot and your buddies. The police will be hot on your tail, so drive carefully and inconspicuously until you reach the hideout and, if everything went to plan, safety.

06 Lay low

The police aren't going to give up on solving the crime any time soon, so make sure to stay in your hideout until the heat is off. Train robberies attract plenty of public and media attention, so it could be a matter of months or even years until you can roam freely. You may have wads of cash, but your life will never be the same again.

---

4 FAMOUS... TRAIN ROBBERS

BUTCH CASSIDY
1866-1908, USA
Accompanied as ever by the Sundance Kid, the famous American outlaw formed the Wild Bunch and halted a train in Wyoming in 1899.

JESSE JAMES
1847-82, USA
The renowned bandit Jesse James turned his attention to trains when he loosened a section of track, toppling a locomotive.

JOHN RENO
1839-95, USA
John and his brother Sim carried out one of the first train robberies, escaping with $10,000 in gold coins and $33 in notes.

GEORGE PARROT
19TH CENTURY, USA
George's gang planned an audacious heist on the Union Pacific Railroad, but they were foiled by workers before the train was dislodged.

© Ed Crooks

HENRY STARR

Film-maker, thief, killer, and one of the West's most successful yet contradictory outlaws.

enry Starr has been immortalized as one of the last Old West outlaws, a symbol of his dying breed. In almost thirty years of robberies and shootouts, first on horseback and later using the new motorcars, Starr established an enduring legend.

Starr blended crime and prison with brief spurts of honest living, but he always returned to robbing, running, and hiding from the law. Bankers feared him, judges and lawmen hated him, yet many ordinary people admired and even supported him. Shortly before his final robbery, Starr summed up his attitude to the outlaw life: "I love it. It is wild with adventure."

He was born into an outlaw family near Fort Gibson, Oklahoma, on December 2, 1873, learning the criminal trade from childhood. His father George, grandfather Tom, and uncle Sam were all criminals. Sam's wife (and Henry's aunt by marriage) was the legendary Belle Starr.

Henry didn't think much of Belle, though, regarding her as crude and obnoxious, and always quick to distance himself from her. All in all, the Starrs were a tough, ruthless, and lawless family of full-time felons. Henry Starr described his grandfather in chilling terms: "Known far and wide as the Devil's own. In all matters where law and order was on one side, Tom Starr was on the other."

Before achieving statehood in 1915, Oklahoma and the Indian Territory were virtually separate entities from the USA, hotbeds of violence and crime. While Oklahoma had an established government and legal system in its own right, the Indian Territory was under federal jurisdiction.

The Indian Territory was then nicknamed "Land of the six-gun" and "Robber's Roost." Sparsely populated, its wide-open landscape was almost custom-made for outlaws plying their trade. Even after becoming part of the state of Oklahoma it continued breeding and sheltering outlaws, men like Raymond Hamilton and Charles "Pretty Boy" Floyd. The Starrs felt perfectly at home.

Henry Starr entered crime at a young age – aged only sixteen he pled guilty to smuggling whiskey into the Indian Territory, a federal crime. Arrested again aged twenty-one for horse theft, Starr faced a more serious problem. In Oklahoma, horse theft was a capital offense. If convicted, he would hang. Hanging wasn't attractive, but jumping bail and outlawry certainly were. Perhaps he thought his only option was jumping bail and becoming a full-time felon. Or, perhaps he was always likely to follow the family profession.

Starr formed his first gang in 1892. Operating in the Indian Territory, it robbed a string of train stations and stores. The hauls weren't big, a few hundred dollars at most, but they were learning their craft. It wasn't long before they tried something bigger.

That something bigger turned out to be the Caney Valley Bank in Kansas on March 28, 1893. Starr's gang rode away with $4,900. Around a month after Caney Valley, they robbed their first train at Pryor Creek. They seemed well on their way, but fate threw a spanner in the works. During their spree, Starr had killed Deputy US Marshal Floyd Wilson and the law wanted him to hang. Arrested in Colorado Springs, Starr

The Outlaw Queen

Henry wasn't the family's only outlaw. Father George, grandfather Tom, and uncle Sam were outlaws as well. Sam's wife was Belle Starr, the legendary Outlaw Queen. In a time when women were usually outlaws' wives and/or girlfriends, Belle was far more.

Born in Carthage, Missouri, on February 5, 1848, Belle knew Frank and Jesse James and the Younger brothers. Learning outlawry from her first husband, Jim Reed, she married Sam Starr after Reed's death in 1874. Reportedly a crack shot even on horseback, Belle was known for wearing two pistols with cartridge belts slung around her waist. She quickly acquired a lengthy criminal record and an unenviable reputation.

She aided rustlers, bootleggers, and horse thieves, harbored fugitives, and assisted in robberies. But when Sam died in a gunfight, Belle's career also ended. She married Jim Starr, one of Sam's relatives, before being murdered on February 3, 1889.

Belle's death is filled with conflicting accounts of how she died. Blasted repeatedly with a shotgun, the prime suspect was Edgar Watson. A fugitive from a murder charge in Florida and one of Bell's employees, Watson allegedly feared her turning him in. Her murder, however, remains officially unsolved.

Known as the Outlaw Queen, Belle also survived an encounter with the Hanging Judge

While incarcerated, Starr witnessed condemned outlaw Crawford "Cherokee Bill" Goldsby attempt to escape. Starr talked him into surrendering

President Theodore Roosevelt pardoned Starr for persuading Cherokee Bill to surrender. Cherokee Bill was later hanged

"They seemed well on their way, but fate threw a spanner in the works"

was shipped to Fort Smith, Arkansas, home of legendary "Hanging Judge" Isaac Parker. It was an encounter both men later regretted.

Unsurprisingly, he was convicted. Equally unsurprising was Parker condemning him to die. Both Parker and Starr were probably very surprized when Starr's lawyers earned not just a retrial – where he was convicted and condemned again – but then a third trial. Starr, copping a plea, received fifteen years of imprisonment and went to the federal prison at Columbus, Ohio, on January 15, 1898. Arkansas felt Starr had cheated it of justice. The paths of Arkansas and Starr, however, would cross again. And it wouldn't end well for either of them.

Before that, Starr found another way to escape punishment. While awaiting trial at Fort Smith, old acquaintance and fellow outlaw Crawford "Cherokee Bill" Goldsby was awaiting execution for murder. Trying to shoot his way out with a smuggled pistol, Goldsby was trapped and Starr spotted his chance.

First he persuaded the guards to let him talk to Goldsby, and then he managed to persuade Goldsby to surrender without further bloodshed. On March 17, 1896, aged only twenty, Goldsby was hanged. Starr's lawyers ensured President Theodore Roosevelt heard of Starr's heroics. On January 16, 1903, Starr left Columbus with a presidential pardon. Once again, he'd beaten the odds.

It wouldn't last. Starr went straight, abandoned crime, got married, and fathered Theodore Roosevelt Starr. Unfortunately, Arkansas hadn't forgotten or forgiven. He was arrested pending extradition over an 1893 bank robbery. Facing prison or the gallows, Starr again became a fugitive. As he later put it: "I preferred a quiet and unostentatious interment in a respectable cemetery rather than a life on the Arkansas prison farm."

Given the horrors of Arkansas' prisons that's no surprise, but Arkansas begged to differ. Fleeing into the Osage Hills, Starr went on to rob banks in Colorado and Kansas before hiding out in Arizona and New Mexico.

Starr now tasted betrayal. He wrote to an old friend in Tulsa, Oklahoma, who promptly informed the authorities. Starr was arrested and extradited to Colorado for the Amity bank robbery. On November 24, 1908 he pled guilty. If he thought confessing would earn leniency, he was very disappointed – instead he drew seven to twenty-five years in Canon City prison. Undaunted, Starr became a model prisoner and a trusty inmate, studied law in the prison library, and wrote his memoir, *Thrilling Events: Life of Henry Starr.* Colorado's state governor saw him as deserving parole after less than five years.

This time it was Colorado's governor who felt betrayed. Starr, paroled provided he remain in Colorado for at least five years, immediately vanished. Returning to Oklahoma, the most lawless phase of his career was about to begin.

Between September 8, 1914 and March 1, 1915, fourteen Oklahoma bank robberies were attributed to Starr's gang, costing $28,000 in stolen money and damages. On March 27, Starr's men did what no other gang had – they pulled off two simultaneous bank robberies in the same town.

Condemned for murdering Deputy US Marshal Floyd Wilson, Starr was lucky to escape Fort Smith's notorious gallows

Starr started his career robbing banks on horseback, but he conducted his last robbery in 1921 in a car

Isaac Parker, the Hanging Judge

Based in Fort Smith, Arkansas, Isaac Parker became as much a legend as some of the lawmen he employed and outlaws he sentenced. Feared by criminals for his stiff sentencing, Parker became known throughout the West as the Hanging Judge.

To be fair to Parker, his reputation came when the gallows weren't solely for murderers. Horse theft, cattle rustling and numerous other crimes then carried the death penalty. In a time when crime was rife and law enforcement often improvised, justice had to be swift and often ruthless. Parker was no different to other judges of his era; he was simply better known.

During his twenty-one years on the bench, Parker tried a staggering 13,490 cases, condemning 160 defendants to death. Of those, only seventy-nine were executed. Henry Starr certainly wasn't intimidated by Parker's reputation.

Sentenced by Parker to hang for murdering Deputy US Marshal Floyd Wilson, Starr made himself abundantly clear:

"Don't try to stare me down. I've looked many a better man than you in the eye. Save your wind for your next victim. If I am a monster, you are a fiend, for I have only put one man to death, while you have slaughtered many with your jawbone."

Known to subsequent generations as the "Hanging Judge," Isaac Parker's firm hand became a symbol of frontier justice

The James-Younger Gang never tried a double-hitter. The Dalton Gang had tried one in Coffeyville, Kansas, on October 5, 1892, where four of them were killed. Nobody had succeeded, but Henry Starr was about to.

Stroud, Oklahoma, earned its unwilling place in criminal history when Starr's men robbed the First National Bank and Stroud National Bank at the same time. Most of the gang shot their way out with $5,815, but Starr and Lewis Estes weren't going anywhere. Both wounded in the gunfight, they were captured.

Starr drew another long sentence – twenty-five years in the Oklahoma State Penitentiary at McAlester. But he had yet another successful ploy to match.

Again a model prisoner, he also lobbied the press and public with his patented "Crime does not pay" routine. He spoke to the press, other inmates, prison staff, and anyone else who might be convinced. Speaking to one reporter from his cell, Starr stated: "I'm forty-five years old and seventeen of my forty-five years have been spent inside. Isn't that enough to tell any boy that there's nothing to the life I have led?"

Amazingly, it worked. Paroled on March 15, 1919, Star again went straight. He spent the next two years living an honest life. He produced and starred in the 1919 silent movie *A Debtor to the Law* to further his outward repentance, earning an offer of movie stardom, but it came to nothing. Starr, fearing publicity might cause the state of Arkansas to extradite him from California, turned it down and returned to Oklahoma.

Neither the repentance nor Starr's life lasted very long. He quickly returned to crime, formed yet another gang, and continued as he always had. This time, though, it would be different. At Harrison, Arkansas, on February 18, 1921, Henry Starr would finally meet his match.

The People's State Bank looked like an easy target, but it wasn't. Former bank President W.J. Myers had rigged a "bandit trap," booby-trapping the vault door with a shotgun for any would-be robbers. Starr, not knowing the trap was set, never saw it coming. Abandoned by his gang and mortally wounded, Starr was captured. It was obvious he wouldn't live to stand trial.

Starr died on February 22 with his wife, son, and mother at his bedside.

Starr stands out for the length of his career, the amount of money he stole, the Stroud robberies, and bridging the gap between horses and getaway cars. He lasted longer, stole more, and killed less than almost all of them. And he remained unrepentant to the last. The day before he died, Starr boasted, "I've robbed more banks than any man in America!"

THE DALTON GANG

Crime was a family affair for the fearsome brothers. Loyalty was their strength, and ego their downfall

The story of the Dalton Gang is one of injured pride, ego, and ultimately violence and death. Related to the notorious Younger brothers, Jim and Cole, through their mother Adeline, they were raized on tales of their cousins rampaging through the Missouri back country, robbing and killing as they went. Only active between March 1890 and May 1892, the Dalton Gang's reign as outlaw legends was brief and bloody. Since then, they have been immortalized in films, dime novels, and a hit song by The Eagles, the sentimental "Doolin Dalton."

Like the James-Younger Gang and Henry Starr, their story was a family affair. Eldest brother Frank had been a Deputy US Marshal serving under Judge Isaac Parker. Sometimes, when extra help was needed, Frank brought his younger brothers into his posses. Brave and tough, he died in a gunfight on November 27, 1888. The Daltons, arch-outlaws, actually began as lawmen. They were the classic gamekeepers-turned-poachers.

His brothers continued "lawing" until 1890. They'd had been lawmen for some time but, when their employers didn't pay them, they abruptly quit and became outlaws. Outlaws and lawmen had similar skills and the risks were much the same, but crime paid better. Skilled riders, trackers, and gunmen with a chip on their shoulder, the Daltons forgot about enforcing the law. The law, however, wouldn't forget them. It wouldn't forgive their changing sides, either.

It wasn't as unusual as it might seem for lawmen and outlaws to switch sides. Some, like the Daltons, abandoned law for crime. Henry Newton Brown, on the other hand, went from outlaw to lawman to outlaw again. A veteran of New Mexico's legendary Lincoln County War in which Billy the Kid was prominent, Brown later became a deputy sheriff in Texas while named on two murder warrants in New Mexico before returning to outlawry, dying from wounds sustained via a shotgun blast in 1884.

In Pawhuska, then part of Indian Territory, the early Dalton Gang was born. Aside from Bob and Emmet Dalton, Charley Pierce, George "Bitter Creek" Newcomb, and "Blackfaced" Charlie Bryant were the original members. Bill Powers, Dick Broadwell, Gratton "Grat" Dalton, and Bill Doolin were all recruited later.

Their first robbery was of a gambling house in New Mexico's notorious Silver City. In the 1870s, Billy the Kid had called it home. In the 1890s, Butch Cassidy's gang got to know every gambling parlor and saloon. In between these two eras, the Daltons arrived.

Grat would probably have joined the gang earlier if not for being in California at the time. While visiting brother Bob, the pair were accused of robbing a Southern Pacific train at Alita on January 6, 1891. The evidence was slim, and Bob was acquitted.

Grat, however, had other ideas. Unwilling to stand trial and risk a lengthy prison sentence, he promptly escaped. He was quickly recaptured, given a twenty-year sentence and escaped again, this time while on a train heading for prison. After stealing the keys to his handcuffs, Grat

The Dalton Gang was mainly known for robbing banks and trains throughout the Wild West

Catastrophe at Coffeyville

To outdo the Youngers, the Daltons attempted something the James-Younger Gang never did: two simultaneous bank robberies in the same town. They entered Coffeyville on October 5, 1892 to rob the C.M. Condon Bank and the First National. Leaving their horses in a nearby alley proved lethal. Coffeyville was their hometown, and as known outlaws, they were recognized almost immediately.

Buying time, a bank teller claimed the safe was on a time lock. It wasn't. A similar ruse had caused the destruction of the James-Younger Gang at Northfield, Minnesota in 1876, and the Daltons fell for it too. With ten minutes to prepare, local people

inflicted a hail of lead on them. Cornered in "Death Alley," the gang attempted to shoot their way out. They failed.

Grat Dalton, Dick Broadwell, and Bill Powers were mortally wounded. Broadwell escaped, later found dead outside the town. Grat and Town Marshal and Charles Connelly died killing each other. Already wounded, Bob Dalton died where he lay, brother Emmett beside him. Emmett tried and failed to save him. Already shot several times, Emmett then took a shotgun blast in his back. Later pardoned after fourteen years of imprisonment, he was the only Dalton who survived Coffeyville.

Bill Power, Bob Dalton, Grat Dalton, and Dick Broadwell's bodies were publicly displayed

Emmett was the only Dalton to survive Coffeyville. He served a long prison sentence before being pardoned

freed himself before jumping off the moving train and into the San Joaquin River. Having landed safely in water instead of on rocky ground, Grat then fled. Reunited with his brothers, he joined the gang as well.

Between May 1891 and July 1892, the Daltons robbed four trains within Indian territory. They managed something bigger at Lillietta, also in Indian territory, taking $10,000 before a final robbery at Red Rock. Splitting up after the Red Rock robbery, Charlie Bryant was arrested. While being escorted by Deputy US Marshal Ed Short, Bryant stole a gun and tried to escape. In the ensuing gunfight, Short and Bryant killed each other. Bryant was the Dalton Gang's first casualty – and he was far from their last.

Their attempt to rob a railroad car at Adair, Oklahoma, on July 14, 1892 turned into an epic shootout. Spotted while unloading the car, they exchanged over 200 shots with eight railroad guards. None of the gang were injured, but several local citizens were. Two doctors, Goff and Youngblood, were both hit by stray bullets, from which Goff died. Captain J.J. Kinney of the railroad police and Captain LaFlore of the Cherokee Indian police were also wounded. The railroad company responded with unusually generous rewards – $5,000 for the capture and

conviction of each individual member of the Dalton Gang.

After Adair, the Dalton Gang dropped out of sight but not out of mind. Bob Dalton had plans, and they would seal the Daltons' legend, though not in the manner any of them would have wanted. The Daltons were preparing the riskiest and most audacious heist of their career, one that would carve their names into Old West history: they were going to raid the bank at Coffeyville.

Little is recorded of the gang until their disastrous raid on Coffeyville in October 1892. After the slaughter of the gang while trying to rob two banks at the same time, the remaining members went their separate ways for a while. Bill Dalton hadn't been at Coffeyville, and nor had George Newcomb and Charley Pierce. They reportedly joined the Wild Bunch, also known as the Doolin-Dalton Gang, under the co-leadership of Bill Doolin and Bill Dalton.

It's said that Bill Dalton was involved in a spectacularly bloody shootout at Ingalls, Oklahoma on September 1, 1893, in which

"Bryant was the Dalton Gang's first casualty – and he was far from their last"

three Deputy US Marshals were killed. Some sources also credit him with robbing the First National Bank in Longview, Texas, on May 21, 1894. Bill, the last Dalton still alive and free, didn't last much longer. Tracked by a posse to Ardmore, Oklahoma, Bill died on June 8, 1894 in a hail of bullets. Strangely, nine of the Deputy US Marshals who killed him were indicted for murder, but they were never tried for Dalton's death. George Newcomb and Charley Pierce, who'd joined the Doolin-Dalton Gang with Bob, were killed by bounty hunters on May 5, 1895.

Bill Doolin, late of the Wild Bunch/Doolin-Dalton Gang, barely outlived his former allies. By the end of 1894, most of his gang had been captured or killed by the Three Guardsmen. The Guardsmen (Bill Tilghman, Chris Madsen, and Heck Thomas) had destroyed the Doolin-Dalton Gang permanently.

Caught by Tilghman, Doolin managed to escape on July 5, 1896. At Lawton, Oklahoma, on August 24, another Guardsmen finally put the last nail in the gang's coffin, slaying Doolin with a shotgun blast. Having done more than anyone

Bill Dalton was also an outlaw. He didn't ride with his brothers, preferring Bill Doolin's Wild Bunch

With a shotgun and six-shooter, Thomas became legendary for helping tame the wild frontier. He killed Bill Doolin, along with many others

else to destroy the Dalton Gang, Bill Doolin's nemesis was none other than Heck Thomas.

There has been speculation (but no evidence) that a sixth outlaw was at Coffeyville, supposedly Bill Doolin. This alleged accomplice's job was to mind their horses, but instead ran from the firefight and escaped. Given Doolin's willingness to face gunfights without hesitation, this is unlikely.

If a sixth man was present, it almost certainly wasn't Doolin. Nor was it likely if it had been *that* Bill Dalton that Charley Pierce and George Newcomb would have let him get away with it. They wouldn't have formed the Doolin-Dalton Gang with him as coleader, either. It's far more likely that Doolin would have been found dead if he'd been found at all.

Emmett Dalton survived the disaster at Coffeyville, the only Dalton there who did. He was tried and sentenced to life imprisonment at the notoriously tough Kansas State Penitentiary. After serving fourteen years of his life term, Dalton was released and eventually pardoned. He spent the remainder of his life in California as a real estate agent, author, and actor. He died in 1937, long after most of the outlaws and lawmen of his era had themselves passed into history.

The outlaws' dream of being first to rob two banks simultaneously had died at Coffeyville, so it seemed. Not until March 27, 1915 would another Oklahoma badman do what the Daltons couldn't and the James-Younger Gang never tried.

The James-Younger Gang were destroyed after a Northfield bank teller lied about the vault having a time lock. Given time to prepare, local citizens shot them to pieces. Bob Dalton, for all his desire to outdo them, fell for the exact same trick, with the exact same brutal outcome befalling him.

Henry Starr did manage a double-hitter at Stroud Oklahoma, robbing the First National and Stroud National Banks. That said, it didn't do him any good either. Wounded in the robberies and abandoned by his cohorts, Starr found himself in prison. But while he is remembered for his dubious achievement, the Dalton Gang was destroyed and then immortalized by their failure.

A silent filmmaker was near Stroud at the time of the robbery, shooting *The Passing of the*

> One of the Dalton brothers, Emmett, wrote a book about their exploits called *When The Daltons Rode*

Oklahoma Outlaws. On hearing of the double robbery, he took his film crew with him and hurried to the scene, hoping to film a real bank robbery as it happened. He was too late to get any footage, but the filmmaker's name was familiar to Starr and the Dalton Gang alike. It was retired Marshal Bill Tilghman, captor of Bill Doolin, avowed enemy of the Dalton Gang and formerly one of the Three Guardsmen.

© Getty

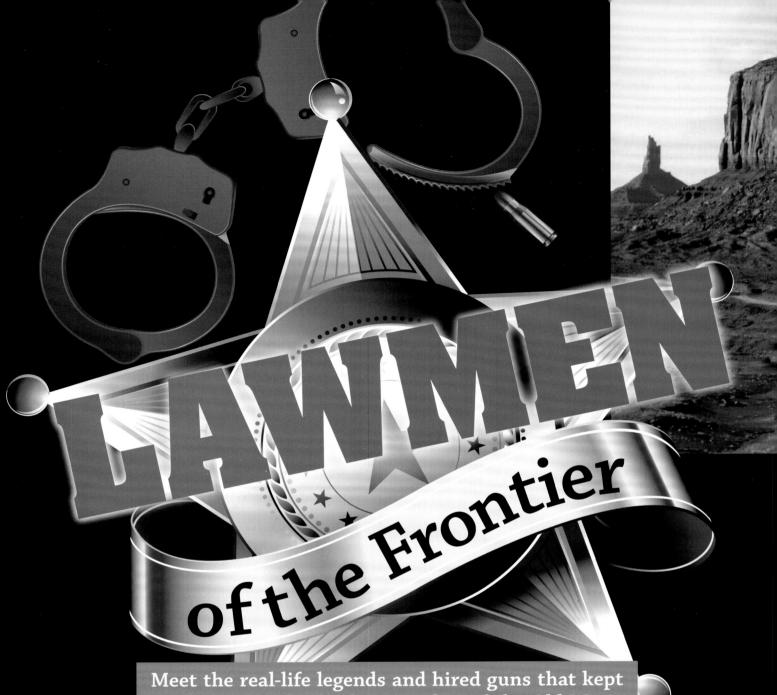

LAWMEN
of the Frontier

Meet the real-life legends and hired guns that kept the peace in the farthest reaches of the Old West

It was a time of gamblers, gunslingers, and legendary lawmen. A time when law enforcement was simpler and often far more brutal. A time when badge-wearing, gun-toting lawmen became legends in their own time. Spectacular shootouts like the OK Corral entered history and immortalized in dime novels and Hollywood movies for years to come. Outlaws became folk heroes shrouded in myths portraying them as far better (and sometimes far worse) than they really were. Welcome to the Old West.

Extending America's western frontier was like opening Pandora's box. It brought huge advances in technology and enormous social change as people flooded west to seek their fortunes. But as always, with the honest citizens came the criminals and gunslingers.

Conmen traded land they didn't own, mines that didn't exist, and cattle bought from rustlers. Gamblers played (and often cheated) wherever games were tolerated. Thieves robbed banks, trains, and stagecoaches almost at will. Freelance gunmen, the dreaded gunslingers, killed for anybody who paid enough. Enter the lawmen, bringing law to the lawless.

Criminals like Jesse James, Billy the Kid, and Arizona's notorious "Cowboys" were overnight sensations. Equally legendary were lawmen like Wyatt Earp, "Bat" Masterson, and Pat Garrett. But, far from the clean-cut image of films like *Shane* and *High Noon*, the distinction between cops and robbers wasn't always as clear as it might seem.

Some blurred the line between lawman and lawbreaker. Earp was a brothel bouncer before becoming a lawman. Deputy US Marshal John "Doc" Holliday was a dentist in Georgia before tuberculosis and scandal saw him head west. Holliday is remembered as Earp's friend, entering the OK Corral out of loyalty to him. Before arriving in Tombstone, however, Doc was already accused of at least a dozen killings.

Misinformers from the Pinkerton Detective Agency

Texas Rangers in the 1860s

Tombstsotone, Arizona, was the location of the famous gunfight at the OK Corral

Canadian Mounties were ruthless but well disciplined

The second half of the 19th century saw mass migration westward, bringing irrevocable change and rich pickings for criminals. Banks, trains, payrolls, mines, and stagecoaches were all fair game. As the huge ranches blossomed, cattle rustling and horse theft became profitable for those prepared to risk being shot.

Facing a crime wave, local law enforcement faced a multitude of problems. Firstly, lawmen in these fledgling frontier towns were grossly understaffed and poorly paid, while facing both outlaws' guns and criticism from town officials if they seemed weak on crime or overly heavy-handed. What's more, their jurisdiction was limited. Anyone could break the law, then cross the nearest county or state line when pursued. But the local sheriff wasn't legally allowed to keep up the chase.

With established law often unavailable – and its enforcers often corrupt – mobs often enforced their own rules. Frontier justice often involved a prisoner, a length of rope, and the nearest available tree. Without stern law enforcers, mobs even took prisoners from jails solely to hang them high.

Facing a breakdown in law and order, state and national organizations were needed. The Texas Rangers, the Northwest Mounted Police, the United States Marshals Service, and the Pinkerton Detective Agency made their names in this era and they still exist today, albeit in very different forms. All of these institutions have their own distinct lineage and place in American history, so let's take a look at them and their key players.

"Mobs even took prisoners from jails solely to hang them high"

US MARSHALS

YEARS ACTIVE: 1789-present **JURISDICTION:** Nationwide
INFAMOUS COLLARS: "Curly" Bill Brocius, the Mason-Henry Gang, the Purdy Gang, Crawford "Cherokee Bill" Goldsby

The US Marshals Service is America's oldest law enforcement body, founded during George Washington's presidency. Many marshals have become legends, including Wyatt Earp, his brothers Virgil and Morgan, Doc Holliday, Bat Masterson, Dallas Stoudenmire, and Bass Reeves. At a time when frontier justice frequently involved a bullet or a noose, it was their job to force law on the lawless.

Dodge City, Tombstone, Abilene, Deadwood, and many other towns saw justice served with six-shooters and shotguns. Unlike state and local police, the US Marshals had national jurisdiction and any state or county without its own lawmen could request one. Feared by outlaws, they often enforced the law using Frank Hamer's methods — with a .45 in the gut.

The most famous marshal is undoubtedly Earp, whose feud with Arizona's notorious Cowboys gang and their gunfight at the OK Corral have become a part of American folklore. However, Earp wasn't the clean-cut, all-American hero you might expect. Working as bouncer, pimp, and gambler before becoming a marshal, Earp crossed the line between lawman and vigilante after his brothers Virgil and Morgan were shot by

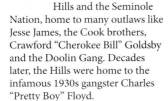

Wyatt Earp's early life has been censored to make his story more family friendly

the Cowboys. Virgil lost the use of one arm. Morgan died.

Earp began his "Vendetta Ride," during which he killed the Cowboys he believed responsible: Frank Stilwell, Florentino Cruz, Johnny Barnes, and "Curly" Bill Brocius. Afterwards, he left Arizona and law enforcement forever.

Another group of marshals, Heck Thomas, Bill Tilghman, and Chris Madsen became known as the Three Guardsmen. They policed what was then the vast Oklahoma Territory, which included the Cookson Hills and the Seminole Nation, home to many outlaws like Jesse James, the Cook brothers, Crawford "Cherokee Bill" Goldsby and the Doolin Gang. Decades later, the Hills were home to the infamous 1930s gangster Charles "Pretty Boy" Floyd.

The Three Guardsmen handled the Doolin Gang simply and brutally. Members who surrendered were arrested — those who resisted died. The Cook brothers also fell before the marshals while Goldsby was hanged at Fort Smith, Arkansas, in March 1896, aged only twenty. Defiant to the end, his last words were, "I came here to die, not make a speech."

Goldsby might have died along with many other outlaws, but the US Marshals live on.

Bill Tilghman was known for his fast hand and sharp eye

ALL ABOUT THE BASS

Deputy US Marshal Bass Reeves isn't as well remembered as Wyatt Earp, but he was equally remarkable. Reeves worked mainly in Arkansas and the Indian Territory. He had learned to speak several Native American languages while hiding out among several tribes as a fugitive slave.

After abolition, Reeves joined the US Marshals in 1875 and worked with them for thirty-two years. He's credited with over 3,000 arrests and fourteen kills during his long career. Reeves even brought his own son to justice for murder, allegedly demanding he be the one to do it.

As a skilled detective and marksman who could converse with Native Americans and – according to contemporary accounts – rode about on a white horse, it has been argued that Reeves may have been the basis for

the Lone Ranger. However, as a pioneering figure during an era of endemic racism, Reeves certainly deserves to be remembered as a legend in his own right.

Reeves was the first Black marshal west of the Mississippi River

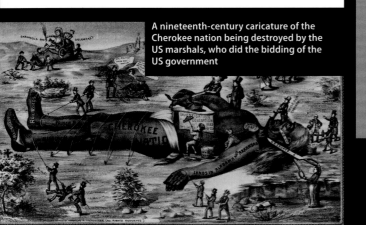

A nineteenth-century caricature of the Cherokee nation being destroyed by the US marshals, who did the bidding of the US government

NORTHWEST MOUNTED POLICE

YEARS ACTIVE: 1873-present JURISDICTION: Originally the Pacific Northwest, now all over Canada INFAMOUS COLLARS: The MacLean brothers, Louis Riel, Ernest Cashel

On the head
Mounties used to wear spiked helmets, again modeled on a cavalryman's, but it was replaced by the light brown "ranger hat" that is familiar today.

Sturdy jacket
Originally based on the uniforms of English cavalrymen, the red coat is still standard uniform for Mounties.

Shooting gun
Commonly thought to be a rifle, the gun slung across the saddle is actually a carbine, a shorter, lighter weapon chosen for convenience and speed. Mounties have also always carried handguns – while today they favor automatic pistols, revolvers were regulation issue.

Suitable footwear
The black trousers and boots remain part of Mountie uniform, though spurs are now seldom worn and horses are rarely ridden.

The Northwest Mounted Police (NWMP) formed in 1873 and were called a police force to sooth American fears about troops building up on their border. But the then governor general of Canada made no bones about what was expected of them: "While nominally policemen, the men will be dressed in a scarlet uniform and possess all the characteristics of a military force." Modeled on the British Army cavalry and Royal Irish Constabulary, the NWMP were a disciplined paramilitary charged with securing the Northwest Territory for settlers.

Tough policing was seriously needed. Canada bought the Northwest Territory from the Hudson Bay Company in 1870 but the region's isolated wilderness meant it was essentially lawless. This culminated in the Cypress Hills Massacre of 1873, which saw a party of drunken traders and hunters kill at least twenty Assiniboine Natives, claiming they had stolen a horse.

To get to the Northwest Territory, 300 NWMP officers and men endured a grueling, two month, 800-mile march across untracked prairie in 1874. The NWMP early activities included ending the whiskey trade and enforcing agreements with the First Nations people. The Great Sioux War of 1876 saw many Native Americans flee to Canada and the NWMP policed their stay. By 1879, many had returned home, but some refused. When food supplies were

stopped, they endured months of starvation before surrendering to the US Army at Fort Buford in July 1881.

Domestic problems included the McLean brothers: Allan, Charles, and Archie. They terrorized British Columbia in the late 1870s, stealing anything they could. Captured after murdering two men, including an NWMP officer, they were hanged at New Westminster in 1881.

With the McLean crisis over, another almost immediately began — the Second Riel Rebellion in 1885. The NWMP helped crush the uprising and Louis Riel was hanged on November 16, 1885. Other notable collars included horse thieves James Gaddy and Moise Racette, both of whom were hanged in 1888 for murdering a NWMP constable.

By far their biggest challenge was the Gold Rush. In 1895, gold was discovered in the Klondike region of Yukon. Thousands came seeking their fortunes and criminals soon followed. But the NWMP enforced the law and customs duties, expelled undesirables and gold rush far more peaceful than what California experienced in the 1840s.

Ironically, policing the gold rush saved the NWMP. Its disbandment was being discussed at the time, but glowing reports saw the plan deferred and then abandoned entirely. The NWMP endures as the Royal Canadian Mounted Police, better known as the Mounties.

TEXAS RANGERS

YEARS ACTIVE: 1835-present **JURISDICTION:** The state of Texas, including the Texas-Mexico border
INFAMOUS COLLARS: John Wesley Hardin, Billy Thompson, Sam Bass, Bonnie and Clyde

The Texas Rangers are probably some of the best-known lawmen in the business. Founded in the 1830s and today part of the Texas Bureau of Investigation, they've tackled every kind of felon. Their jurisdiction covers the whole of the state of Texas including the Mexican border, which was a hotbed of crime and disorder.

In keeping with the times, their early methods were usually violent. As Ranger Captain Frank Hamer bluntly put it, "We're here to enforce the law, and the best way to do it is a .45 slug in the gut."

In many ways, Hamer practiced what he preached. By the time he ambushed Bonnie and Clyde in May 1934, he'd already killed a total of 53 men, been shot approximately seventeen times, and left for dead four times. He was nothing short of your typical old-school ranger.

Recruitment was based on demand. In times of crisis, as many as 300 to 400 men could be employed. When times were easier, rangers were simply laid off — governors could hire and fire them at their convenience and often did. Seldom a permanent job, it was almost always a dangerous one.

John Horton Slaughter served as a Texas Ranger, Arizona sheriff, and US marshal

The Texas Rangers made their name and legacy during the Old West era, but it came at a price. To date, 105 rangers have died in the line of duty, although this is less than one percent of the individuals who have served.

When not tackling outlaws and cattle rustlers, the rangers defended the Texas-Mexico border against renegade Native Americans and Mexican bandits. In fact, the organization was founded by prominent colonist Stephen Austin in 1823 to deal with the threat of the Native American Comanche tribe, who raided extensively all along the border using hit-and-run tactics.

Paid only $1.twenty-five a day with a $10 monthly bounty in property, rangers had to provide their own horses and guns. They were skilled horsemen, trackers and marksmen and every man was fearless without being reckless. Above all, their loyalty to their oath and each other was sacrosanct. Not just law enforcers, the rangers have become a part of North American history and legend.

Packing a Paterson
The Texas Rangers were one of the first to embrace the Colt Paterson .36 caliber five-shot revolver as it meant they didn't have to reload as often during a fire fight.

Mexican headgear
While often depicted wearing stetson hats, in the nineteenth century most Texas Rangers preferred to wear broader-brimmed sombreros to better keep the sun out of their eyes.

Lone star badge
From 1875 onwards, Rangers adopted badges to identify themselves. Invariably made from a Mexican silver coin, they were cut into a star shape modeled on the state flag.

No uniform
Rangers initially had to supply their own weapons and horses and wore plain clothes. To this day, they have no formal uniform but are required to dress in a "western" style.

TWO PRESIDENTS UNDER THE GUN

Without a doubt the most important case in their history, the Texas Rangers managed to foil an attempt to assassinate American president Howard Taft and Mexican president Porfirio Díaz at the same time. The leaders were to have their first summit meetings in El Paso, Texas, and Ciudad Juárez, Mexico, in October 1909. Tensions were high and security involved thousands of troops and lawmen patrolling on both sides of the border.

Private Moore of the Rangers and adventurer Frederick Russell Burnham noticed a man loitering by the El Paso Chamber of Commerce along the route of the presidential procession. Suspicious, they took him aside and searched him. They discovered a loaded palm pistol, a single-shot weapon designed to be concealed in the user's palm with only the barrel visible. They foiled the plan just in the nick of time. Taft and Díaz were reportedly only feet away when the would-be assassin was thwarted.

THE PINKERTON DETECTIVE AGENCY

YEARS ACTIVE: 1850-present **JURISDICTION:** Nationwide
INFAMOUS COLLARS: Adam Worth, the Reno Gang, the Molly Maguires

The NWMP and US Marshals began as official law enforcement bodies. The Texas Rangers, originally paramilitary, became an official body. The Pinkerton Detective Agency, however, remains a private company with far less public oversight and a much darker past.

The agency's founder, Scottish immigrant Allan Pinkerton, famously foiled a plot to assassinate President Abraham Lincoln at his inauguration in 1861. However, his agency became synonymous with union busting using very dubious methods.

"By the mid-1850s a few businessmen saw the need for greater control over their employees; their solution was to sponsor a private detective system. In February 1855, Allan Pinkerton, after consulting with six Midwestern railroads, created such an agency in Chicago," explains Frank Morn, a criminal justice historian.

Pinkerton's Pennsylvania campaign typified his attitude to unions and strikers. In the 1870s, agent James McParland infiltrated the Molly Maguires, a group of Irish-American agitators in Pennsylvania's coalfields. McParland's testimony saw several Mollies hanged and many jailed. But before pursuing prosection, McParland attempted to intimidate the Mollies, sending masked men to beat them up in their homes. Later, on July 6, 1892, 300 Pinkerton detectives from New York and Chicago were sent to protect its Pittsburgh mill. This resulted in a fire fight in which sixteen men were killed and twenty-three others were wounded. It took two brigades of the Pennsylvania militia to restore order.

The agency also hunted outlaws with decidedly mixed results. The Reno Gang were smashed after numerous shootouts. Butch Cassidy evaded Pinkerton and left the country, dying in Bolivia beside Harry "Sundance Kid" Longabaugh. Pinkerton's hunt for Jesse James was disastrous.

After Jesse's gang killed agents Joseph Whicher and Louis Lull in March 1874, Pinkerton declared a personal vendetta. In January 1875, his agents raided the James homestead, throwing an incendiary bomb into the building. Jesse's mother, Zerelda, lost an arm and his brother Archie, aged only fourteen, died. Pinkerton publicly denied intentional arson but his private letters clearly state his intent to "burn the house down."

Business suffered accordingly and worse was soon to follow. The 1893 Anti-Pinkerton Act outlawed government employment of private detectives and mercenaries, specifically naming Pinkerton's agency: "No employee of the Pinkerton Detective Agency, or similar agency, shall be employed in any Government service or by any officer of the District of Columbia." All told, the Pinkertons' history isn't as clean-cut as it seems.

SCHOOL FOR STRIKE-BREAKERS

Employed by factory owners, undercover Pinkertons tried to influence labor union decision-making, forcing out union officials and replacing them so that they could alter union policy. Agents tried to create internal strife whenever possible, setting rival factions within unions against each other. If strikers committed crimes like sabotage, undercover agents gathered the evidence. Many people were jailed as a result and some were even executed.

Pinkerton security guards would also protect workers refusing to support strikes, often providing armed escorts into picketed workplaces. Violence was commonplace. These security guards were also often provocative and confrontational, frequently encouraging violence and blaming striking workers for the bloodshed.

Pinkerton men at the 1892 Homestead Strike, as depicted on the cover of Harper's Weekly

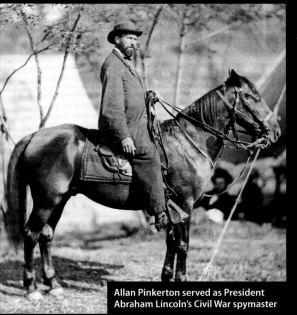

Allan Pinkerton served as President Abraham Lincoln's Civil War spymaster

A Pinkerton flyer appealing for information on a suspect

PINKERTON'S NATIONAL DETECTIVE AGENCY.
We never sleep.

PRINCIPAL
Geo. H. Bangs, Gen'l Supt.
Robert A. Pinkerton, Supt. 66 Exchange Place NEW YORK.
Benj. Franklin, Supt. 45 South Third Street.
F. Warner, Supt. 191 & 193 Fifth Avenue PHILADELPHIA.
W.A. Pinkerton, CHICAGO.
Clarence A. Seward, Attorney and Counsel for the Agency, 29 Nassau St. New York.

NEW YORK, Feb. 11, 1878.

WILLIAM F. REILLY absconded from New York, February 2d, 1878, having FORGED his employer's name to checks drawn on various Banks for $15,000.

On leaving New York he took with him his younger brother, EDWARD A. REILLY, and a companion named LOUIS CARLIN.

The following are their descriptions:

WILLIAM F. REILLY, twenty-two years of age, five feet seven inches high, erect, medium size and well built, straight-limbed, full face, fresh complexion, rosy cheeks, brown hair thick and short, wore small light moustache and little side whiskers, features regular, pretty full broad forehead. Is of Irish descent.

EDWARD A. REILLY, sixteen years of age, five feet nine inches high, slim but strongly built, large for his age, sloping shoulders, head slightly forward, medium rather pale, long face, heavy dark hair rather short, dark

WYATT EARP

With his own and his family's lives threatened by a murderous band of outlaws, one man took the law into his own hands and formed a posse to track them down, becoming a hunted outlaw himself.

Four gunshots splintered a dry and dusty night in Tombstone, Arizona. A man, wandering from the town's central Crystal Palace Saloon back to the Cosmopolitan Hotel, suddenly felt time slow to a crawl as his back and arm were lit up in a blaze of agonizing pain. The contact of three loads of double-barrelled buckshots slammed into him like a runaway freight train. The force of the impact sent him crashing back into the side of the Crystal Palace. In excruciating pain, he stumbled towards the Cosmopolitan, blood dripping from him onto the baked earth. Drawing upon his last reserves of energy, he managed to reach the hotel's entrance and fall through its door – a moment later, everything was black. Across the street on the upper floor of an unfinished building, the assassins slipped away into the night.

The morning after, on December 29, 1881, Tombstone's deputy town marshal Wyatt Earp sent a telegram that read: "Virgil Earp was shot by concealed assassins last night. His wounds are fatal. Telegraph me appointment with power to appoint deputies. Local authorities are doing nothing. The lives of other citizens are threatened. Wyatt Earp."

For weeks, Wyatt, his brothers, and their friends had been receiving death threats for their role in the shootout at the OK Corral, a gunfight that had seen a number of infamous outlaws taken out. The critical condition of Virgil convinced him that everyone he knew and loved

had been marked for death. Unfortunately, while the lawman knew those responsible, he was powerless to act, with the sheriff of Tombstone, Johnny Behan, openly hostile to the Earps. Behan was close friends with William "Curly Bill" Brocius whom Earp believed had his brother's blood on his hands.

The tall, pale, and serious-looking Wyatt, with his rough and gravelly voice, was going over the head of Behan to US Marshal Crawley P. Dake, a man who had the authority to grant him deputizing powers to assemble a posse capable of bringing the assassins to justice. The question was whether or not Dake would free his hands and if so, how quickly his confirmation would reach Tombstone. With the assassins still at large, the danger to the Earps and their friends was high. Luckily for Wyatt, he soon received a return telegram. In it, Dake officially bestowed deputizing powers on Wyatt and issued a mandate that he was free to pursue the assassins at his discretion.

Back at the Cosmopolitan, local doctor George E. Goodfellow amazingly announced that Virgil would live, although his left arm would be permanently crippled. Upon finally waking from his coma and being told about his crippled arm, Virgil showed the characteristic Earp grit by telling his wife Allie: "Never mind, I've got one arm left to hug you with."

While relieved that his brother had survived, hatred for the assassins had begun to take hold

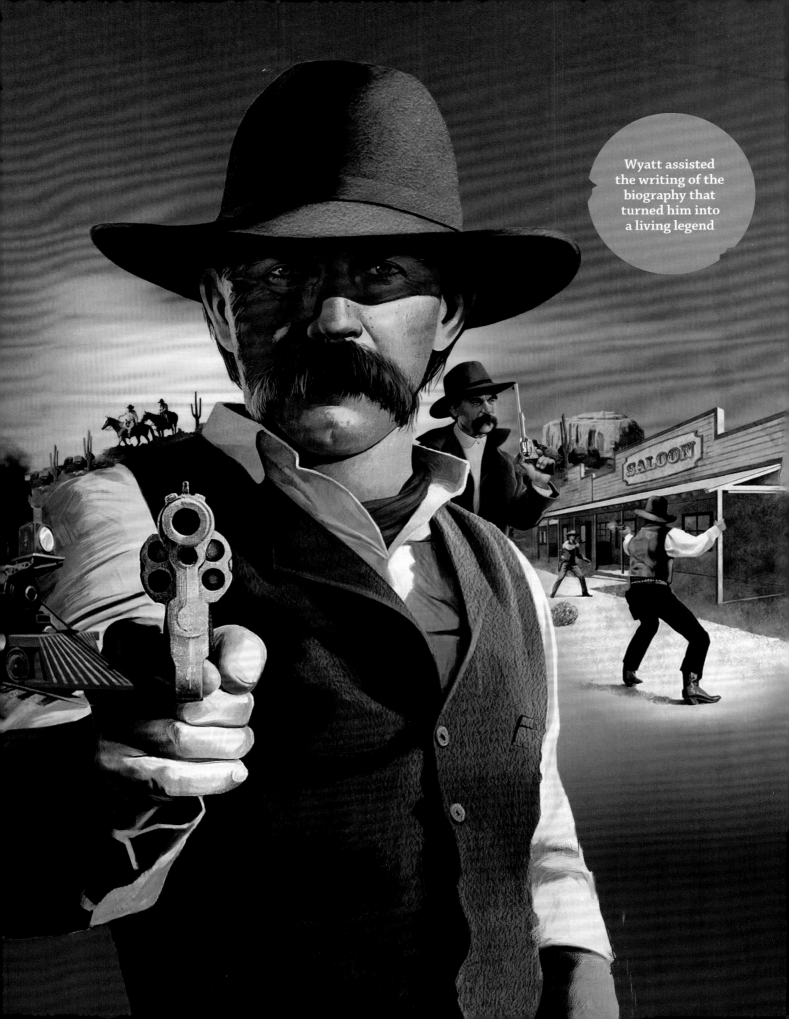

Wyatt assisted the writing of the biography that turned him into a living legend

of Wyatt, with him thinking of little other than revenge. He also knew who could help him get it. His old ally Doc Holliday would ride with him, as would his other brother Warren Earp, but for a job like this he needed ruthless professionals. Sherman McMaster and Jack "Turkey Creek" Johnson were first on his list – tough men who had what it takes to kill a man. Joining McMaster and Johnson would be Charles "Hairlip Charlie" Smith and John "Texas Jack" Vermillion, who had checkered pasts but experience of battle.

Three months passed after Virgil's shooting with no major activity. One of the Wild West's greatest lawmen hadn't been idle, though, as by March 18, 1882, he had his posse gathered in Tombstone while his brother Virgil was making his first tentative steps out of his sickbed. It seemed things were falling into place for Wyatt. He just needed to ensure his brother's safe passage out of Arizona and the vendetta ride could begin.

However, his plans were shaken to their foundations as the very night Virgil started walking again, his younger brother Morgan was set upon at Tombstone's Campbell & Hatch Billiard Parlor. He was shot through the establishment's window, the bullet shattering his

The vendetta ride posse, June 1883. From left to right: W. H. Harris, Luke Short, Bat Masterson, and seated Charlie Bassett, Wyatt Earp, Frank McLain, and Neal Brown

"Wyatt rushed to the parlor where he was forced to listen as his brother slowly bled to death. The outlaws had gone after two of his brothers"

EARP'S VENDETTA POSSE

JOHN "DOC" HOLLIDAY
1851-87
A trained dentist, professional gambler, and sharp-shooting gunfighter, Doc Holliday was one of Wyatt Earp's best and oldest friends, famously fighting with him at the shootout at the OK Corral. By the time of his death five years after the vendetta ride, Holliday had survived eight gunfights, killed six men, and wounded countless others.

JOHN "TEXAS JACK" VERMILLION
1842-1911
A close friend of Doc Holliday, Texas Jack was renowned throughout the Old West for his gunfighting abilities and ice cold demeanor when under fire. He played a key role in the closing Iron Springs gunfight of the vendetta ride, fighting fiercely and fearlessly even when his horse was shot dead from under him during the confrontation.

DAN "TIP" TIPTON
1844-98
An experienced sailor and gambler, Dan Tipton was one of the people present when Wyatt Earp's brother Morgan was assassinated at the Campbell & Hatch Billiard Parlor in Tombstone, Arizona. He rode with Earp for the first part of the vendetta ride, witnessing the gunning down of outlaw Florentino Cruz at Pete Spence's woodcamp.

spine and sending him shuddering back into a billiard table. Wyatt rushed to the parlor where he was forced to listen as his brother slowly bled to death. The outlaws had gone after two of his brothers, injuring one and killing the other. Wyatt swore that he would bring those responsible to justice.

The following day he decided that, regardless of Virgil's still-weak state, he had to get him out of Arizona now or he would be the next to be taken out. At the same time the coroner Dr. D.M. Mather held an inquest into Morgan's death and discovered that Marietta Duarte, the wife of well-known outlaw Pete Spence, knew something and was ready to talk. Duarte told Matthew that the day before Morgan's assassination she had overheard her husband talking with Florentino "Indian Charlie" Cruz. Apparently, Morgan had walked by and she had heard Spence say to Charlie, "That's him, that's him."

Duarte also said that this same night, Indian Charlie and Frank C. Stilwell came to Spence's house, armed with pistols and carbine rifles, and that they all talked outside for a while in hushed tones. The following morning, when Marietta confronted Spence about the night's activities, she recounted that Spence hit her and threatened to shoot her if she spoke to anyone about what she had heard. Spence, Stilwell, and Cruz were now the prime suspects in Morgan Earp's murder.

Duarte was called to testify this in court and did so, Wyatt looking on from the rear of the courthouse. However, thanks to the then-antiquated legal system, Duarte's testimony was dismissed because a spouse could not testify against her husband. Learning of the judge's decision to free the men Wyatt knew the law could not be relied on to bring the outlaws to justice – he had to kill them all himself.

Arrangements were made to escort Virgil and his wife to the train station in Contention City, so that they could leave the state. Upon arriving, news was received that Stilwell and others were hunting Virgil and waiting in Tucson – the next stop on an intended trip to California – to murder him. As such, Wyatt and his men remained with Virgil up to Tucson.

Before he became a man of the law, Wyatt Earp worked numerous jobs, including a buffalo hunter and saloonkeeper

In the Wild West saloon, bars were often where vendettas were settled

SHOOTOUT
AT THE
OK CORRAL

6 Tom and Billy bleed out
By the time the shooting stopped, Ike Clanton had fled the scene, Frank McLaury lay dead, and Tom McLaury and Billy Clanton were wounded. Despite being moved to a nearby house, both Tom and Billy would bleed out from their wounds.

1 A threat too far
In the preceding days and weeks running up to the gunfight, dangerous outlaw Ike Clanton had repeatedly threatened the Earp family and their close friend Doc Holliday. Tired of threats, the Earps moved to bring the cowboy and his gang in to jail.

When and where did it take place?
Wednesday, October 26, 1881 in Tombstone, Arizona.

Who was involved?
On one side were the Earp brothers Virgil, Morgan, and Wyatt, and Doc Holliday. They went up against Billy Claiborne, Ike and Billy Clanton, as well as Tom and Frank McLaury.

Who died?
Billy Clanton, along with both Tom and Frank McLaury.

What happened next?
The fight led to a bitter feud that set in motion the events that would end with Wyatt Earp's vendetta ride.

Tombstone, Arizona, 1881

After spending a night in a nearby hotel before escorting Virgil and his wife to the train the next morning, Wyatt spotted two figures lying in wait on a nearby flatcar; Stilwell and accomplice Ike Clanton. Years of experience as a lawman mixed in with the culminate rage of months of death threats, and living in fear and Wyatt Earp ran full speed, shotgun in hand, at the men. Seeing Wyatt and Doc Holliday approaching, Stilwell and Clanton turned to run, but Stilwell tripped and fell. Scrambling around in the dust of the train yard, he attempted to regain his footing but it was too late – Wyatt was on him. A double-barrelled shotgun pointing directly at his chest at point-blank range, Stilwell caught a glimpse of the burning hatred within Wyatt's eyes before both barrels were unloaded into his torso.

Stilwell's short scream was immediately terminated with the blast, with six buckshot holes blown through his body and powder-burned holes on the back of his coat. Drawing his .44 Schofield Smith & Wesson revolver from his holster, Wyatt carefully aimed for Stilwell's head and then fired a single round into his skull. Leaving the corpse to grow cold in the early morning sun, Wyatt and his posse watched as the train with Virgil and his wife on slowly pulled out of the station, bound for California and safety.

4 A double-barrelled death

After two opening revolver shots, one from Billy Clanton and one from Virgil, the latter hitting Frank McLaury in the stomach, Doc Holliday moved around Tom McLaury's horse and surprized him with a double-barrelled shotgun blast. Tom tried to escape down the street but collapsed.

3 Fast on the draw

Upon discovering the cowboys, Virgil Earp shouted, "Throw up your hands, I want your guns!" Frank McLaury and Billy Clanton moved to draw and cock their six-shooters. Virgil yelled, "Hold! I don't mean that!" but it was too late and the shooting began.

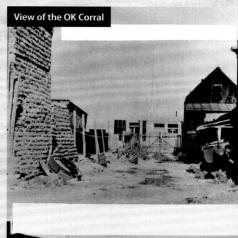

View of the OK Corral

2 Not OK

The location of the shootout at the OK Corral was actually not directly at the building, but in a narrow lot six doors west of its rear entrance. When the Earps and the Clanton gang ▮▮▮ off, they were only about 6 feet from each other.

5 McLaury gunned down

A chaotic exchange of gunfire occurred, with Billy Clanton shooting Morgan Earp across the back, wounding his shoulder, and he himself being hit in the wrist. Frank McLaury exc▮▮▮▮ some shots with Doc Holliday but was shot through the head and killed instantly.

WANTED
The outlaws marked for death

WILLIAM "CURLY BILL" BROCIUS 1845-82

A violent criminal, cattle rustler, and assassin, Curly Bill was the leader of the outlaws responsible for the murder of Wyatt Earp's brother Morgan. He was known as "Arizona's most famous outlaw" and spent most of his time leading up to the vendetta ride robbing stagecoaches and threatening rivals with a bloody death.

PETE SPENCE 1852-1914

Pete Spence was a well-known outlaw in Arizona, robbing stagecoaches and rustling cattle. He was a friend and business partner of fellow outlaw and killer Frank Stilwell, who, along with Spence, was a key suspect in the assassination of Morgan Earp.

FRANK C. STILWELL 1856-82

A miner and livery stable owner who was known to partake in illegal activities, Stilwell was famously identified as one of the outlaws who had ambushed and murdered Morgan Earp. Lack of evidence saw Stilwell walk free of any punishment, placing him high up on Wyatt Earp's vendetta kill list.

The gang made their way back to Tombstone, but back in Tucson the remains of Stilwell had been discovered and his killing linked to the Earp posse. Tucson Justice of the Peace Charles Meyer issued arrest warrants for all five members of the posse and sent a telegram back to Tombstone, stating that Sheriff Behan should arrest them. What Meyer couldn't have known, however, was that the telegraph office manager was a friend to the Earp family and upon receiving the telegram, showed it to Wyatt when he rode into town.

The gunslinger knew that if Behan saw the telegram, he would try to stop the vendetta posse in its tracks, so he began preparing a quick exit. But Behan had rushed to the hotel and found the men he was looking for in the lobby, heavily armed and about to leave. Walking straight up to Wyatt he told him that he was to accompany him back to the sheriff's office. Wyatt ignored him and walked outside.

They were met outside the hotel by further members of the posse, John "Texas Jack" Vermillion and Dan "Tip" Tipton, Charlie Smith, Fred Dodge, Johnny Green, and Lou Cooley. Continuing to ignore an increasingly irate Behan, they saddled up and rode out of Tombstone.

The following morning, on March 22, Wyatt rode into Spence's woodcamp in the South Pass of the Dragoon Mountains. A quick inspection of the area revealed that Spence wasn't there – in fact, he had become so paranoid that Wyatt was

> ## "As Wyatt pressed down on Cruz's wound with his spurred boot, a scream curdled out of Cruz into the pass and he shouted the names of the killers"

Wyatt's boyhood home

OK Corral casualties – Tom and Frank McLaury and Billy Clanton in their coffin after being killed at the famous gunfight

A photo of Wyatt Earp, circa 1882

going to kill him that he had handed himself in to Behan's custody for protection. Wyatt was unaware of this and so decided to make one final search of the premises to make sure Spence wasn't hiding like the coward he knew he was. He suddenly saw movement, a figure running out to the rear and diving into the scrub. It wasn't Spence though, it was Florentino "Indian Charlie" Cruz, Spence's right-hand man.

Wyatt drew his pistol but couldn't get a clear shot, so he called for his men. Holliday, McMaster, and Johnson were the fastest, drawing and firing from multiple positions at the fleeing Cruz, who was hit simultaneously in the arm, thigh, and pelvis, bringing him crashing into the dust. Cruz's cries of anguish echoed throughout the pass as he started to bleed out, all the time attempting to crawl into cover. Wyatt was on him quick as a flash though and Cruz started begging for his life. When questioned about the assassination of Morgan, he confessed that he had been the lookout. As Wyatt pressed down on Cruz's wound with his spurred boot, a

A Desperate Fight Between Officers of the Law and Cow-boys—The Killed and Wounded—Failure of Lord & Williams.

TOMBSTONE, A. T., October 26th.—This morning the City Marshal, V. W. Earp, arrested a cow-boy named Ike Clanton, for disorderly conduct, and he was fined twenty-five dollars and disarmed in the Justices' Court. Clanton left, swearing vengeance on the Sheriff and Marshal Earp and his brother Morgan who tried to induce Claxton to

The gunfight at the OK Corral made the news

HUNTING A LAWMAN
The sheriff chasing down Wyatt Earp

A key player not just in Wyatt Earp's vendetta ride but also the famous shootout at the OK Corral, Johnny Behan was the sheriff of Cochise County in Arizona Territory during both. After the climactic gunfight at the Corral, Behan famously testified against the Earp family, saying they precipitated the shootout and therefore murdered three outlaw cowboys in the encounter. The Earps were later exonerated, however, and so started a bitter feud between them and Behan.

While he was known to think himself a model of law and order, Behan in fact had a checkered life, with his wife leaving him in June 1875 for taking a mistress and sleeping with prostitutes. He was also particularly violent towards women, threatening them consistently, both verbally and physically. Behan also liked to associate and deal with known outlaws while off official business, dealing with cowboys such as Ike Clanton, Johnny Ringo, and William Brocius, all three who were instrumental in the maiming of Virgil Earp and the murder of Morgan Earp.

Following Behan's famous confrontation with Wyatt Earp in the Cosmopolitan Hotel, Tombstone, and then failed pursuit of Wyatt and his vendetta posse, Behan fell into another feud with his own deputy Billy Breakenridge. Breakenridge accused Behan of misappropriation of illegal monies and after an investigation Behan was shown to have set aside $5,000 from unknown sources while sheriff. While Behan escaped jail, he failed to be renominated as sheriff of Cochise County and was stripped of his rank and authority months after Wyatt left the state.

Behan was stripped of his rank soon after the Wyatt's vendetta ride

LAW AND ORDER – WILD WEST STYLE
Was there any system of justice in the American Old West?

The American frontier was huge and there was no standardized law enforcement agency keeping control in the Wild West. As such, criminals found many opportunities to rob pioneer families, while what law there was found it difficult to track them down and bring them in, let alone provide concrete evidence that would see them sentenced in court. It was this system that infamous cowboys such as Jesse James, Billy the Kid, and Butch Cassidy thrived.

The result of this lawlessness and lack of authority led to many people taking the law into their own hands – as evident by Wyatt Earp's vendetta ride – with the law's apparent impotence to combat outlaws driving them to take extreme measures. This led to a culture of feuds, bounties, and vengeance killings, with rival groups taking turns to avenge each other's latest illegal act. The natural conclusion of this ramshackle tit-for-tat system of justice was that it often led to violence for mere perceived threats, rather than real acts of criminality. The end point for anyone successfully apprehended by law or outlaw was death, typically by shooting or hanging.

Further, the line between legal and illegal, good and bad, justified and cruel, was blurred in

A horse thief being hanged in the American Old West

the Old West, with outlaws in one state perceived as respected lawmen in the next. Sheriffs, who are often depicted in films as bastions of honor and virtue, were often ex-outlaws themselves who had gained their position through violence and threats, ruling their territory like Medieval barons. It was only when the USA became developed enough to establish a true federal system of law and order in the late 19th century that crimes like horse stealing, highway robbery, duelling, and cattle rustling were effectively combated.

scream curdled out of Cruz into the pass and he shouted the names of the killers. William "Curly Bill" Brocius. Frank Stilwell. Hank Swilling. Johnny Ringo. As he said each name, a death sentence was passed on them.

Cruz started shouting that Wyatt had got what he wanted and he should leave him alive and send him back to Tombstone. There was only one place Wyatt was going to send Cruz – straight to hell. Drawing his pistol, he placed it to the side of the assassin's head and, punctuated only by a final scream from Cruz, pulled the trigger. A single trail of gunsmoke from his pistol rose slowly into the air. One down, three to go.

So, it had been Brocius who had orchestrated the murder. He should have known that his old enemy from the OK Corral was the mastermind behind his family's enduring misery. Wyatt and his posse saddled up their mounts and headed straight for Brocious' old prowling ground, the Whetstone Mountains.

The posse searched the surrounding area for the next two days, to no avail, eventually arriving at Iron Springs in the Whetstone Mountains. The area looked to be empty when they stumbled onto a group of cowboys cooking dinner alongside the spring. It took only a split-second for Wyatt to identify Brocius and in a heartbeat he dismounted from his horse, grabbed his

Before he became a lawman, Wyatt Earp was one of the co-owners of the Oriental Saloon

shotgun and burst around a ridge and down into the men's camp with Texas Jack, Doc Holliday and McMaster hot on his heels. Wyatt walked toward purposefully Brocius, his long trench coat flapping behind him in the wind.

Panic broke loose in the camp, with the outlaws all scrambling for their weapons. Like a

rattlesnake, Brocius weaved to his own shotgun and turned and fired at the advancing Wyatt, but missed the avenging town marshal. Texas Jack drew his dual pistols and began firing at the outlaws. Brocius' men fired back, rounds hitting Wyatt's coat and even Texas Jack's horse, which was killed instantly. Doc Holliday, McMaster and

MAP OF THE VENDETTA RIDE
Follow the key events of Wyatt's vendetta ride

MEXICO

1. Frank Stilwell taken out in Tucson
After escorting his recovering brother Virgil to Tucson so that he and his wife could leave the state for their own safety, Earp intercepts would-be assassin Frank Stilwell and kills him in the Tucson train yard.

7. Curly Bill taken out
"Curly Bill" Brocius is discovered twenty miles west of Tombstone with his gang. After an intense firefight, Brocius is gunned down by Wyatt. His other men are either shot or flee the scene.

GULF OF CALIFORNIA

ARIZONA

5. Florentino executed in the South Pass
Traveling to Pete Spence's wood camp in the South Pass of the Dragoon Mountains in search of the murderer, Wyatt and his posse discover his accomplice instead, Florentino "Indian Charlie" Cruz. Cruz, after confessing who was behind Morgan's murder, is executed by Wyatt.

Phoenix

6. Outlaws tracked to Whetstone Mountains
Wyatt, now aware that Morgan's murder had been orchestrated by "Curly Bill" Brocius, starts what a two-day search of the Whetstone Mountains, known stomping ground of the outlaw.

Tucson

4. Behan deputizes a rival posse
Sheriff Behan, whose long-standing feud with Wyatt had just been made worse by Wyatt's casual dismissal of him as he left town, takes pleasure in assembling his own rival posse to bring him and his men in and sets off in pursuit.

NEW MEXICO

9. Vendetta posse breaks up
In early April 1882, Wyatt Earp's posse head east out of Arizona, stopping in Silver City, New Mexico, and then Albuquerque. None of them are ever seen in Tombstone, Arizona again.

8. Wyatt seeks refuge
Wanted by Behan's posse for a growing number of killings, the Earp posse seek refuge and end up at the Sierra Bonita ranch of wealthy and prominent rancher Henry C. Hooker.

Silver City

3. Vendetta posse leaves Tombstone
Wyatt takes the law into his own hands, deputizing a posse. He ignores Sheriff Behan's repeated attempts to bring him in for the Stilwell shooting.

Tombstone

2. The law fails the Earps
Returning to Tombstone, Wyatt watches outlaw cowboys Pete Spence, Frank Stilwell, and Florentino Cruz escape from the law.

An illustration of Wyatt Earp winning a duel in Dodge City

"Like a rattlesnake, Brocius weaved to his own shotgun and turned and fired at the advancing Wyatt, but missed"

Johnson moved to cover and started shooting while Texas Jack dashed to his fallen horse in an attempt to retrieve his rifle.

During the chaos, Wyatt had never taken his eyes off Brocius and calmly advanced on him. Time slowed and Wyatt raized his shotgun, aimed directly at Brocius at point-blank range, and watched as the killer of his brother was blown in two. Seeing their leader dead, the rest of Brocius' party fled, but not before Wyatt had continued his vengeful rampage by killing Johnny Barnes with a gunshot round to the chest and wounding Milt Hicks with another shot.

The rest of Wyatt Earp's vendetta ride ran its course in the only way it could. Wanted by the law, Wyatt and his posse could not return to Tombstone. As such, after making a couple of stops at safe houses, most of the group headed east out of Arizona, riding out of the state with the Sun on their backs. Behan never did catch them and after arriving in Albuquerque, New Mexico, they went their separate ways. Vengeance had been delivered with a efficiency and brutality that would permanently affect the lives of all the men involved and cement their reputation as legendary figures. Justice – Wild West style – had been served.

10 DEADLIEST GUNSLINGERS IN THE WEST

JAMES "WILD BILL" HICKOK
1837-76

Wild Bill Hickok – real name James Butler Hickok – was the best sharpshooter and gunfighter of his day. Famously, Hickok was involved in the first-ever recorded quick-draw duel, with him gunning down a gambler called Davis Tutt Jr. in the town square of Springfield, Missouri. Hickok is also recorded as shooting an outlaw called David McCanles with a single bullet from 225 feet away – quite a remarkable achievement with the pistols of that time.

KILLS: 36

Did he ride off into the sunset? Hickok was shot through the back of the head by gambler Jack McCall while playing five-card draw at Nuttal & Mann's Saloon in Deadwood, Dakota Territory.

BILLY THE KID
1859-81

The gunslinger – real name William H. Bonney – killed many men during his short lifetime, with many saying it was twenty-one;, one kill for each year of his life. Often depicted as a bloodthirsty raving killer of a man, surviving testimony from people who knew him said in reality he just repeatedly ended up on the wrong side of the tracks, killing other men who were worse than himself. Regardless, due to his excellent marksmanship and wily nature, Billy became infamous across the USA, something only exacerbated by a daring escape from jail and years spent on the run.

KILLS: 15-26

Did he ride off into the sunset? Bonney was shot dead by Sheriff Pat Garrett on July 14, 1881.

> "Within one year, Stoudenmire had killed six men in shootouts and executed a would-be assassin"

JOHN WESLEY HARDIN
1853-95

Hardin had his first kill registered at the tender age of fifteen, and his life consisted of a series of run-ins with outlaws and lawmen alike. While Hardin was known as a good shot, it was his cunning in combat that earned him a deadly reputation, often killing men after confrontations in cold-blooded, unseen ways. His most famous kill was Sheriff John Helms on August 1, 1873. Hardin was eventually captured and spent seventeen years in Huntsville Prison before being released on February 17, 1894.

KILLS: 27-42

Did he ride off into the sunset? Hardin was shot through the back of the head in the Acme Saloon, Texas, by lawman John Selman Sr. on August 19, 1895.

KING FISHER
1854-84

Fisher was a celebrated gunslinger, racking up double-digit kills by the age of thirty. He was known to carry twin ivory-handled pistols and to dress in bright-colored clothes. His most memorable trait, though, was his brutality in combat. The most famous example of this was in his fight with a rival bunch of Mexican cowboys, clubbing one to death with a branding iron, outdrawing and shooting another and then executing the remaining two.

KILLS: 14

Did he ride off into the sunset? Fisher was shot thirteen times at a theater in San Antonio, Texas, in a revenge killing.

TOM HORN
1860-1903

Horn was at one time a lawman, scout, soldier, hired gunman, assassin, and outlaw, fluidly shifting from one side of the law to the other. During his eventful life, Horn reportedly garnered fame for his tracking abilities, bringing many outlaws to justice and then, once his appetite for blood became too problematic – he was linked to the unlawful murder of seventeen people – he had to turn to mercenary work, fulfilling contract killings with brutal efficiency. His legacy of murder only came to a close when he was captured after his killing of a fourteen-year-old boy in 1901.

KILLS: 35-50

Did he ride off into the sunset? Horn was captured, tried, and hanged in Cheyenne, Wyoming, on November 20, 1903.

JESSE JAMES
1847-82

Along with his brother Frank, Jesse led a gang that robbed banks, trains, and stagecoaches. Before turning to crime, Jesse had been a guerilla fighter in the Confederate Army, but when the Union triumphed in the American Civil War, he was left disenchanted. James famously shot a clerk while holding up the Daviess County Savings Association bank in Gallatin, Missouri, living permanently on the run along with his gang from the event until his death. After James' death, rumors spread that he had survived, but there is no evidence to suggest this was true. Frank James, on the other hand, slipped the noose, living to the age of seventy-two and dying years later in 1915.

KILLS: 1-5

Did he ride off into the sunset? James was shot through the back of the head by fellow outlaw Robert Ford – who hoped to cash in on his bounty – on April 3, 1882.

CHEROKEE BILL
1876-96

The outlaw actually named Crawford Goldsby was known for his fast and itchy trigger finger. In a period of two years from the age of eighteen, Bill along with his gang robbed, pillaged, maimed, and killed anyone who stood in their way, with Goldsby earning the reputation of one of the meanest outlaws of the Old West. Goldsby even shot and killed his own brother-in-law Mose Brown in an argument over a simple bunch of hogs. Despite the terror he inflicted, two years later he was caught and imprisoned, later going on to hang for his various crimes.

KILLS: 7

Did he ride off into the sunset? At the age of just twenty, Goldsby was hanged as a convicted murderer at Fort Smith, Arkansas.

JIM "KILLER" MILLER
1866-1909

Legend has it that Miller survived more duels than any other person. The most famous duel was with Pecos Sheriff George A. "Bud" Frazer, where Miller was set on by Frazer and shot four times in the chest. His gang rushed him to a doctor where it was revealed he had been wearing a steel plate under his clothes across his chest, which saved his life. Two years later, he tracked Frazer down and executed him with a shotgun.

KILLS: 14

Did he ride off into the sunset? Miller was dragged from prison and hanged by a lynch mob on April 19, 1909.

ROBERT CLAY ALLISON
1840-87

While Allison did not rack up the largest body count in the Old West, the way in which he killed was brutal. Allison cut the head off a man and displayed it on a pole outside a saloon, hung another publicly after gunning him down over a minor disagreement, and executed many others with point-blank headshots. On January 7, 1874, Allison accepted an invitation to eat with a known gunman called Chunk Colbert, despite knowing that Colbert was trying to kill him. While eating the meal, Colbert tried to draw on Allison, however he was too slow and shot through the head by Clay.

KILLS: 6

Did he ride off into the sunset? Allison fell from a wagon and broke his neck on July 3, 1887.

DALLAS STOUDENMIRE
1845-82

Stoudenmire was one of the most feared gunslingers of his day, with him ruling the rough and violent city of El Paso, Texas, with an iron fist. Shortly after arriving in El Paso, Stoudenmire would be involved in one of the most famous gunfights of the American Old West – the Four Dead in Five Seconds shootout. Within one year, Stoudenmire had killed six men in shootouts and executed a would-be assassin – the latter sent to the grave with eight gunshot wounds.

KILLS: 10

Did he ride off into the sunset? His luck ran out in 1882 when he was killed in a shootout.

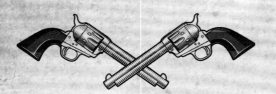

GANGSTERS & THE MOB

78

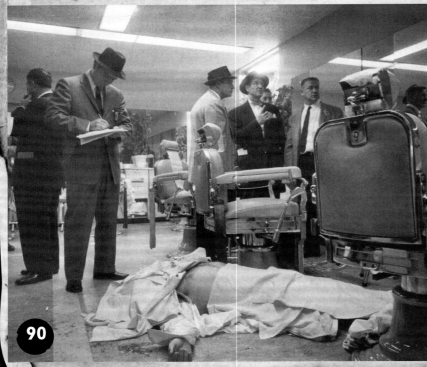

90

56

PUBLIC ENEMIES
AMERICA'S MOST WANTED

The Crime Wave made celebrities of America's outlaws. They robbed, kidnapped, and killed their way across America, lived fast, and died young.

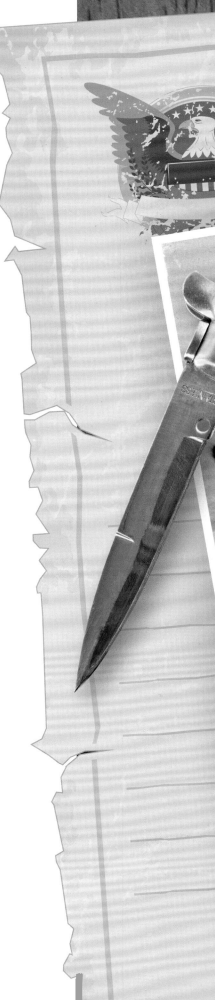

The early 1930s brought chaos and crisis to America. 1929's Wall Street Crash created the Depression. Prohibition was intended to inaugurate a new, clean-living era, but instead it handed America's alcohol business entirely to gangsters. Racketeers made millions while thousands died from toxic homemade booze. Gangsters and citizens alike died in droves as rival crime-lords battled for supremacy.

The Roaring Twenties also created a different breed of gangster. Racketeers like Al Capone concentrated on gambling, bootlegging, extortion, drugs, and prostitution. The "yeggs" or "yeggmen" ripped through state after state robbing, kidnapping, and killing almost at will. An Indiana bank one morning, an Illinois kidnapping that afternoon. The authorities seemed powerless to stop them.

Some, like Bonnie and Clyde, were responding to poverty and desperation. For John Dillinger, it was a profession. For criminals like

Lester Gillis, a.k.a. "Baby Face" Nelson, it was a lucrative way to punish a society they despised. Almost all their lives were short, their ends seldom merry. Most would end their days in prison or a hail of lead.

The Old West outlaws had been content with their six-shooters, Winchester rifles, shotguns and horses. Yeggs, however, had much better tools. Revolvers were largely replaced by automatic pistols. The Winchester gave way to the Tommy gun and Browning Automatic Rifle. Bulletproof vests were fashionable and horses were replaced by cars, which were much faster. Sawn-off shotguns, however, remained popular. America had never seen such outlaws. Never again would they wreak such havoc and bring so much slaughter.

But the Crime Wave certainly wasn't an isolated event – nor even necessarily an event in its own right. The period between 1920 and 1935 could instead be considered as the Golden Age of lawlessness and the Crime Wave merely

> **Some gangsters like Sam "Samoots" Amatuna really did carry Tommy guns in violin cases**

its crescendo. It wasn't the most violent period of history, merely the most publicized. The new breed included Bonnie and Clyde, John Dillinger, the Barker-Karpis Gang, Charles "Pretty Boy" Floyd and, "Baby Face" Nelson.

Some, like Ma Barker and Bonnie and Clyde, were portrayed as being criminal masterminds they definitely weren't. Others, like John Dillinger, were natural criminals wanting easy money and lasting fame. Born without money or connections, they were people for whom the American Dream would remain exactly that without drastic action. While handing America's booze business to the underworld, Prohibition did something far worse – it inspired in many Americans a complete disrespect for the law. Some almost considered it their duty to drink illegally. The Prohibition era recast gangsters, especially bootleggers, from public enemies to public servants.

Meanwhile, an economic meltdown left millions destitute. As it worsened, banks foreclosed loans, bankrupted businesses, and repossessed homes. Many people saw bankers as natural enemies and outlaws as heroes. If nothing else, people like Dillinger were seen as honest crooks unlike the bankers they robbed. That and their media-friendly exploits entranced a population desperately wanting entertainment. Dillinger's mentor Harry Pierpont, when tried for murder, bluntly told the prosecutor, "I'm not like some bank robbers, I didn't get myself elected president of the bank first." Millions of Americans felt the same. Some, broke and desperate, decided to act.

Dillinger was one of them. He bore a grudge against the law after mugging a shopkeeper in 1924. Offered leniency by the judge in return for a guilty plea, Dillinger drew between nine and twenty years. Convinced the law was out to get him, he used his time learning a more lucrative craft – armed robbery. Paroled from Indiana State Penitentiary in May 1933, Dillinger had learned from some of the toughest yeggs around. Pierpont, Ed Shouse, Russell Clark, Walter Dietrich, and Charles Makley were all seasoned pros. Fellow alumnus Homer van Meter joined them later. In return for their joining the first Dillinger Gang, Dillinger arranged their escape. Robberies provided the money and guns were smuggled into the prison. On September 26, 1933, ten inmates escaped and the first Dillinger Gang was ready to go.

Dillinger, however, had been arrested the previous day. Springing him in Lima, Ohio, on October 12, Pierpont murdered Sheriff Jess Sarber. After robberies in Wisconsin, Illinois, Ohio, Indiana, and Dillinger's first murder (Patrolman William O'Malley), the gang fled for Florida and then Arizona. It proved a bad idea; in Tucson, the gang was recognized and arrested in January 1934. Dillinger was extradited to Indiana's "escape-proof" Crown Point Jail for murdering O'Malley. Pierpont, Clark, and Makley went to Ohio for murdering Sheriff Sarber. Both states had the electric chair and fully intended to use it.

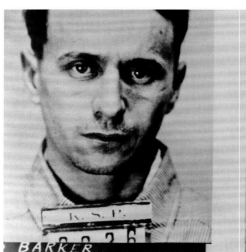
"Baby Face" Nelson killed three FBI agents, still the record number killed by a single felon

Dillinger didn't stay long. A smuggled pistol and sheer bravado saw him escape on March 3. Stealing Sheriff Lillian Holley's car, he headed for Chicago. It proved a fatal mistake. No matter what Dillinger did, the FBI couldn't intervene until he committed a federal crime, much to their frustration. Driving a stolen car across a state line invited the G-Men to enter the fray. Hoover immediately put a $15,000 bounty and shoot-to-kill order on Dillinger.

Dillinger soon formed a new gang. Homer van Meter, Tommy Carroll, and John "Red" Hamilton joined him. So too did the notorious "Baby Face" Nelson. No gang member liked or trusted Nelson. They feared his hair-trigger temper and resented his ego. Van Meter had feuded with Pierpont and now he feuded with Nelson.

The "G-Men" hunting him were mainly law graduates and accountants, mostly without any policing experience. It showed in their pursuit of Dillinger, which was at times farcical. That said, they were still learning their craft against seasoned career criminals, and learning fast. Epic blunders like their chaotic raid on Wisconsin's Little Bohemia Lodge on April 22, 1934 were harsh lessons, but necessary.

The gang escaped Little Bohemia, Nelson murdering one FBI agent and wounding another. Three innocent bystanders were shot. With every failure, the Bureau was increasingly humiliated but even more determined to destroy Dillinger. The tide of public opinion had also started turning. Van Meter, Carroll, and Hamilton fell in gunfights, one after another. At Mason City, Iowa, in March 1934, bystanders attacked the gang and Dillinger was wounded. At South Bend, Indiana, on June 30, bystanders again attacked them. This time, Nelson went berserk even for him, spraying bullets in all directions. Several bystanders were wounded and one police officer, Howard Wagner, was shot dead. It was their last heist. The Dillinger Gang then scattered, never to reform. Dillinger himself had only weeks to live.

The gang leader's end came in Chicago, somewhere he visited regularly. Too regularly, as it turned out. Calling himself Jimmy Lawrence, Dillinger lived quietly. He was often at Chicago's cinemas and regularly visited local brothel madam Ana Cumpănaș (alias "Anna Sage"). Cumpănaș knew his true identity and, facing deportation to Romania for brothel-keeping, had cut a deal with FBI inspector Sam Cowley. July 22, 1934 would be John Dillinger's last picture show.

Sage and employee Polly Hamilton visited the Biograph Theater with Dillinger to watch *Manhattan Melodrama*. A gangster movie starring Clark Gable, it ends with Gable's character facing the electric chair. Acting on Sage's tip-off, FBI agents planned a similar end for Dillinger. Sage wore an orange dress that evening for easy identification, and as the trio left the Biograph, agents moved in.

Dillinger, realizing he'd been betrayed, ran. Agents Clarence Hurt and Charles Winstead immediately opened fire and Dillinger was shot dead. Amid the chaos, bystanders, realizing what they'd just witnessed, claimed souvenirs by dipping handkerchiefs in his blood. The notorious public enemy was gone.

Pierpont and Makley didn't last much longer. Condemned, they tried escaping the Death

Ma Barker and son Fred were killed in Florida in January 1935. Ma's influence on the gang is staggeringly overstated

BARKER

KATE BARKER

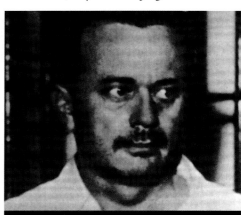
Arthur "Dock" Barker joined Karpis at Alcatraz. He was shot dead attempting to escape the Rock in 1939

House at Ohio State Penitentiary in September 1934. Makley was shot dead and Pierpont crippled. He was carried to the electric chair on October 17, only days after his thirty-second birthday. Nelson, whose violent nature guaranteed his early death, became Public Enemy Number One after Pretty Boy Floyd was killed by FBI agents on October 20, 1934. He reigned for only a month before the FBI killed him, too, on November 27.

Dillinger was perhaps the most infamous public enemy, but only one of many. The Barker-Karpis Gang was equally vicious without the enduring infamy. Barker brothers Arthur and Fred, with Fred Goetz, Volney Davis, Bryan Bolton, and their probable leader Alvin "Creepy" Karpis committed a string of armed robberies and murders. According to the director of the FBI, J. Edgar Hoover, they were led by Kate "Ma" Barker, who taught them every form of violent crime. According to most more objective sources, though, Hoover used her as a scapegoat to explain FBI agents killing her and Fred in Florida in 1935. As fellow yegg Harvey Bailey put it, "That old woman couldn't plan breakfast."

Like Dillinger and the Barrow Gang, they exploited fast cars, automatic weapons, bulletproof vests, inexperienced FBI agents, and crossing state lines to evade capture. Unlike the others, they were also kidnappers, demanding large cash ransoms on pain of death. Raized in Tulsa, Oklahoma, the Barkers were all juvenile delinquents and petty crooks. Ma always proclaimed their innocence and obstructed efforts to catch them, but it's highly unlikely that she was anything more than a willing accomplice and no evidence exists of her active participation. Very few sources support Hoover's assertion.

Between 1932 and 1936, the Barker-Karpis Gang robbed banks, post offices, and payrolls, stealing several hundred thousand dollars. They

WANTED

JOHN HERBERT DILLINGER

On June 23, 1934, HOMER S. CUMMINGS, Attorney General of the United States, under the authority vested in him by an Act of Congress approved June 6, 1934, offered a reward of

$10,000.00

for the capture of John Herbert Dillinger or a reward of

$5,000.00

for information leading to the arrest of John Herbert Dillinger.

DESCRIPTION

Age, 32 years; Height, 5 feet 7-1/8 inches; Weight, 153 pounds; Build, medium; Hair, medium chestnut; Eyes, grey; Complexion, medium; Occupation, machinist; Marks and scars, 1/2 inch scar back left hand, scar middle upper lip, brown mole between eyebrows.

All claims to any of the aforesaid rewards and all questions and disputes that may arise as among claimants to the foregoing rewards shall be passed upon by the Attorney General and his decisions shall be final and conclusive. The right is reserved to divide and allocate portions of any of said rewards as between several claimants. No part of the aforesaid rewards shall be paid to any official or employee of the Department of Justice.

If you are in possession of any information concerning the whereabouts of John Herbert Dillinger, communicate immediately by telephone or telegraph collect to the nearest office of the Division of Investigation, United States Department of Justice, the local addresses of which are set forth on the reverse side of this notice.

June 25, 1934

JOHN EDGAR HOOVER, DIRECTOR,
DIVISION OF INVESTIGATION,
UNITED STATES DEPARTMENT OF JUSTICE,
WASHINGTON, D. C.

Dillinger's infamy left him the most notorious man in America, wanted in seven states and by the FBI.

Lester Gillis, a.k.a. "Baby Face" Nelson. Homicidal Gillis happily killed for killing's sake. No brutality was off limits to him.

Henry Methvin, last of the Barrow Gang. His father Ivy assisted Bonnie and Clyde's ambush to protect his son

also committed numerous murders, including suspected informants and gang members considered untrustworthy. In 1935, Karpis even robbed a train in Garretsville, Ohio, and Chicago's Federal Reserve Bank netted a big score in September 1933. Their largest robbery was in Concordia, Kansas, in 1932, taking $240,000.

They earned considerably more from kidnapping. In Minneapolis, Minnesota, they abducted brewery heir William Hamm on June 15, 1933. The $100,000 was quickly paid, securing Hamm's release. The kidnapping occurred only two days before the Kansas City Massacre, which boosted Hoover's efforts to make the FBI credible crime-fighters.

On January 17, 1934, the day after Clyde's Eastham Prison raid, the Barkers abducted Edward Bremer, manager of the Jacob Schmidt Brewing Company, demanding $200,000. Coming so soon after 1932's Lindbergh

Safe Havens: A Gangster's Paradise

Crossing state lines was one way to evade capture. Constant movement was another. Gangsters with money and connections had another option: safe havens operated by corrupt cops, politicians, and local gangsters. If they could afford steep fees they could live, openly and unmolested, in towns where cops were as crooked as robbers.

Hot Springs, Arkansas was effectively a gangster's paradise run by transplanted New York gangster Owny "The Killer" Madden. With Madden's approval, fugitives could live there in peace unless federal agents found them. Local police were largely on Madden's payroll, even chief detective "Dutch" Akers.

St. Paul, Minnesota was run by Harry Sawyer out of his notorious "Green Lantern" tavern. Gangsters like Dillinger and the Barker-Karpis Gang lived there quite openly. Through Sawyer and corrupt police and politicians, fugitives knew the deal – if they paid up and committed no crimes within or near St. Paul, they had little to worry about.

Joplin, Missouri was equally notorious, although less attractive following the Barrow Gang's shootout there in April 1933. Joplin's arrangement wasn't as formal as those of St. Paul or Hot Springs. The risk of honest police actually policing the town made it less of a safe haven.

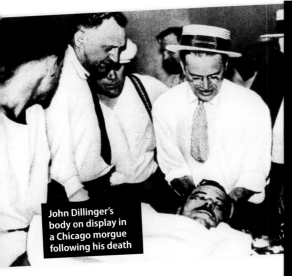
John Dillinger's body on display in a Chicago morgue following his death

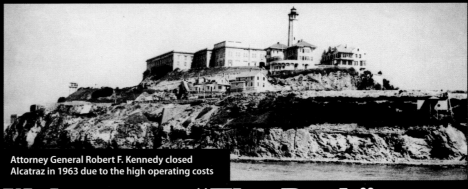
Attorney General Robert F. Kennedy closed Alcatraz in 1963 due to the high operating costs

kidnapping and almost coinciding with Eastham and Kansas City, the Barker-Karpis Gang found themselves hunted everywhere.

Regular robberies increased their take and their mounting body count. Heists, shootouts, and murders in North Dakota, Minnesota, Kansas, Illinois, Nebraska, Missouri, New Jersey, and Ohio cost over a dozen lives. When Karpis was finally captured in New Orleans in April 1936, he was accused of committing at least nine murders personally and implicated in at least sixteen. If captured, they risked execution in at least seven states.

The gang was ruthless in killing police officers and sometimes bystanders, but they were perhaps most ruthless towards their own accomplices. Underworld doctor Joseph Moran and gang member Arthur Dunlap died as suspected informers. The gang was fully prepared to kill even their own if they came under suspicion.

Law enforcement was equally ruthless – especially the FBI. Every public enemy caught or killed was grist to Hoover's mill and the Barker-Karpis Gang was no exception. Hoover's publicity machine trumpeted FBI successes as loudly as

Welcome to "The Rock"

Originally a fort and military prison, Alcatraz opened in August 1934 as America's first supermax penitentiary. Alvin Karpis, George "Machine Gun" Kelly, Al Capone, Arthur "Dock" Barker, and many others served time there. Perhaps its most famous inmate was murderer Robert Stroud, also known as the "Birdman of Alcatraz."

Alcatraz offered only maximum security, minimum privileges, and harsh discipline. Minor infractions earned ordinary solitary confinement in D Block, and serious infractions earned complete darkness in cells nicknamed "The Dark Hole" without even a bed. In its early years,

underground dungeons were used, prisoners sometimes chained to their damp, cold, dark walls and beaten with knuckledusters and blackjacks.

Alcatraz's regime was intended expressly to break inmates. Regardless of notoriety, inmates' mugshots didn't have names, just numbers. They gained nothing by conforming, but suffered for disobedience. Between 1934 and 1938, under the "silent system," even talking without permission earned solitary confinement.

Dozens went mad – in the early years, over thirty inmates were certified and suicide wasn't unusual. The sustained mental cruelty probably caused

the "Battle of Alcatraz" in 1946, a failed escape-turned-bloodbath. Three inmates and one guard died while eleven inmates and guards were injured and two inmates, Miran Thompson and Sam Shockley, were executed.

A penal failure and financial sinkhole, Alcatraz was finally closed on March 21, 1963. While the prison had been open, thirty-six inmates had made fourteen escape attempts, twenty-three were caught, six shot dead, two drowned, and five went missing, presumed drowned. Today it's Northern California's most popular tourist attraction, receiving over 1 million visitors a year.

"Pretty Boy" Floyd, one of the last public enemies. Implicated in 1933's Kansas City Massacre, Floyd died in questionable circumstances

possible. Slain gangsters made for good column inches and newsreels, the bodies of Dillinger and Pretty Boy Floyd being publicly displayed. The Barker-Karpis Gang was luckier than most. Most were taken alive with the notable controversial exceptions of Fred and Ma.

In January 1935, they were tracked to a secluded house near Oklawaha, Florida. The shootout lasted several hours with Ma and Fred fighting even after tear gas was fired through the windows. When police and FBI agents finally entered the building, Ma and Fred were both dead. Hoover claimed Ma had died shooting beside her son. This has always been fiercely debated, with Hoover being accused of lying to increase public support for his Bureau.

Ma and Fred went to their graves. Surprisingly, most of the gang went to prison. Arthur "Dock" Barker was captured in Chicago in January 1935 with Bryan Bolton. Dock died in 1939 trying to escape Alcatraz. Also on the Rock was Bill Weaver, who died of a heart attack in 1944. Volney Davis and Harry Campbell served decades before their release and disappearance into obscurity.

The last to be caught was Alvin Karpis. By then, the G-Men were mopping up the last of

Armour-piercing "cop killer" bullets like the Super .38 and .357 Magnum were originally invented for cops to use against robbers

America's public enemies and Karpis' arrest in New Orleans in April 1936 was even marked by the personal appearance of FBI chief J. Edgar Hoover himself. Stung by political criticism of his never having personally arrested anyone, and with his fitness to run the Bureau being questioned, Hoover claimed that he personally arrested Karpis. But Karpis disagreed, stating that Hoover actually only appeared after agents had detained and disarmed him. As he later put it: "If that version of my arrest is any criteria, you know, as to the contents of this book, oh boy, they should put it right on a shelf for fairytales."

Karpis rejoined the remaining gang members in Alcatraz in 1936, serving twenty-six years there and becoming its longest-serving inmate. Transferred to McNeil Island, he was finally released in 1969 after thirty-three years of imprisonment. Harvey Bailey went to Alcatraz in August 1933. He was in prison until 1965.

By 1936, the public enemies were effectively finished, most of them imprisoned or dead. It's a measure of their enduring status that the FBI Academy shooting range is still haunted by one. Targets used by today's trainees still bear the face of a former Public Enemy Number One and celebrity gangster – John Dillinger.

HUNTING THE PUBLIC ENEMIES

Hoover transformed the FBI, running it as though it was his personal fiefdom

J. Edgar Hoover

Hoover transformed the FBI (then the Bureau of Investigation) from a ramshackle, corrupt, incompetent organization into the institution it is today. Using Scotland Yard as a template, Hoover was a feared disciplinarian, firing agents for the slightest infraction. He wasn't always liked by politicians or even his own agents.

Frank Hamer (top left) led the six-man ambush posse that finally ended Bonnie and Clyde's career

Frank Hamer

The archetypal Texas Ranger, Hamer had a sharp mind and a fast gun. Active between 1905 and 1932, he came out of retirement specifically to hunt Bonnie and Clyde after the Eastham prison break in January 1934. They were the fifty-third and fifty-fourth felons Hamer killed during his career.

"By 1936 the public enemies were finished"

Purvis (left) with FBI Director Hoover. Once Hoover's favorite, he fell out of favor with his long-time boss

Melvin Purvis

An FBI agent since 1927, Purvis hunted Dillinger, Baby Face Nelson, and Pretty Boy Floyd. He was accused of brutal interrogations and feuded with Hoover after Dillinger's death. He was also accused of ordering agent Ed Hollis to shoot Floyd after he'd been wounded and disarmed. Purvis resigned in 1935

Cowley (left) and "Ed" Hollis (right) were killed by Nelson at the Battle of Barrington. Nelson died hours later

Samuel Cowley

Cowley arranged Anna Sage's betrayal of Dillinger and was one of three FBI agents murdered by Baby Face Nelson, dying beside agent Ed Hollis. Nelson, also mortally wounded, died hours after the shootout on November 27, 1934, nicknamed the "Battle of Barrington." Cowley was one of Hoover's most trusted aides when he died.

How to ESCAPE ALCATRAZ

The island prison was renowned for its ill-fated jailbreaks,
San Francisco Bay, California, USA, 1934-63

Originally set up as a naval defense post in the 1850s, Alcatraz became a fortified, high-security prison in 1934. Situated just over a mile offshore from San Francisco, California, the prison became known as "the prison service's prison," and took on violent and dangerous criminals from other penitentiaries in the US.

Despite its fortress-like security, escape attempts still occurred. Of the thirty-six prisoners who tried to escape on fourteen occasions (including two men who tried twice), twenty-three were caught, six were shot, and two drowned. The remaining five men were never found, and are still listed as missing and presumed drowned. Alcatraz closed on 21 March 1963 due to running costs.

Raft
The raft was glued together using a "vulcanization" method, by pressing the glued rubber against the prison's steam heating pipes.

Paddles
The raft and paddles were inspired by an article in *Popular Mechanics*. The magazine was later found in a cell.

Tides and currents
The water around Alcatraz is very cold, and the tidal currents strong. The escaped inmates in the raft were never found.

Life vest
Fabricated using the same technique as the raft, life vests were also inflated using a modified accordion-like instrument as a pump.

Escapees
Frank Lee Morris, John William Anglin, and Clarence Anglin escaped on the night of June 11, 1962. Another inmate was in on the plan but failed to get out of his cell.

Supplies

PAINT

TOOLS

HOMEMADE PERISCOPE

50 PRISON-ISSUED RAINCOATS

PADDLES

01 Gather associates
For the best chance to make your escape, you'll need some trusted friends, as this will take teamwork. When you're confident in your associates, spend time going through your plan and ironing out the weak spots. Spend the rest of your time watching the guards and learning their movements inside out so you're prepared when the time comes for action.

02 Collect tools
You'll need as many tools as possible for cutting, drilling, sculpting, and sewing. Take and conceal whatever you're able to get away with, and find a sensible hiding place that won't arouse suspicion. Be resourceful – when the vacuum cleaner breaks, you can steal one of the motors when you repair it to make a motorized drill.

How Not to Flee From the Rock

There are plenty of failed escape attempts from the prison on The Rock, with the most bloody being the Battle of Alcatraz. On May 2, 1946, bank robber Bernard Coy initiated a carefully planned escape attempt with four accomplices. After watching the guards closely, he scaled a wall and slipped through bars to enter the Gun Gallery, arming him and other inmates. The prisoners locked Alcatraz guards in cells, but failed to find the key to the recreation yard that was the crux of their escape plan. As the alarm was raized, the warden sent in teams to recover control of the cellblock. What followed was forty-eight hours of bloody battle, with shots ringing out between guards and prisoners. The marines were called in to use explosives to regain control. There were five casualties, three conspirators and two prison guards. The remaining conspirators, Thompson and Shockley, received the death penalty in December 1948.

03 Widen vent holes

Carefully and methodically chip away at the cement around the vent grills to widen the holes. Plan the times you work and make sure someone keeps watch. When you eventually chip through the walls, slip through and plan your route out of the cellblock. You'll need to do the same to the vent at the top of the cellblock in order to gain access to the roof.

04 Make a lifelike dummy

Begin to make the decoys to ensure you're not missed when you make your escape. Use soap, toilet paper, and whatever else you can find to sculpt some fake heads. Paint them pink using materials from the prison art kits, and steal human hair from the barber's for the head. If you like, name your dummies "Oink" and "Oscar."

05 Prepare a "raft"

Carefully steal some glue from the glove shop, and procure as many prison-issued raincoats as possible. Some inmates will donate them but some you'll have to steal. Build an inflatable raft – about two yards by four – as well as some paddles. Use the same techniques to make life vests to boost your chance of survival in the cold San Francisco Bay.

06 Escape at night

Straight after lights out, slip through the hole in your cell. Meet your accomplices, but don't wait for anyone if they haven't escaped in time. Scale the plumbing to the top of the cellblock, head across the roof, and climb down to the ground near the entrance to the shower block. Launch the raft at the shore and you're off the island.

FOUR FAMOUS ALCATRAZ PRISON INMATES

AL CAPONE
CHICAGO, ILLINOIS, 1899-1947

The notorious mob boss and gangster, also known as "Scarface," was imprisoned in Alcatraz in 1934 as #AZ85. He served four years on The Rock, the last of which was spent in the prison hospital.

GEORGE "MACHINE GUN KELLY" BARNES
MEMPHIS, TENNESSEE, 1895-1954

Bootlegging, armed bank robberies, and kidnapping with his favorite weapon, a Tommy gun, Kelly and his wife lived a life of crime. He was finally incarcerated in 1934.

JAMES "WHITEY" BULGER JR.
BOSTON, MASSACHUSETTS, 1929-2018

The former boss of the Winter Hill Gang in Boston was imprisoned for nineteen murders as Alcatraz inmate #AZ1428 in 1959, based on grand jury testimony from former associates.

ROBERT STROUD
SEATTLE, WASHINGTON, 1890-1963

Locked up in solitary confinement, Stroud became known as the "Birdman of Alcatraz" because he raised canaries in his cell. He even wrote two books about them.

AL CAPONE

Arriving in Chicago as a minor league mobster, Al Capone helped build an empire of prostitution, bootlegging, and murder that made him a notorious household name.

he needle skipped as the gun barked twice in the killer's hand, the record player screeching into the silence of the restaurant's corridor as its owner crashed to the floor, blood pooling out onto the polished tiles. Giacomo "Big Jim" Colosimo, his body cooling from its exit wounds, had recently left his wife, filing for divorce and skipping town to marry a nineteen-year-old cabaret singer. His ex-wife, Victoria Moresco, or one of her brothers, was the prime suspect in this crime of passion, but the police knew enough to pay a visit to two of Colosimo's associates – the genial Johnny Torrio and his sidekick, the disquieting Alfonse Capone, three nasty scars on his cheek contorting as he smiled. "Big Jim and me were like brothers," claimed Torrio. "Mr Colosimo and me both loved opera," added Capone. "He was a grand guy."

Colosimo's murder on May 11, 1920 is still regarded as unsolved, but perhaps it's a crime that the Chicago Police Department chose to leave that way. For nearly a decade, Colosimo had ruled Chicago through hard graft and intimidation – running over 100 brothels with his wife – and extorting protection money from most of the city's illegal gambling dens. The profits he made snaked through the entire city, supplementing the meager wages of the cop patrolling on the street corner and boosting the bank account of the city's two-time mayor, William "Big Bill" Hale Thompson.

Chicago was a rough town. Booming in the early 1920s thanks to heavy industry and cheap labor, the Windy City was a Wild West frontier town with chimney stacks instead of cacti and bullet-riddled Model-T Fords in lieu of horses. "She was vibrant and violent," wrote local journalist Robert St. John, "stimulating and ruthless, intolerant of smugness, impatient with those either physically or intellectually timid."

Capone had arrived in Chicago from New York in 1919 to work for his old friend Torrio, who had earned Colosimo's trust by chasing off a rival extortion racket and stuck around as the boss' second in command. Capone soon put the feared reputation he had enjoyed back home to work as a debt collector, seeing firsthand how Colosimo's operation held a stranglehold over the underworld; gambling dens that refused to pay up for Big Jim's protection would either find themselves the subject of a convenient police raid or a visit from Capone, who was more than happy to break a few legs with a swing from his baseball bat.

CAPONE IN NEW YORK

Born in 1898 in a run-down district of Brooklyn to Italian immigrants Gabriele and Teresina Capone, Al Capone's life of crime began early, brawling with street gangs and running errands for mobsters. One, a young rising star called Johnny Torrio, would loom larger in his life later on.

Capone soon found work with Frankie Yale (born Francesco Ioele), a vicious thug with links to Torrio. Working as a barman in Yale's bar, the Harvard Inn – a notorious haunt of prostitutes and gangsters – Capone got the vicious scars on his face when he leered at one mobster's sister, "Honey, you got a nice ass and I mean that as a compliment, believe me."

The furious Frank Galluccio called Capone out and slashed him three times across his cheek with a knife. He needed thirty stitches, but he was lucky the hoodlum had been drinking because Galluccio was aiming for his jugular. In the bar he also picked up syphilis, which eventually caused his death, but may have affected him even earlier. Neurosyphilis attacks the brain and the spinal column, and can cause violent mood swings, delusions, and megalomania.

Johnny Torrio

Even after handing control over to Capone after he was shot, Torrio was still involved in organized crime and became a close associate of Lucky Luciano and other mob bosses.

Capone learned his trade in 1910s New York

Compared to the claustrophobic Big Apple, where half a dozen gangs butted heads over a block at a time, Torrio and Capone found Chicago fertile for expansion, as the only thing that stood in their way was their own boss.

In January 1920, the rules of the game changed again as the 18th Amendment to the US Constitution came into effect. Also known as the Volstead Act, which prohibited the production, transportation, and sale of alcohol – but not the consumption – Prohibition meant a huge swathe of the population were suddenly transformed into potential customers. Torrio and Capone saw that this was a revenue stream with the potential to dwarf even prostitution and racketeering, but to their dismay Colosimo was having none of it. When Colosimo was conveniently removed from the picture, John "The Fox" Torrio became the boss of the Chicago Outfit, and by his side stood Al Capone.

With Torrio's blessing, Capone set about covertly reopening the breweries and distilleries that had been forced to close by the Volstead Act, setting up an ambitious distribution network to the city's mean speakeasies with the help of his older brothers Ralph and Frank Capone. "Nobody wanted

Prohibition," he said. "This town voted six to one against it. Somebody had to throw some liquor on that thirst. Why not me?"

The loyal Ralph was put in charge of one of the Chicago Outfit's legal enterprises, a soft-drink bottling plant that earned him the nickname "Bottles," while Frank honed a reputation for savagery that overshadowed even Al's. Estimated to have been responsible for 300 deaths, Frank infamously advized his little brother that "you get no talk back from a corpse."

It was happening under Johnny Torrio's command but there was no doubt that bootlegging was Al Capone's kingdom, and he was soon to pay for it in blood as 1923 finally saw the downfall of Chicago's sticky-fingered mayor, Big Bill Thompson. The Democrat William Emmett Dever was voted in on a pledge to sweep the gangs from the city, and Torrio entrusted Capone with an urgent relocation to Cicero – the fourth largest city in Illinois – which was just outside of Chicago and the legislative reach of "Decent Dever."

While Torrio and Capone had ruled their criminal empire largely as Colosimo had – with money in the right pockets and threats whispered in the right ears – the takeover of Cicero was

How America Swam with Booze

1. WHISKY ON THE BOARDWALK

Ships laden down with whisky from Canada would anchor off the coast of New Jersey, well beyond the maritime limit patrolled by the US Coast Guard. Smugglers would sail out to pick up the crates of booze and New Jersey's vast coastline became something of a free-for-all, with rival gangs hijacking each other's shipments. The hedonistic boardwalk resort of Atlantic City became the major gateway with the town's Irish-American racketeer Enoch "Nucky" Johnson taking a major cut before it moved onward to Capone in Chicago or other mobs in New York and Jersey City.

2. RUM FROM THE CARIBBEAN

With Prohibition, Cuba emerged as a hedonistic getaway from the newly "dry" US to the Bacardi-soaked Caribbean. Traffic flowed both ways, however, with "rum runners" smuggling from Cuba, Jamaica, and the Bahamas into South Florida, Texas, and Louisiana.

In Texas, Galveston was soon to become the major entry point, supplying the rest of Texas and much of the Midwest. Dubbed the "Free State of Galveston," brothers Sam and Rose Maceo ruled the local vice trade and successfully held off competition from Capone and New York boss Albert Anastasia.

3. A LAKE OF WHISKY

Although Ontario had its own temperance laws, it didn't ban distilling alcohol – leading to a flow of hooch across Lake Michigan and up the Detroit River from Windsor to Detroit. With illegally obtained papers saying their final destination was Venezuela, they would quietly off-load their cargo in Motor City instead. Detroit had been "dry" well before Prohibition and the Purple Gang tightly controlled the rum-running trade and were major suppliers to Capone's Chicago Outfit.

4. MULES FROM MEXICO

Mass smuggling of US goods into Mexico was turned completely on its head thanks to Prohibition. Now homemade tequila and mescal was smuggled in the opposite direction by mule in groups of three or four, often crossing rivers at night, or by truck and car along dusty and isolated roads.

Texas's 800-mile Mexican border was simply too wide to be adequately policed, and cat-and-mouse chases between the smugglers and Texas Rangers became the stuff of legend.

5. MOUNTAIN MOONSHINE

While champagne, gin, rum, and whisky were available to those with the cash to cover its dangerous distribution, the poorer had to be taken care of too and moonshine cut the costs significantly.

Rural communities in the Appalachian Mountains and the Midwest had a tradition of home brew, but now a market opened up for their moonshine.

Stills could explode and quality control was poor and potentially life-threatening – but moonshiners often expanded their operations into barn-sized breweries.

---

an overt display of force, as Capone set about rigging the mayoral election for the mob's pet politician, Joseph Z. Klenha.

On the eve of the 1924 mayoral election, Frank Capone burst into the office of the Democrat candidate for Cicero with some of his thugs, beating the hopeful to a pulp with their pistol butts, trashing his office and firing their revolvers into the ceiling as a preamble for the next day's takeover. As cold, gray April 1 dawned, Capone hoods stormed into the polling stations to screen voters, snatching their ballot papers to ensure they were ticking the right box. Officials with the guts to intervene were dealt with; a Democrat campaign worker was shot in the legs and dumped in a cellar, two men were shot in the street, and another had his throat cut.

Eventually, a desperate judge bussed in seventy Chicago police officers, deputized on

the spot into the Cicero Police Department, to restore order. As the rain started to fall, Frank Capone found himself in a firefight outside a polling station. Opening fire on an approaching police car, he was gunned down by the startled cops but it was too late – the town belonged to the Chicago Outfit. Frank got a funeral fit for a war hero, with $20,000 worth of flowers placed around the silver-plated coffin and over 150 cars in the motorcade.

Despite the appalling bloodshed in the takeover of Cicero, Al Capone had been something of an enigma to the press. However, as he got his hands dirtier and dirtier and frequently acted unstably – a possible consequence of syphilis contracted back in New York – his name was beginning to be heard outside of darkened back rooms where shady men made deals. A few weeks after Frank's body hit the

pavement, small-time burglar "Ragtime" Joe Howard was enjoying a drink in a bar, when two men entered. Witnesses, who quickly forgot all the other details, recalled him say a friendly "Hello Al," before he was shot point blank – four rounds into his cheek and two into his shoulder. Nobody saw anything, nobody recognized the man, but the police knew who was responsible and so did the press, so for the first

ST. VALENTINE'S DAY MASSACRE

A step-by-step account of the day when seven men were gunned down in cold blood

STEP 1 — GIVING THE NOD

Mobster and boxer "Machine Gun" Jack McGurn, a survivor of an attack by the rival North Side Gang, approaches Al Capone in his Miami winter home. He proposes a plan to take out the North Side leader, George Clarence "Bugs" Moran, and his lieutenants.

THE LOOKOUTS

McGurn stations lookouts – the brothers Harry and Phil Keywell, both members of the allied Purple Gang – in an apartment opposite Moran's headquarters, a nondescript garage behind the offices of SMC Cartage Company at 2122 North Clark Street.

STEP 3

STEP 5 — THE AMBUSH

Four gunmen in a stolen police car – two of them wearing police uniforms – burst in. Believing this to be a routine raid, the six members of the North Side Gang and two of their associates surrender and allow the "policemen" to remove their weapons from them.

THE SET-UP — STEP 2

On February 13, 1929, McGurn has a booze hijacker approach Moran about selling him some top-end whisky for the bargain price of $57 a case; they arrange to meet in the morning. He adds that the whisky is stolen from Detroit's Purple Gang – suppliers to Capone's mob.

STEP 4 — TRAP CLOSES

On February 14 at 10:30 a.m. the North Side Gang gather at their garage HQ, expecting a shipment of Old Log Cabin Whiskey. McGurn's scouts think they spot Moran arriving – it's Albert Weinshank, wearing the same-colored coat and hat as his boss.

LUCKY ESCAPE — STEP 6

Moran and Ted Newberry arrive late through a side street in time to see the police car pull up and wait it out in a café. Spotting another mobster, Henry Gusenberg, they warn him off, while a fourth survivor also arrives late. He notes down the car's license plate and skedaddles.

Murder weapon

Fitted with either a twenty-round box or the iconic fifty-round circular drum, the Thompson Submachine Gun could fire between 800 and 900 rounds a minute, allowing its wielder to spray his enemy with the entire magazine in a matter of seconds. Though retailing for $200 at a time when a car cost $400, it used ubiquitous .45 ammunition and could be easily broken down for transport and reassembled in under a minute. Effective at a range up to 150 feet, the Tommy gun was perfect for close-range firefights across streets and the marble counter of the speakeasy. It quickly became a cultural symbol of gangsters in the 1920s, so much that when the police started recruiting their "G-Men," they made sure to equip them with Tommy guns of their own.

Victims

Four unfortunate victims of the massacre

John May

Not a member of the North Side Gang, May was a mechanic who worked on their cars and occasionally as muscle. May was trying to stay out of trouble, but the demands of seven children left him with no other option but to take work from the mob.

Peter Gusenberg & Frank Gusenberg

Hitmen for the North Side Gang, the Gusenberg brothers entered the criminal underworld in their teens. They took part in a drive-by shooting of Capone's HQ in 1926 and killed two of his allies in 1928.

Adam Heyer

Moran's business manager and North Side Gang accountant, Heyer owned the lease on the gang's headquarters. Described as a snappy dresser, Heyer had been in prison twice – once for robbery and once for running a confidence game.

Police investigation

The hunt for the killers

Frank Gusenberg lived on for hours despite being riddled with wounds, but sticking stubbornly to the mob's code of silence, he refused to admit he'd even been shot, let alone who'd done it, before he died. The Chicago Police Department quickly announced that they believed Capone associates John Scalise, Alberto Anselmi, Jack McGurn, and Frank Rio were responsible, but the case floundered due to lack of evidence and McGurn skipped town with his moll.

In frustration, the police began its retaliation efforts by shaking down Detroit's Purple Gang on the basis that Moran's mob had recently been hijacking their liquor shipments. On February 22, the burned remains of the police Cadillac were found, but it was impossible to pin it on either Capone or the Purple Gang, while the two murder weapons later turned up in a police raid on the Michigan home of bank robber and hitman Fred "Killer" Burke in November that same year.

Burke, who led a vicious gang that Capone called his "American boys," was finally arrested in March 1931, attempting to rob a bank in Kirksville, Missouri, and died in prison in 1940

from diabetes. Having killed a Michigan police officer, the Chicago police were unable to extradite him to Illinois and his role in the St. Valentine's Day Massacre went unexamined.

Meanwhile in a completely unrelated case, the FBI had finally pinned down the ruthless Barker-Karpis Gang of bank robbers and kidnappers, when one of their members – Byron "Monty" Bolton – confessed to the St. Valentine's Day Massacre and implicated Burke. Having no jurisdiction over the case, the FBI suppressed the information but it finally leaked to the press, adding to the already considerable confusion and the mystery of the entire case.

Suspects

Who might have pulled the trigger?

John Scalise and Alberto Anselmi

John Scalise and Alberto Anselmi

Capone's most feared hitmen, the Sicilian-born "murder twins" were believed to be responsible for the death of North Side Gang boss – and Moran's predecessor – Dean O'Banion in 1924, as well as a failed attack on Moran and the murder of two police officers in June 1925. Both were sent to prison, but released a year later.

Frank Rio

One of Capone's most loyal and dependable bodyguards, Italian-born Rio had been arrested twice, once for handling stolen furs and once for the daylight robbery of a mail train, but intimidation and bribery of judges helped him escape conviction, earning him the nickname "Slippery" Frank Rio.

---

time, Capone's mugshot appeared on the front page.

In private, Capone's gang whispered that Howard had stuck up Jack "Greasy Thumb" Guzik for $1,500, boasting he had "made the little Jew whine." Guzik was Capone's trusted money man, responsible for regular payoffs to cops and judges. Soon the name "Scarface" began to stick, needling away at Capone's vanity – he never allowed the left side of his face to be photographed – and he began to lash out at the flickering flash bulbs of the photographers.

There were far more immediate threats than damning headlines, though. The predominantly Irish-American North Side Gang run by Dean O'Banion controlled the breweries and the bootlegging in Chicago's North Side and had resisted all of Torrio's efforts to bring them to heel. Alliances and truces had dwindled and fallen apart, but the last straw came on May 19, 1924 as O'Banion finally relinquished his share of the Sieben Brewery to Torrio. As soon as Torrio and his boys – joined by their allies in Little Sicily's "Terrible Gennas" – showed up, a conveniently timed police raid swept in and the boss was left with a $5,000 fine and a nine-month jail sentence. "Deany was all right," smirked Capone, who took over the day-to-day running of the mob while Torrio served his sentence. "But like everyone else, his head got away from his hat."

One day, while O'Banion clipped chrysanthemums in his flower shop, Schofields, Mike "The Devil" Genna, John Scalise, Albert Anselmi, and Frankie Yale strode in. As O'Banion and Yale shook hands, Scalise and Anselmi fired two bullets into his chest and two into his throat. As he lay on the floor in a pool of blood and petals, he was shot in the back of the head for good measure. He had been dealt with.

George Clarence "Bugs" Moran took over the North Side Gang and nursed their grudge, moving the headquarters from Schofields to the garage that would become the site of the shocking St. Valentine's Day Massacre in 1929, the culmination of a brutal and bloody five-year gang war between the Chicago Outfit and the North Side Gang.

Upon his release, Torrio kept a low profile – safe in the knowledge that with Capone in the hot seat, he'd be less of a target. For all of the Fox's wiles, he just hadn't reckoned on how personal this war had become. Returning from a day shopping with his wife on the morning of January 24, 1925, gunfire lit up the street from a blue Cadillac lurking on the curb, shredding shopping bags to confetti. Blood mingled with the groceries from a litany of wounds as Johnny Torrio stared at the sky, the shrieking of Anna Torrio strangely distant. As Bugs Moran stood over him, blocking the crisp winter sun, his revolver levelled at Torrio's skull – the gun clicked on empty and the would-be assassins fled.

Capone's ascendancy was immediate as Torrio underwent emergency surgery. Capone slept by his mentor's bedside – the men of the Chicago Outfit standing guard around the clock, eyeing each disinterested nurse and flower-clutching day visitor

"His revolver leveled at Torrio's skull – the gun clicked on empty and the would-be assassins fled"

Victims of the St. Valentine's Day Massacre

"Capone moved his headquarters into Chicago's Lexington Hotel, taking over the fourth and fifth floors"

Five Facts About Scarface

- Capone's specially outfitted, bulletproof Cadillac was seized by the US Treasury Department in 1932. It was later used by the government as President Franklin Roosevelt's limousine.

- Even though he is synonymous with Chicago, he only lived in the city for twelve years of his life.

- Allegedly, he had never heard of Eliot Ness, the government agent sent to bring him to justice.

- The man who helped America swim in booze during Prohibition's favorite drink was Templeton Rye whisky.

- His men carried out most of the deaths he is responsible for, but Capone is still thought to have killed more than a dozen men personally.

suspiciously. "It's all yours, Al," said Torrio eventually. "Me? I'm quitting. It's Europe for me."

With the Fox quietly returning to Italy, Capone moved his headquarters into Chicago's Lexington Hotel, taking over the fourth and fifth floors where he held court like an emperor. A concrete vault was installed in the basement and a secret staircase hidden behind a mirror in one of his bathrooms, just one part of a web of tunnels that would allow him a quick escape.

Rising late most days, he took his time pouring over the morning papers like a statesman before dressing himself in expensive, finely tailored suits. Early afternoon, Capone moved into his study in another suite where petitioners waited anxiously for favors and his patronage. Nobody talked about the "Free Kingdom of Torrio" anymore. No, now the press called Cicero the "Capital of Caponeland."

Capone began to court newspaper men, handing out expensive cigars and inviting them to lavish parties, where the lord of the Chicago underworld played billiards with boxers, baseball players, and the notoriously corrupt mayor

of Chicago, Big Bill Thompson, miraculously re-elected in 1927.

"Public service is my motto," Capone explained to attentive reporters in December 1927. "Ninety-nine percent of the public in [Chicago] drink and gamble and my offense has been to furnish them with those amusements. My booze has been good and my games on the square."

Already, the public had some sympathy for the bootleggers and Capone took hold of the notion and twisted it into the specter of Robin Hood, portraying himself as heroic outlaw giving the people what they wanted. The bigger Capone's business became, the more intricate and vulnerable the network of mobsters, bribes, and alliances required to sustain it. But it soon got to a point where the endemic corruption of Chicago's law and government simply couldn't be ignored.

In the wake of the shocking St. Valentine's Day Massacre, Herbert Hoover was elected president of the United States on an anti-corruption platform. His first move was to dispatch Prohibition agent Eliot Ness and a handpicked team of incorruptible "Untouchables" to clean up Chicago's streets by raiding Capone's speakeasies and stills, and more importantly, it transpired, a team of International Revenue Service agents headed by accountant-turned-lawman Frank J. Wilson with a mandate

Capone with family and friends at a picnic, Chicago, 1929

CAPONE AND ALCATRAZ

What was he sentenced for?

Capone was sentenced to eleven years for three counts of tax evasion in 1927-29 and two counts of failing to provide tax returns in 1928-29 as his lavish lifestyle and lack of legitimate income was used against him. eleven further counts of tax evasion and 5,000 violations of the Volstead Act were dropped out of fear the prosecution would be unable to get a conviction.

How was life for him in jail?

Initially, Capone served his sentence in Atlanta, Georgia, continuing to rule his crime empire by proxy, bribing guards with thousands of dollars hidden in the hollow handle of a tennis racket to be able to communicate with the outside world. He was then sent to the newly opened Alcatraz, where his link to the outside world was finally severed.

What was his defense?

Capone's legal team originally struck a deal with the prosecution to admit to the lighter charges and serve between two and five years so business would be able to go on as usual. However, when details leaked to the press, the outrage was so great that the deal was immediately canned and the judge threw the book at him.

Was Alcatraz a "hard" prison?

Capone's letters were censored, newspapers banned, and all magazines had to be at least seven months old. He was only allowed visits from immediate family, who would be separated from the one-time king of crime by a sheet of glass.

What happened at trial?

The jury was suddenly exchanged for another in the court by Judge Wilkerson when the police learned of a plot from Capone's mob to bribe them. The new jury, all from rural Illinois, were sequestered overnight to keep them out of the Chicago Outfit's reach. Wilkerson sentenced Capone to eleven years, $50,000 in fines, court costs of another $30,000, and no bail.

Why was he released?

Capone was released into the care of his family on November 16, 1939, due to brain damage caused by neurosyphilis. By 1946, he was deemed to have the intelligence of a 12-year-old, suffering from delusional fits, raving about communists and plots to kill him. Capone had a stroke on January 21, 1947, and just four days later on January 25, he suffered a fatal heart attack, aged forty-eight.

to turn over Capone's finances for something that would stick in court.

"Every time a boy falls off a tricycle, every time a black cat has gray kittens, every time someone stubs a toe, every time there's a murder or a fire or the Marines land in Nicaragua, the police and the newspapers holler, "Get Capone!" raged Chicago's premier gangster in his penthouse. "I'm sick of it."

As the gangster was having a tantrum, one of the men tasked with bringing him to justice was having second thoughts. "Doubts raced through my mind as I considered the feasibility of enforcing a law which the majority of honest citizens didn't seem to want," Ness admitted in his autobiography. "I felt a chill foreboding for my men as I envisioned the violent reaction we would produce in the criminal octopus hovering over Chicago, its tentacles of terror reaching out all over the nation. We had undertaken what might be a suicidal mission."

While Capone wallowed in fine silks and syphilitic megalomania in his penthouse, Ness and his Untouchables began nipping at his heels – shutting down eighteen stills and arresting fifty-two bootleggers in a single night. In the first six months alone, Ness' daring raids had cost the Chicago Outfit an estimated $1,000,000, as well as some loyal lieutenants, who now languished in jail for violations of the Volstead Act. He shrugged off Capone's clumsy attempts at bribery, as well as two assassination attempts.

It was only ever an irritant, taking chunks out of his income and his pride – but to a mobster as egotistical as Capone, such defiance drove him into a rage. It was a fury Ness gleefully exploited – parading captured vehicles outside his hotel and taunting him on the phone. However much Ness might have damaged his ego, the real danger came from fraud investigator Frank J. Wilson as he poured over reams of paperwork.

In May 1927, the US Supreme Court's "Sullivan decision" had reversed a bizarre legal loophole that meant gangsters were legally exempt from having to register illegal income on their tax returns on the basis that it would violate their Fifth Amendment rights. Manly Sullivan, a Chicago bootlegger whose trial lent the decision its name, received a landmark conviction for tax evasion.

That same year, the Chicago Outfit's income was an estimated $108 million. Capone simply had to be next. Facing a possible thirty-four-year jail term from Wilson's tax case and Ness' Prohibition case, the former would stick and the latter wouldn't, but that scarcely mattered. It was the end of Capone's empire of crime, brought down not by gunfire, violence, and police raids, but by the simple, dry truth of the balance sheet. The reign of Chicago's public enemy number one was over.

BUGSY SIEGEL

The story of a gangster, Las Vegas, and the Flamingo Hotel.

When Benjamin "Bugsy" Siegel landed in Las Vegas in 1945, bringing with him a whirlwind of under-the-table deals, the feds were paying attention. It's not as if Vegas, which by the 1930s had grown from an abandoned Mormon fort into a desert waterhole frequented by fly-boys from the local United States Air Force base, was operating under the radar of the authorities. Since gambling was legalized in Nevada in 1931, there had been a low hum of criminal activity in what would become the jewel in the state's crown. Al Capone and his brother Ralph had even made plans to run their own casino there in the early days, and some think they had a hand in the Pair-O-Dice Club, Vegas' very first casino on the famous Strip. But the bright-light city-to-be hadn't seen the likes of Siegel before. This cat was connected to every East Coast mobster worth knowing. He was cunning, had a hair-trigger temper, a gift for violence, and was fiercely intimidating.

These talents made him a natural leader of Murder Incorporated, the ruthless hitmen-for-hire enforcement arm of Meyer Lansky and Charles "Lucky" Luciano's National Crime Syndicate. Moreover, Siegel was an archetypal Hollywood gangster of his generation – a devilishly handsome, magazine-cover hero with piercing blue eyes who matched his silver-screen looks with effortless charm. Bugsy made sure that he was seen in the trendiest nightspots and restaurants, he schmoozed with film stars like Clark Gable, and enthusiastically revelled in his criminal celebrity status. He was also a big hit with the ladies.

While the West Coast Hollywood playboy lifestyle undoubtedly suited Siegel, there was an (il)legitimate reason for his move to California. He could see a very lucrative future for the mob in the dustbowl of Las Vegas, and while his partners several thousand miles to the east weren't as convinced of the investment, Siegel was in good standing with bosses like Lucky Luciano and his old friend Lansky. They were willing to bet heavily on his success, which would ultimately pay off for the mob, if not for Bugsy himself.

Siegel had already muscled in on the Las Vegas race wire service via one of Meyer's lieutenants, Moe Sedway, and by early 1945 it was returning a tidy sum of about $twenty-five,000 ($330,000 today) a month. The deal was simple: Vegas bookies gave a cut of their profits – no argument – in return for betting odds and reliable data on winners. Siegel was expanding into the southwest via Phoenix bookmaker

Gus Greenbaum and was in the process of creating a bookmaking empire with a veneer of legitimacy, while he skimmed thousands of dollars away under the table. This inevitably put him into contention with former bootlegger and extortion racketeer Jack Dragna, the "Capone of Los Angeles." There was no love lost between these two characters. But as Siegel was the representative of the powerful Luciano crime family and golden boy of the East Coast crime syndicate, Dragna was forced to give way after Lucky Luciano himself advized him that it would be in his "best interest" to defer to Siegel. As it turned out, it really was: Siegel immediately moved in on the LA bookmaking scene and "convinced" bookies on his turf to pay tribute to Dragna, further lining his wallet.

Siegel also set up a Mexico-California drug trade, blackmailed Hollywood film companies by organizing union strikes, and "borrowed" hundreds of thousands of dollars from celebrities he had befriended, safe in the knowledge they wouldn't ask a reputedly violent mobster for it back.

The upshot of all of this criminal entrepreneurship was

that by the time Siegel had begun pulling strings to build a hotel-casino in Vegas, he was an influential man on the west coast with more than a few aces up his sleeve. He was very wealthy, but most of his money was dirty. So, with some laundered seed capital from his friends in New York, he moved into suite 401 of the Last Frontier Hotel while he looked for a potentially profitable investment. The El Cortez Hotel & Casino was picked up for $600,000 in late 1945 and sold in July 1946 for $766,000. Not a bad return in six months at all, even for this high-rolling gangster. Siegel's ambitions grew as he eyed up his next investment, which would see his name made synonymous with the most iconic hotel and casino in Las Vegas' history. But for the first time in his criminal career, Bugsy would find the cards stacked against him.

Billy Wilkerson was a prominent Vegas nightclub owner who founded the *Hollywood Reporter*, an entertainment trade rag that he used to list suspected communist sympathizers (the foundation of what would be the infamous Hollywood blacklist). Wilkerson had picked up thirty-two acres of cheap desert about a half mile from the Last Frontier

and was planning on building a more European style of hotel-casino, a class above the spit-and-sawdust saloons and tables of the old Strip. But iron, bricks, and basic building materials had been sucked up by Uncle Sam during World War II and the construction business had far higher overheads than they had before the war.

Wilkerson quickly found himself in over his head and $400,000 short of finishing his dream. He sought investors and found an eager Benjamin Siegel, posing as a respectable businessman, with the cash and charm to win him and his "investment partners" two-thirds of a stake in the project – the glitzy Flamingo Hotel and Casino, supposedly named after Bugsy's leggy firebrand of a girlfriend, Virginia Hill. By the time Wilkerson realized exactly who his new partners were, it was too late to pull out.

During this time, and in the prelude to the second Red Scare, FBI director John Edgar Hoover was focusing the efforts of the agency on political subversives but he could hardly allow a high-profile mobster to gain a foothold in Vegas on his watch. Siegel was already under scrutiny, but Hoover wanted to up the ante. In a memorandum to the attorney general written on July 18, 1946, he put

> Siegel played a big role in creating the Las Vegas that everyone knows today

By the time this first mugshot of Bugsy was taken in 1928, the twenty-two-year-old was already a wealthy bootlegger

The Flamingo was already turning a profit when Siegel died, but its veneer of respectable gambling brought a higher class of client and even bigger profits in the 1950s

The Story of Vegas

Discovery
Mexican merchant Antonio Armijo stumbles upon the valley with his caravan, while looking for a trade route to Los Angeles. He calls it Las Vegas, which means "The Meadows" in Spanish. **1829**

Army Fort
In preparation for the war brewing with the Mexicans, John C. Fremont is sent into the valley to gather forces and create an outpost fort that remains for a generation. Vegas' famous Fremont Street is named after him. **1844**

Mormon Fort
Years later, twenty-nine Mormon missionaries from Utah led by William Billinghurst occupy the fort with the intention of making it a Mormon stronghold. It was abandoned a year later after finding difficulties surviving in the desert heat. **1855**

"Las Vegas Rancho" The fort changes hands a few times until Archibald Stewart is given it in lieu of a debt and his wife becomes its first postmaster. The land is irrigated and over the next decade farmers move in. Las Vegas is permanently settled. **1881**

City
Las Vegas rapidly grows with the railroad that has been built to run through it bringing hundreds of settlers. It's finally made a city after 108 acres of what is now downtown Vegas is snapped up by buyers. **1905**

forward a case for more intense surveillance on the mafioso: "In the course of the above investigation, we have ascertained that Benjamin "Bugsy" Siegel, notorious racketeer with underworld connections on the west and east coasts and Las Vegas, Nevada, will again visit the latter city within the next few days and reside at the Last Frontier Hotel there in Suite 401. As previously pointed out, we are desirous of following Siegel's widespread activities and, therefore are requesting authority to place a technical surveillance on his telephony at the Last Frontier Hotel which will be Las Vegas 1800. At this time, I also with [sic] to point out that Siegel, because of his far-flung interests, is almost in constant travel status, thereby making it extremely difficult at times to follow his activities and anticipate his movements. It is recommended, therefore, that authority be granted to cover any hotels, residences, or places of business which might be used by Siegel in his journeys throughout the country. I strongly feel that this type of coverage is necessary if we are to establish his racketeering connections."

The FBI was cleared to bug rooms and tap phones, and the Suite 401 phone tap proved particularly fruitful: Siegel was recorded

discussing his interests in Vegas with the east coast and his lieutenants. The FBI now had hard proof that the mob was looking to stick around. Still, the feds barely had any real case against him, so Hoover played a trump card that nearly bust Bugsy.

Walter Winchell was a big-time broadcaster with a popular fifteen-minute Sunday national radio gossip program, and on July 14, 1946, he exposed Siegel's hand to the nation with this simple statement: "According to the FBI, a prominent west coast racketeer is endeavouring to muscle a prominent west coast publisher out of his interest in a west coast hotel."

Siegel was livid. His attempt at legitimacy was being put into jeopardy along with the hotel, gambling, and liquor licences he was in the process of securing for the Flamingo. He had one of his men phone Winchell and put the heat on him, and Winchell folded under the indirect wrath of an angry mob boss. "Winchell identified his source as the director," so goes the FBI summary of the phone tap that took place in the "Boiler Room" of Las Vegas 2460, the "Las Vegas" club. "When he learned that Siegel and [CENSORED] were involved, exclaimed, "God, what a mistake I made. I may have caused them

(Siegel and [CENSORED]) to lose their hotel licenses."" Although no one knows for sure, the name censored by the FBI is thought to be that of a high-ranking member of the Chicago outfit.

The Suite 401 tap subsequently recorded a fuming Siegel making audacious statements to his girlfriend. "Let [him] tell me where he got it from," he spat, referring to none other than J. Edgar Hoover, before he ranted on about having his men bring Hoover to him and getting him to squeal about where he got his information from. A lot of bluster from a man known to have a short fuse, for sure. But when one of the most powerful and feared underworld figures in the United States threatens violence against the director of the FBI, even empty threats are taken seriously. The conversation was duly detailed in three pages of typewritten memo by special agent A. Rosen and airmailed to FBI headquarters in Washington.

Bugsy had been respected among his peers for being gutsy, but now he was overplaying his hand. At 9:30 a.m. on July 21, 1946, he sought to reassure Meyer Lansky: "Oh, the guy called me up. I knew I had something to tell you." Siegel concluded the conversation by passing the FBI situation off almost as an afterthought.

Siegel's girlfriend, Virginia Hill: she had to appear before the Kefauver special committee in 1951, which was investigating organized crime across the USA

● **Gambling Outlawed**
Nevada is the last state to ban gambling, even flipping a coin for a drink, from its bars and public places. But Vegas continues to prosper. **1910**

● **Siegel's Vegas**
Bugsy first starts visiting California in the early 1930s after several attempts on his life back east. He has much of his business in Los Angeles at the time, but the casino scene in Vegas is an attractive one to the entrepreneurial crook. **1933**

● **Bugsy Siegel Shot**
After a disastrous opening, Benjamin Siegel is killed by an unknown hitman. He lived to experience just a taste of success with his hotel and casino, the Flamingo. **1947**

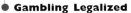

● **Gambling Legalized**
After relaxing gaming laws over the previous few decades, gambling is finally decriminalized in the Silver State, and Nevada cities, including Vegas, become a boomtown for casinos. **1931**

● **Hoover Dam Built**
It took five years and $49 million to build the Hoover Dam across the Colorado river. Workers are restricted from visiting Vegas while they are involved with its construction. **1936**

● **Nuclear Testing**
The infamous Nevada test site opens with the first of more than 100 nuclear explosions. With a clear view from Vegas, the city's sky bars do a roaring trade in "Atomic cocktails" with a view of the mushroom clouds. **1951**

Bugsy's Rant

Incensed by Winchell, Siegel vents his anger to his girlfriend, unaware the FBI is listening

BUGSY SIEGEL: We'll make him bring Hoover in front of me and let that ████████r tell me where he got it from... I said tell that dirty son of a b████ you may say don't give me a license here and we go in and spend 3 million dollars, every nickel we possess. He thinks it's Meyer and I in there... Winchell apologized forty times, said 'I would never do a thing like that.' He said all right, █████████████you're a friend of mine but these two either fellows are dearer friends to me in there, he said, and me especially is a very dear friend of mine, wouldn't do a thing in the world to hurt him, said I want you to see the letter when you get back. Jesus Christ – but I know it all instigated from him see. He just have given it to him, to give to Hoover, see. He called and said I get the letter just now, you should see the front of it – right there in front of what you call it, the senator, that contract we signed. Yeah but Winchell's liable to cop. I'll knock his ██████ eyes out – just like this – God damned right... But now he's got this God damned letter a block long from Winchell.

VIRGINIA HILL: That means you won't get a license?

SIEGEL: What?

HILL: What kind of license, honey?

SIEGEL: Say I came in after it and through him or something they refuse to give me a gambling licence, what am I gonna do with the hotel, stick it up my ass?

HILL: Well, why don't you get them? Then once you get them–

SIEGEL: Well, they always revoke them – get them, never mind about that, say whatever they want. If there is no connection in this town to get these things they can put you out of business, honey. Why to [sic] you think I work so much time with ███████? Give them money and this and that. Although it is legitimate business but still, you know, these ██████ when you have a license...

[The sound of a child entering the room can be heard]

[Call ends]

The last original structure of the Flamingo was torn down in 1993 and a garden built in its stead: despite Siegel's notoriety, he was given this memorial in recognition of his vision of the famous hotel

Finland Awarded 1952 Olympic Ga
'BUGSY' SIEGEL MURDER
Senate Labor Fight Rages on After All-Night S

The murder of one of the most feared gangsters in the country sparked decades of mystery about who pulled the trigger

No one outside of the mob saw his death coming, though Bugsy must have had an inkling that there were those who either saw him as a problem or would profit from his death

"Last night, he read me a letter he just got from Winchell. He (Winchell) says in the longest day he never dreamed it was him or I. He said, "I want you to understand that the other fellow is even a better friend than you are. I'd never done that in a million years. The man who I thought it was is [CENSORED]." He said, "I went right back to my man that gave it to me," and then it tells him it's Mr Hoover, you understand? And bowled the by-Jesus out of him. He says, "I want you to tell my mutual friend that when I come out I will explain the whole thing," you couldn't give me a million dollars to do that. He (Winchell) said I would never do that because he went on to tell him how it might have hurt me up here. But I found out that it's still him. So I'll tell you when I see you."

Perhaps, in the creation of his west coast empire more than 1,800 miles from his bosses, Siegel had forgotten who he was working for, because Lansky's curt and guarded responses to Siegel suggested he wasn't buying it. Winchell later told Hoover that he never sent a letter of apology to anyone, so maybe the New York kingpin saw right through Siegel's bluff.

Still, Bugsy was to get away with a lot more before his east coast partners called in their debts. Las Vegas summers can easily see the temperature rise above 100 degrees Fahrenheit, and by August 1946, Siegel was feeling the heat in the Mojave. His wire service, Trans-American, was experiencing difficulties and profits would slump for the next few months, leaving him to face another awkward phone call with Lansky. He was also in the process of a messy divorce with his first wife and the FBI was looking into getting him on a government fraud rap, as Siegel tried to get the Flamingo built as quickly and cheaply as possible. Bribing officials and breaking rules to get his way was second nature to Bugsy (after a bit of old-fashioned thuggery, that is) and he'd been wriggling his way through the red tape of the Civilian Public Administration (CPA).

Apparently, the Las Vegas community didn't think much about a lavish new mobster-run hotel-casino in their midst, either. An angry Richard King wrote this article for the August 1, 1946 issue of the *Las Vegas Tribune*: "The Flamingo, giant gambling resort now under construction on Highway 91, at a cost estimated to reach the $3 million mark, promises to be the biggest and most elaborate club in the country. Under normal conditions, construction of this type may be tolerated and by many welcomed as an additional enterprise to put Las Vegas on the map. At present, however, construction of another gambling resort of such magnitude is causing much unfavorable comment, especially among veterans who have been trying vainly to purchase building materials for homes that they feel they are entitled to build for their families. Contractors and building supply houses state they do not have any materials to build homes. But, somehow, builders of gambling clubs seem to have no trouble whatsoever getting anything they want…"

That $3 million (more than $36 million today) turned out to be a conservative estimate. Problem was, while Siegel had the right idea of a glamorous Vegas with the mob running the show, he wasn't really the right guy to execute this vision. He skimmed money off anywhere he could, even as his own construction crew moved expensive building materials in through one door and out the other, only to sell it back to the project the next day. His budget was beginning to spiral out of control, Clark County was refusing to grant him his gambling and liquor licences, and the feds were now investigating him for bribery. Apparently, Siegel was wryly bribing CPA officials with beer.

It took another four months before he finally got his licences in order, and the Flamingo Hotel and Casino could open to a bumpy start. Siegel wanted an early launch to recoup any revenue he could for what was threatening to be a $6 million white elephant, but the hotel was still unfinished and fate paid a cruel part in the December 26, 1946 flop. Lightning had prevented planes full of gamblers from taking off in Los Angeles, so many of Siegel's guests didn't arrive. Guest suites hadn't been completed yet either, so when

the entertainment – which included comedian and musician Jimmy Durante and the Xavier Cugat band – for the "West's Greatest Resort Hotel" concluded, guests and gamblers had to return to rival Vegas casinos where they were able to gamble and drink all night before retiring to their suites.

A storm was brewing back east, too. Siegel's old friend Lansky was holding the Cosa Nostra at bay, but his investors were growing impatient. The Flamingo had to close again just a month later, but reopened in March 1947, and by May, it was finally in profit to the tune of $250,000.

Some suspect that this was too little, too late for Bugsy. On the evening of June 20, 1947, the casino don was reading the newspaper in the living room of Virginia Hill's mansion in Los Angeles when an unknown assassin fired a volley from a military carbine, striking him twice in the right side of his head. In a gruesome twist, the newspapers made much of the fact that Siegel's left eyeball had been blown out of the socket and was found on the far side of the room.

The fate of the Flamingo and the mob's future in Vegas mirrored that of Bugsy's. Lansky took over management of the luxury hotel, its success was ensured, and the mob made a killing skimming off the weekly take. Who'd have thought? Turns out, Bugsy was right about the place all along. The years that followed would see the Cuban Revolution oust the Mafia from their casino interests in Havana and the US turn to the Bright Light City for its kicks, where Lansky and his associates were already casting long shadows in the desert.

Who Killed Bugsy?

No one knows who whacked Siegel, but there are several parties who had good reason to want him dead

01 Mob "Housekeeping"
The Havana conference of December 1946 brought the old world Cosa Nostra and US Mafia leaders together to discuss business, mob rules, and settle any beef. Bugsy wasn't invited – partly because he had his hands full with the opening of the Flamingo. But there was another reason, some think: Luciano and company wanted to discuss what to do with the increasingly cocky Siegel and the money pit he had built in the desert.

02 Preemptive Strike
Bee Sedway, the wife of Siegel's lieutenant and partner in the Flamingo Moe Sedway, revealed in a recent interview that Siegel had threatened the life of her husband. He said, "I'll have Moe, chop his body up and feed it to the Flamingo Hotel's kitchen garbage disposal," after discovering that Moe was sending details of the Flamingo's botched accounts back to Lansky. Bee called her lover up, a man named Matthew "Moose" Pandza, and begged him to protect her husband.

03 A Woman Spurned
Siegel and his girlfriend Virginia Hill had a tempestuous relationship. She was possessive and would fly into a jealous rage if Bugsy spoke to other women. She was as crooked as him, too, so when she left for Switzerland and withdrew $2.5 million Bugsy had deposited into a Swiss bank account, it didn't take the mob money men long to trace it back to the Flamingo. Was she covering her tracks?

Following Bugsy's death, business at the Flamingo picked up and by 1947, gaming tables such as this "Bird Cage" were turning a nice profit

MACHINE GUN KELLY

Once a small-time crook in the US Prohibition era, this Memphis-born mobster became embroiled in a high-profile kidnapping which saw him ingrained in criminal history.

Entering the world as George Kelly Barnes on July 18, 1895, the young boy who would grow up to become one of America's most infamous outlaws was raized in a traditional American household in Memphis, Tennessee. Kelly was given ample opportunities to better himself, but when he enrolled at Mississippi State University in 1917 as an agriculture student, his prospects cascaded downhill.

The teenager was a lackluster student, constantly in trouble, working off the demerits and warnings he had acquired. Still a teenager, he fell in love with Geneva Ramsey, and in what seemed a rash decision, Kelly dropped out of school, his heart set on marriage. They had two children and Kelly worked as a taxi driver to make ends meet. Despite his efforts, Kelly earned a pittance, and with financial strain and Kelly's keeping of bad company constantly at the forefront of his marriage, he and Geneva separated.

On the brink of unemployment, Kelly seized an opportunity to make some cash and began associating with small-time criminals. Bootlegging in the Prohibition era was a way many criminals made a buck, scamming the strict system that had restricted the sale of alcohol. It was in bootlegging that Kelly finally found he was able to make some money. Following a series of arrests for illegal trafficking, Kelly packed up his life and headed west. Swapping his identity for an alias, George R. Kelly, he felt this was the only way to prevent police from catching up with him and to preserve his respectful family name.

By the time of his first prison sentence in 1928 for smuggling liquor into an Indian Reservation, Kelly had built a reputation as a veteran gangster. His empire would have to wait, however, while he served a three-year sentence at Kansas' Leavenworth Penitentiary. Behind bars, Kelly made friends with other criminals, most notably the leaders of the bank-robbing Holden-Keating Gang, Francis Keating and Thomas Holden, who he allegedly helped to escape from prison. Supposedly a model inmate, Kelly was released from prison early but unable to stay out of trouble, finding himself in hot water with the law once again. He was sentenced to a stretch several months long inside a New Mexico prison for a similar bootlegging-related offense.

Fresh out of prison and looking for a new venture, Kelly headed to Oklahoma City in 1930 where he became associated with "Little Steve" Anderson, a small-time criminal and bootlegger. When Kelly set eyes on Anderson's mistress, Kathryn Thorne, he fell in love again. A Texas gal, Kathryn was a bodacious and vivacious twenty-six-year-old woman and a seasoned criminal, having racked up multiple convictions for crimes including robbery and prostitution, and was even suspected of killing her third husband Charlie. Almost instantaneously the pair became inseparable, and in September 1930 they were declared husband and wife at a ceremony in Minneapolis, Minnesota, before traveling to St. Paul, Minnesota, where Kelly met up with his prison pals Keating and Holden. With his pals in force, Kelly carried out lucrative bank robberies in

Kelly changed his name after leaving Memphis in an attempt to protect his family name if he was ever apprehended

A Handsome Ransom for Ulscher

You will pack two hundred thousand dollars ($200,000.00) in used genuine federal reserve notes of twenty dollar ($20.00) denomination in a suitable light-colored leather bag and have someone purchase transportation for you, including berth, aboard train #28 (the sooner) which departs at 10:10 p.m. via the M. K. & T. lines for Kansas city, MO (Missouri).

You will ride on the observation platform where you may be observed by someone at some station along the line between Okla. City and K. C. MO. If indication is alright, somewhere along the right-of-way you will observe a fire on the right side of track (facing direction train is bound). That first fire will be your cue to be prepared to throw bag to track immediately after passing second fire.

Remember this: if any trickery is attempted you will find the remains of Urschel and instead of joy there will be double grief, for someone very near and dear to the Urschel family is under constant surveillance and will likewise suffer for your error.

If there is the slightest hitch in these plans for any reason whatsoever, not your fault, you will proceed on into Kansas City, MO. and register at the Muehlebach Hotel under the name of E.E. Kincaid of Little Rock, Arkansas, and await further instructions there.

The main thing is do not divulge the contents of this letter to any law authorities, for we have no intention of further communication. You are to make this trip Saturday, July 29, 1933.

Kelly dabbled in bootlegging, bank robberies, and kidnapping

Kelly was in and out of prison a few times; his first sentence was three years for smuggling liquor

Kelly met his second wife while she was the mistress of another criminal, "Little Steve" Anderson

multiple states, the resulting loots worth tens of thousands of dollars.

There is an age-old saying that professes that "behind every great man is an even greater woman," and Kathryn's influence on her husband's reputation as a hardened criminal was certainly substantial. Purchasing a Thompson sub-machine gun for Kelly, she taught him how to shoot it, offloading his bullet casings onto other associates, purring that it was a "souvenir" of her husband's success. With his new weapon becoming an integral part of his crimes, Machine Gun Kelly was born. In 1932 came the Great Depression, and funds inside bank safes began to dry up. After hearing that the Barker-Karpis Gang had scored $100,000 in ransom money for a kidnapping plot, the Kellys and their criminal associate Albert Bates began plotting.

The evening of July 22, 1933, at around 11:15 p.m., wealthy oil tycoon Charles Urschel, his wife, and their friends Mr. and Mrs. Jarrett were playing bridge on the screened porch of their Oklahoma City residence when two men, one armed with a machine gun and the other with a

> His wife, Kathryn Kelly, was the one who bought him the machine gun from which he would get his nickname

pistol, opened the screen door. The men standing before them demanded the oil man reveal himself to them, but when neither party spoke, the armed intruders were undeterred. "Well, we will take both of them," they said, hauling Urschel and Jarrett from the home. Placing them in the back of the Chevrolet sedan they had arrived in, they sped off. Almost immediately, Urschel's wife called the director of the Federal Bureau of Investigation, J. Edgar Hoover, to report what had happened. Officers were quickly dispatched to the Urschels' home, where they began their investigation.

Hours later, Jarrett returned to the Urschel residence. He explained to the authorities and Urschel's distressed wife that he and his companion had been driven to the outskirts of the city. After having identified that he was not Urschel, the masked intruders had pulled him from the car, taken $50 from his wallet, warned him not to reveal the direction the kidnappers had gone and abandoned him at the side of the road, heading south with their victim in tow.

Over the next few days, anonymous letters and phone calls provided leads that, although followed up, proved to be of little value until the kidnappers made contact on July 26. A package, addressed to a friend of the kidnapped victim, J.G. Catlett, contained a handwritten letter from Urschel requesting Catlett to act as an intermediary for his release. Also inside the package was a typewritten note from his kidnappers demanding that he immediately leave for Oklahoma City, with a separate typewritten letter addressed to a Mr. E.E. Kirkpatrick. Catlett was warned against communicating with the Urschel family.

The letter to Kirkpatrick demanded a $200,000 ransom for Ulscher and details of exactly how he would hand it over to them. Two days later, Kirkpatrick checked into a specified hotel under an alias that the kidnappers had provided. The telephone rang at 5:30 p.m., and the voice on the other end of the line told him to leave the hotel, describing a location where he could deliver the cash into their hands. Shortly after 6 p.m., Kirkpatrick found himself face to face with a mysterious man and handed over the money. The figure told him to return to his hotel, and after it had been confirmed that the total sum was accounted for, they would release their prisoner. At 11:30 p.m. Urschel walked

From taxi driver to bootlegger to full lifer, George Kelly Barnes, or Machine Gun Kelly, was one of the biggest names in US criminal history

Kelly is regarded as one of the most notable inmates to have served time inside Alcatraz Prison after he received a life sentence for the 1933 kidnapping of a wealthy oil tycoon

The Bonnie to his Clyde

Born Cleo Mae Brooks on March 18, 1904 in Rockwall, Texas, like her husband, the future Mrs Kelly had a somewhat unremarkable upbringing. At the age of nine, her family moved across town to Coleman. Her mother and father divorced when she was still a child and soon after, her mother, a hotelier, remarried a Fort Worth farmer. Before the future Mrs Kelly married her first husband at the age of fifteen, she had changed her name to Kathryn.

After two years, she and her husband separated. She married for a second time, but again the marriage did not last, and Kathryn moved onto bootlegger Charlie Thorne in 1924. After only three years of marriage, Kathryn was a widow. While her husband's death had been officially ruled a suicide, some couldn't help but notice that the bootlegger Kathryn had vocally and publicly berated just two days beforehand following the revelation he had been cheating on her had been found dead in what were somewhat suspicious circumstances.

A typed note alongside his body had been most questionable, as Charlie was illiterate. Nevertheless the judge deemed Charlie's death self-inflicted. Kathryn was arrested for a robbery soon after, but let off on a technicality. Between her third husband's death and meeting her fourth spouse, Kelly lived the high life of the Roaring Twenties and the Prohibition era.

George (right) and Kathryn (left) Kelly were handed life sentences for kidnapping oil tycoon Charles Urschel and holding him ransom for $200,000. George died behind bars in 1954, while Kathryn was released in 1958

back through the doors of his home. Exhausted, distressed, and relieved to be home safe, Urschel began detailing the nine-day ordeal he had been through. Meanwhile, Bates and the Kellys were already making their way off into the sunset with their money.

Investigating detectives had already been tipped off to the fact that the Kelly duo might be behind the kidnapping as early as two days after Ulscher was kidnapped, but in the interest of keeping him safe had focused primarily on retrieving him as opposed to chasing down crooks. Now that Urschel was home, they focused on his recollections of the people and places he had encountered for the last week and a half.

While on the run with her husband, Kathryn attempted to strike a deal with an FBI agent. In return for a lenient sentence for her and her mother, she would hand Kelly over to them. But the deal never went through. Thanks to Urschel's photographic memory, particularly of one of the buildings in which he had been held, police were able to trace the crime scene back to a ranch belonging to Kathryn's parents near Paradise, Texas. Storming the building on August 12, authorities arrested Kathryn's mother, stepfather, and brother, as well as several of their associates.

The same day, over 1,000 miles away in Colorado, Bates was snared on separate charges. But when detectives discovered him to be carrying money from the kidnapping, they promptly swooped in on him and questioned him about the crime. The Kellys evaded capture for several weeks but with their associates quickly being mopped up by the long arm of the law, it was only a matter of time until police discovered the pair hiding out in Memphis, arresting them during an early morning raid on September 26.

The following month, Kelly, Kathryn, and Bates received their sentences: life in prison. Kathryn's mother and stepfather were also given life in prison for their connection to the crime. Her brother was given a probation of ten years. Almost two dozen other associates related to the kidnapping and the stolen money were also jailed.

During his incarceration, Kelly was transferred to the infamous Alcatraz Prison in California, where he found himself housed with notable inmates including Prohibition Chicago mobster Al Capone. In the final years of his life in the 1950s, Kelly was transferred back to the Kansas prison he had served his first major stint in. Kelly died from heart failure on the day of his fifty-ninth birthday.

©Getty

CHARLES BIRGER

Meet the Prohibition-era gangster who took on the Ku Klux Klan in southern Illinois

The first thirty-eight years of Charles Birger's life were lived in obscurity as he chased the American Dream. Born Shachnai Itzik Birger to a Jewish family in Russia in 1881, they migrated to the United States when Birger was still a young child. They settled in St. Louis, where Charles adopted his Americanized name, but it was a tough introduction to life in the US. The Birger family was poor and, at the age of eight, Charles was sent out to work as a news boy to garner a much-needed wage.

Birger worked in a number of different jobs as he slowly made his way in the world. Employment in a pool hall was followed by a three-year stretch in the US Army, during which Birger was described as a good soldier in the 13th Cavalry. When his military stint was up, Birger put his newfound horsemanship skills to good use, working as a cowboy in South Dakota. He then turned his hand to coal mining before becoming a saloon keeper. Over three decades of hard graft, Birger transformed himself from a poor immigrant child into a small-scale businessman.

Following World War I, Birger saw an opportunity to make even more money – only this time, he would stray into illegality. In 1919, the USA adopted Prohibition, banning the manufacture, transportation, and sale of alcohol. As a saloon keeper, Birger's livelihood was threatened, so he decided to go underground, opening a number of speakeasies and brothels that sold illicit alcohol. After a number of police raids on Birger's bars, the authorities persuaded him to close up shop in Saline County, but Birger merely relocated across the border in Williamson County. He built a new speakeasy, Shady Rest, with a guard post to warn of police raids. Shady Rest was also heavily fortified and adequately supplied to withstand a siege, becoming a place so intimidating that the police decided to stop bothering its owner.

Birger's leather jacket usually concealed two handguns and, when the need arose, he was perfectly capable of using them, as in 1923 when he killed two men in three days. The first, Cecil Knighton, was a bartender in Birger's employment who double-crossed his boss. Although Birger was spotted standing over Knighton's body while holding a shotgun, the jury returned a verdict of self defense. His second victim was a St. Louis gangster named Whitey Doering. Birger was again freed on the basis that the killing was self defense after he claimed that Doering opened fire first – Birger was indeed wounded in the arm and the chest. While recovering in hospital, he made the acquaintance of another local bootlegger, Carl Shelton.

The local juries were willing to acquit such an obviously shady character because he also acted as a public benefactor. Known as a handsome charmer in his hometown of Harrisburg, Birger purchased coal and

BIRGER AND HIS GANG

The Birger gang openly posed with guns for the camera at Shady Rest, knowing the police were powerless to raid the fortified speakeasy

schoolbooks for poor families, and promized them that he would keep violence away from his home patch.

Yet Birger struggled to contain the bloodshed when his corner of southern Illinois drew the unwelcome attention of the Ku Klux Klan. The Klan supported Prohibition, since alcoholism was regarded as an un-American vice that was mainly the preserve of immigrants. For Birger – himself a Russian-born Jew who ran a bootlegging operation – the Klan was an obvious threat.

Illinois Klansmen began forcibly searching houses for alcohol, targeting the homes of immigrants, with rumors of planted evidence and rough treatment. The elected public officials of Williamson County were threatened, driven from office, and replaced by Klan members. The immigrant communities were powerless to stop them – or so they thought.

Birger was determined to drive the Klan from his territory, and combined forces with those of his old hospital mate, Carl Shelton, and the gang he ran with his two brothers. On April 13, 1926, an election day in Illinois, the Birger and Shelton mobs attacked Klan members in Herrin's polling stations, coldly assassinating six of them with Tommy guns and shotguns. The authorities turned a blind eye to the violence – the police refused to respond and the coroner ruled that the deaths were homicides "by parties unknown." The Klan's influence waned in the face of such vehement opposition, and was never again able to challenge the bootleggers.

However, Birger swapped one opponent for another when his alliance between with the Sheltons turned sour. Birger was annoyed when a robbery occurred in his hometown of Harrisburg, and compensated the owner from his own pocket. He suspected that the Sheltons were behind the robbery and, a few days later, the alleged thief was found dead. Tensions escalated and by the autumn of 1926, just six months after the Klan had been run out of town, Birger and the Sheltons were in open conflict.

Both gangs converted trucks into armored tanks from which they conducted drive-by tit-for-tat shootings. The Sheltons even tried to drop bombs made from dynamite and nitroglycerine

Birger, seated center on top of the car, demanded loyalty of his gangsters, but was snitched on over the Price and Adams murders

on Shady Rest from a plane, but the mission was a failure (although Birger's pet dog and eagle were killed). However, the Sheltons returned and in January 1927, Birger's fortified speakeasy was destroyed in an arson attack. Four people perished in the inferno; their bodies were so charred that they were almost unidentifiable, although one was a woman.

Birger was equally prepared to take the offensive. When he heard that the Sheltons' tank was being repaired at a garage owned by Joseph Adams, the mayor of nearby West City, he had his operatives bomb Adams' front porch. A few weeks later, two teenage members of Birger's gang, Harry and Elmo Thomasson, arrived at Adams' house declaring they had a letter from

the Sheltons. As he started to read, the brothers drew their pistols and shot him twice. Adams died minutes later.

For a fleeting moment, Birger thought he had won the violent gang war with the Sheltons. He convinced the authorities that the Sheltons were responsible for the robbery of a post office messenger who was carrying $21,000. Based on Birger's tip-off, the three Shelton brothers were arrested. In the trial they were shocked to see that the star witness against them was none other than Charlie Birger, their rival. The jury returned a guilty verdict, and the Shelton brothers were told that they would spend the next twenty-five years in prison.

"The Sheltons even tried to drop bombs made from dynamite and nitroglycerine"

The Curse of the Noose
Such was Birger's notoriety that even the rope that hung him caused conflict

The noose used to kill Charles Birger was fashioned by George Phillip Hanna, an Illinois farmer and banker who also had the macabre job of the region's hangman. After the length of rope had accomplished its deadly deed, Hanna handed it to James Pritchard, the sheriff of Franklin County who helped bring Birger to justice.

The noose became a morbid family heirloom. In 1996, Pritchard's daughter, Mary Glover, lent it to the Franklin County History Museum. A decade later, Glover's daughter and legal guardian, Rebecca Cocke, requested it be returned, but the

museum put up a fight. Since Pritchard was an employee of the state, they argued, the noose was state property. "It's part of my family's heritage," Cocke stated to newspapers. "If I let it go now, I'll never see it again."

She did see it again, but not for long. Cocke was victorious after a five-year legal battle and the noose was returned to her, but only two days later she suffered a fatal stroke. The rope passed to her son, but he put it up for auction in 2015, where it was bought for $14,000 by an anonymous buyer.

Birger smiled before his execution, but the battles over his noose would leave Sheriff Pritchard's descendents anything but happy

However, Birger's victory was short-lived. Among the murders that occurred during the gang war were those of Lory Price, a corrupt Illinois state trooper who was widely thought to be running a stolen car scam with Birger, and his wife, Ethel. The Prices were initially thought to have been abducted by the Sheltons in an attempt to eliminate a Birger ally, but a former gunman used by Birger turned informant and told the police that Price had been killed in the presence of Birger himself because the policeman knew too much about the criminal organization. Price's body was discovered dumped on farmland, riddled with bullet holes, and the snitch's story gained more credence when he revealed the location of Ethel Price's body in an abandoned mineshaft.

Although Birger was not held to account for the murder of Price and his wife, the killing of an innocent woman turned public feeling against him. When he was arrested for the murder of Mayor Adams, Birger allowed himself to be taken without a fight. It had happened to him many times, and he always escaped without punishment. On this occasion, however, the police made sure to move him to Franklin County, out of his sphere of influence. The decision was ostensibly taken for his own safety, as it was feared he may be lynched due to the ill feeling from the Ethel Price murder, but it also took him away from a friendly jury.

Birger and his two young gang members, Harry and Elmo Thomasson, were found guilty of the murder of Joe Adams. The two shooters were sent to prison, the leniency of their sentence a reward for cooperating and implicating their gang boss. Birger, the mastermind who gave the order, was sentenced to hang. He repeatedly

The Ku Klux Klan was pro-Prohibition, but this brought it into conflict with the immigrants of Illinois

Prohibition's Most Wanted

Prohibition led to a boom in organized crime as entrepreneurial crooks took advantage of a nation's thirst

Arnold Rothstein
Probably the first criminal to realize the potential gains to be made from Prohibition, Rothstein arranged for Canadian liquor to be smuggled across the border and supplied it to New York's gangs. He earned up to $10 million, possibly making him the richest crook in the country.

Al Capone
Capone controlled Chicago's bootlegging outfit. Seemingly safe from arrest due to police corruption, Capone maintained a public image as a modern-day Robin Hood, but fell from grace after the Saint Valentine's Day Massacre of seven rival gangsters. He was ultimately imprisoned for tax fraud.

Carl Shelton
The eldest of the three Shelton brothers who ran a bootlegging outfit in competition with Charles Birger, Carl was the brains of the operation. Released from prison after Birger was arrested, Shelton arranged to split Illinois with Al Capone – north of Peoria belonged to Capone, while south was Shelton territory.

George Kelly Barnes
Better known as Machine Gun Kelly, Barnes was a bootlegger in Memphis and Tulsa. As Prohibition came to an end, he attempted a botched kidnapping of two wealthy Oklahomans, Charles Urschel and Walter Jarrett. After his capture by the FBI, Barnes spent the rest of his life in prison.

appealed the decision, but on April 19, 1928, he became the penultimate man to be executed in public in Illinois.

Birger eventually accepted his death and showed humility. In a newspaper interview from his prison cell on the eve of the execution, he explained, "They've accused me of a lot of things I was never guilty of, but I was guilty of a lot of things which they never accused me of, so I guess we're about even." Birger wore a black hood for the hanging rather than the usual white one, which reminded him of the hated Klan. He

shook hands with the hangman, and his final words were, "It's a beautiful world."

The manner of Birger's death sealed his legend. Was he a Robin Hood figure who helped his community with the proceeds of his crimes, or was he just a violent thug? Was he a gangster with morals, or was his war with the Ku Klux Klan just to save his own skin? Whatever the case, Charles Birger is now the forgotten Al Capone of southern Illinois.

THE CASTELLAMMARESE WAR

Declaring what would become a bloody and violent war on the streets of New York City, Sicilian-born gangsters banded together in a bid to redefine the dynamics of the American Mafia.

The 1920s was a dynamic time for America's central hub of New York City. Prohibition laws had left an exploitable gap in the market for cheap liquor, extortion, and even murder. Crime was a babbling brook running through the city's veins until one day a war, one of the worst in US history, erupted on the sidewalks. Suddenly, the Mafia community became plagued by jealousy, betrayal, and greed in the name of victory and domination.

At the center of this were two warring criminal factions led by their bosses: Italian American mafiosos Joe "The Boss" Masseria and Salvatore Maranzano. Their gangs battled it out killing dozens of men between them, each boss determined to be top dog. The Castellammarese War, named after the victor's homeland, lasted a little more than fourteen months and birthed a new dawn in the gangster era, changing the face of the American Mafia for the next several decades. After more than a year of fighting, the tide left one rival the underdog, slaughtered by his own men and his rivals, with the Mafia in the hands of a new, forward-thinking crime boss.

Born in Menfi in the province of Agrigento, Sicily, Giuseppe (Joe) "The Boss" Masseria came to New York City as a sixteen-year-old boy with few prospects, having escaped a murder charge back in Italy. An immigrant in a foreign land, he joined the Morello crime family, one of the oldest established in the US, which operated out of Harlem and parts of Little Italy in southern Manhattan. Starting out as an enforcer and hitman, he was jailed for three years in 1913 for the burglary of a Bowery pawnshop. Released in 1916, the family had already undergone huge changes and a civil war for which the splintered factions of the family bore grudges and vendettas against their own kind for its outcome.

In 1910, its leader, boss of bosses Giuseppe "the Clutch Hand" Morello, and his coleader Ignazio Sietta were imprisoned for up to three decades on counterfeit charges along with several other allies leaving Morello's half-brothers Ciro, Vincent, and Nicholas Terranova as the presiding heads of the organization. In 1916, the Terranovas were suddenly challenged by their former partners, Brooklyn Camorra. Nicholas was murdered, but within a year the Camorra heads were imprisoned thanks to turncoats, leaving the family to lick their wounds. Salvatore D'Aquila, a Morello captain, broke away from the family, which was dissipating in absence of its leader and formed a rival family.

Because of his perceived wisdom and veteran family status, D'Aquila came to be regarded as a senior adviser among the New York Mafia. It was with D'Aquila's backing that Masseria rejoined the family upon his release from prison and made the head of a splinter faction of the family. Although he had been Morello's ally and a supporter of the Terranova leaders, D'Aquila kept him at arm's length, where he could watch him closely.

In 1920, Morello and Saietta were released from prison early for good behavior. Saietta

The war took place between 1929 and 1931 in New York City and decided the future of the Mafia

A playing card was still in Masseria's hand when gunmen blasted him to death, effectively ending the ongoing war

Castellammarese Clan

A number of men originally sided with Maranzano, making the rival faction of Masseria a force to be reckoned with

Joseph "Joe Bananas" Bonanno
A man with reportedly superior organizational skills and very quick instincts, Bonanno immediately became a protege of Maranzano during the outbreak of the war.

Stefano "The Undertaker" Magaddino
Born in Castellammare del Golfo, Sicily, Magaddino emigrated to the US in 1909, where he became boss of the Buffalo crime family and the the longest-tenured boss in the history of the American Mafia.

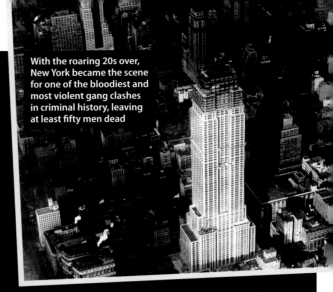

With the roaring 20s over, New York became the scene for one of the bloodiest and most violent gang clashes in criminal history, leaving at least fifty men dead

Joseph Profaci
Italian-born olive oil importer Profaci was rumored to have been neutral during the war. However, other sources have claimed that he was actually firmly aligned with Maranzano.

Joe Aiello
Wanting to kill Prohibition crime boss Al Capone, Aiello went to Masseria for support, which ended in an argument that allegedly played a vital role in the outbreak of the war.

Vito Bonventre
The leader of a group known as the "Good Killers" and part of the Schiro crime family, Bonventre became a target after family members threatened to take out Masseria. Masseria forced Schiro to pay him $10,000 and resign as boss of the family. After this incident, Bonventre was gunned down outside his garage.

"Gangsters began to resent Masseria for his stringent and unwavering ways"

returned to his homeland of Sicily but Morello remained in the US, determined to rejoin the family. D'Aquila sensed that his position as the head of the crime family was about to be threatened, and so ordered the murders of both the former captain and his ally Masseria. D'Aquila's disgraced henchman and long-serving family member Rocco Valenti offered to take care of the hit in a bid to return to favor with the crime boss. While he was supposedly one of – if not the best – hitmen at D'Aquila's disposal, his failed attempts to shoot Masseria resulted in a civil war commencing on December 19, 1921.

The war raged on for less than eight months, ending with Masseria's men shooting Valenti dead. Masseria became the new boss of bosses, having established a new-found respect for himself with the Italian underworld in light, Valenti's failed point-blank assassination, having earned the nickname "the man who can dodge bullets." D'Aquila was shot in 1928, supposedly by his former right-hand man, who became Masseria's underboss – Alfred Mineo. Throughout the 1920s, Masseri ruled with an iron fist, building himself up an empire of loyal Sicilian-born American gangsters, as well as those from the Calabria and Campania regions of southern Italy.

Across the waters, powerful Sicilian mafioso Don Vito Ferro got wind of the rising powers of the Italian-American mafia, and decided to make

a bid for control of its operations in the United States. From his base in the rural Castellammare del Golfo, he sent Salvatore Maranzano to seize control. The well-connected Castellammarese mafioso came to America in 1925, setting up a large alcohol distillery to benefit from Prohibition. He stuck out like a sore thumb, revolting against Masseria's dictatorship.

Maranzano was, on the account of crime boss Joe Bonanno, a "gentleman's gentleman," and according to crime historians, the mobster was a smart, avid reader who had, prior to his gangster days, studied for the priesthood. Masseria was unimpressed with the newcomer, deeming him and his people "country bumpkins" and "hinterland primitives." According to Masseria, the Castellammare people were "incapable of ever assuming responsible roles in the organization's hierarchy."

In New York, Masseria was determined to have the Mafia dance to his own tune. In Carl Sifakis' book *The Mafia Encyclopedia*, he describes Masseria as "a glutton in personal habits, as well as administration of criminal activities." It seems the power began to go to Masseria's head and behind closed doors, other gangsters began to resent Masseria for his stringent and unwavering ways. Times were changing in New York, and Masseria represented everything old and outdated about the Mafia. Sensing the outpouring of dissatisfaction within the

community, Maranzano plotted against Masseria, promising a change to the masses. Unlike Masseria, who demanded huge sums of profits from their exploits and criminal enterprises as tribute, Maranzano promized a fair division of assets and territories.

For some, Maranzano represented the ideals that they so desired when it came to their criminal activity. In Bonanno's autobiography *A Man of Honor*, published in 1983, he explained how the factions had just wanted to be left alone and allowed to carry out their business uninterrupted, unaffected by Masseria.

Giuseppe (Joe) "The Boss" Masseria's old ways of running the Mafia saw him become "Public Enemy Number One" when the promise of a fairer governed system presented itself in his rival, Salvatore Maranzano

Masseria's was ambushed while meeting with Lucky Luciano at a restaurant on Coney Island. No one was ever charged with his murder

The divide in ideas left Masseria loyalists continuously butting heads with new age thinkers wanting to follow Maranzano.

The tensions between the two factions began as early as 1928. One side would target the other's lucratively profitable alcohol trucks, which were racking cash up in light of the Prohibition laws that were rife in America at the time. In response, the other side would target their rival's bars and clubs, smashing them up in retaliation. According to multiple sources, the proverbial opening shots in the war were fired within the Masseria faction, although crime historian Jay Robert Nash claims it was Maranzano who opened the avenues of war for honor's sake. In order to protect and maintain the criminal empire that he had built up, Maranzano reportedly declared war on his rival in February 1930.

That same month, in order to protect his secret allies Tommy Gagliano, Tommy Lucchese, and Dominick "The Gap" Petrilli, Masseria ordered the murder of his lieutenant, Gaetano Reina. Masseria believed that he was conspiring with Marazano and putting the rest of his men at risk. He gave the job to young Vito Genovese. Masseria treplaced Reina with Giuseppe Pinzolo as head of his crew. Reina's murder cost him the support of the Reina clan, who threw their support behind Masseria's rival. Within weeks, two other prominent Castellammarese allies had been shot and killed.

Less than eight months later, on October 23, 1930, Castellammarese ally Joe Aiello, president of the Chicago Unione Siciliana, was gunned down in Chicago, shot at least thirteen times in the street. At the time, it was widely assumed that Al Capone, another Castellammarese ally, had killed him as part of a bitter feud between the two. However, Luciano later admitted that Masseria ordered the hit, which was performed by Masseria ally Alfred Mineo. On February 5, 1931, yet another Masseria loyalist, Joseph Catania, was murdered. New York City Police estimated that as many as fifty men were killed as a result of the war.

Masseria's men were growing tired of the battle. As well as having to constantly look over their shoulders, the violence was bad for business and with no resolution in sight, Charles "Lucky" Luciano, Frank Costello, and Vito Genovese along with a number of other Masseria supporters, began plotting to kill their leader, luring him to a lunch meeting on Coney Island on April 15, 1931. While playing cards with Masseria, Luciano excused himself and went to the bathroom. Suddenly four gunman, believed to be Bugsy Siegel, Albert Anastasia, Joe Adonis, and Genovese, entered the restaurant and murdered him. No one was convicted of Masseria's murder – there were no witnesses, and Luciano had an alibi. With the leader of the rival faction six feet under, the war had finally come to an end. Maranzano was the victor, declaring himself the undisputed leader of the Mafia – but not for long.

> The war was named after the hometown of the clashing bosses – Castellammare del Golfo in Sicily, Italy

Messeria's Men

With so many men at his disposal, Masseria had a viable army to take on Maranzano at the start of the war

Charles "Lucky" Luciano
Masseria's gunman Luciano was a racketeer, extortionist, bootlegger, and drug trafficker and eventually became a renegade of the group, luring Masseria to his death.

Albert "Mad Hatter" Anastasia
A fierce and ruthless mobster and leader of the International Longshoremen's Association, he assured Luciano he would kill anyone who got in his way to reach the top of the mafioso hierarchy.

Vito Genovese
A bootlegger and extortionist, Masseria's enforcer emigrated to the US with his family at the age of fifteen, residing in Little Italy. Joining forces with Masseria, Genovese's main value to him was his propensity for violence.

Alfred Mineo
D'Aquila's former underboss, he supposedly shot his former boss on October 10, 1928 in a bid to show his loyalty to Masseria.

Frank Costello

Bootlegger, businessman, racketeer, and crime boss Frank Costello entered criminal life as a young boy. Adjoining alliances with Luciano to organize Masseria's death in 1931 he then became Luciano's advisor.

Willie Moretti
Costello's right-hand man and cousin, he was famously connected to singer Frank Sinatra's godfather.

Joe Adonis

Born Giuseppe Antonio Doto in the small Italian town of Montemarano near Naples, he was crime boss Frankie Yale's enforcer before his death in 1928. After that, he then joined Masseria's group.

THE RISE AND FALL OF THE NEW YORK MAFIA

The bloody era of the mob war was finally over and a new dawn was on the horizon for the landscape of crime in America – but peace among mobsters was still a distant prospect.

After the final few trickles of blood from the violent Castellammarese War had pooled to a stop, the victorious Salvatore Maranzano established a new secret set up for the gangsters – La Cosa Nostra, he called it. Based on the Sicilian Mafia setup that was thriving across the waters, twenty-four "families" across the US would elect their own boss. Five families were established in New York: the Luciano family under Lucky Luciano, the Mangano family under Vincent Mangano, the Gagliano family under Tommy Gagliano, the Profaci family under Joseph Profaci, and the Maranzano crime family, which he would rule as the capo di tutti capi – "boss of all bosses." A hierarchy was established: heading the family was the boss, with an underboss as second in command, a consigliere or advisor would be the boss' right-hand man, and soldiers would carry out the legwork working for the caporegime beneath the underboss. This hierarchy, along with a core agreement that the families would carry out their business on their own allotted turf was a new beginning for the criminals in the hope that peace would once again be restored.

Unlike real families, rivalry ran deep with few achieving peace for long. Unwilling to serve under Maranzano's rule, Luciano sent five disguized men to his office to murder him, taking his place as the most powerful gangster in the country. The family structure as created by Maranzano was adhered to, but Luciano removed the boss of bosses' status in favor of a Board of Directors ("The Commission") made up of the Five New York Families plus the Chicago Outfit and Buffalo family, with Luciano as Chairman of the Commission.

Joseph Bonanno's crime family was at one stage the most powerful and successful of the Five Families, and prospered in the running of businesses involving loan sharking, bookmaking, numbers-running, and prostitution

BONANNO

TERRITORY: Brooklyn, Queens, Staten Island, Long Island, Manhattan, The Bronx, Westchester County, New Jersey, California, and Florida, as well as ties to the Montreal Mafia in Quebec

Originally, the Maranzano family, headed by Salvatore Maranzano, power was awarded to 26-year-old Joseph Bonanno after his murder. Between 1931-61, the group was the most powerful of the Five Families. However, by the early 1960s Bonanno's position was in peril after the death of his ally, family boss Giuseppe Profaci, and the harmonization of the Lucchese and Gambino clans. What's more, his own faction was beginning to grow discontent with its leader.

To regain control, Bonanno and Profaci's successor Joe Magliocco conspired to wipe out the other bosses. The plot was foiled when the arranged gunman, Joseph Colombo, revealed their plan to The Commission. Bonanno fled the city and disappeared for two years. Undeterred by Bonanno's vanishing act, the panel ordered he be replaced by Gaspare DiGregorio in 1964.

Constant hostilities between Bonanno and DiGregorio loyalists resulted in a four-year war. Dissatisfied with the internal fighting, the panel ordered that DiGregorio be superseded

by Paul Sciacca. Tensions in the family continued to mount until Bonanno announced his permanent retirement in 1968, and Natale Evola was promoted to Bonanno head. Sick of the strained relations of the Bonanno family, it was stripped of its seat among The Commission. Evola died in 1973.

Philip Rastelli took over the Bonanno unit. His close friend Carmine Galante infamously took over the family and orchestrating the murder of eight members of the Genovese clan. He was removed from the family, later shot dead in Brooklyn, and Rastelli was put back in power. In 1981 came the first of what would be two major disgraces to the family name, when it was discovered that undercover FBI agent Joseph Pistone, under the alias "Donnie Brasco," had infiltrated their ranks, resulting in

lengthy sentences for Rastelli and his soldier Benjamin "Lefty Guns" Ruggiero and a second disgraceful removal from the panel. During the September 1986 Mafia Commission Trial, which saw multiple members of the New York Mafia indicted, the Bonannos were the only family to avoid indictment. From behind bars, Rastelli operated as mafioso until he died in 1991 when Joseph Massino was promoted to boss.

In 2004, Massino became the first-ever Mafia boss in the history of the organization to become an FBI informant. For nearly a decade, a number of members served as the family boss, but in 2013, Michael Mancuso, who is currently imprisoned, was named the new official boss of the family.

"FBI agent Joseph Pistone, under the alias "Donnie Brasco," had infiltrated their ranks"

COLOMBO

TERRITORY: Brooklyn, Queens, Long Island, Staten Island, Manhattan, The Bronx, New Jersey, and Florida

In 1928, Lucciano named a young Giuseppe "Joe" Profaci as the head of one of the Five Families. Profaci went on to be one of the longest-serving mafia bosses in history – his reign was virtually unchallenged until the late 1950s. After capo Frank Abbatemarco racked up a debt of over $50,000 from his policy game scheme, Profaci looked to Joseph Gallo, aka "Crazy Joe," to take him out. In exchange for the hit, Profaci promized he would hand over the police racket to Gallo.

After Abbatemarco was shot and killed in Brooklyn on November 4, 1959, Profaci ordered criminal associates and Gallo brothers Larry and Albert "Kid Blast" to hand over Abbatemarco's son, but was refused, so Profaci revoked his promise to Crazy Joe, prompting the first of the three wars to break out among the family. In 1961, Gallo was imprisoned for murder. The following year Profaci died from cancer, ending the first war, leaving Joe Magliocco as Mafioso leader.

Looking for allies, it was Magliocco who looked to Joseph Colombo to take down the leaders of the major crime families as part of a conspiracy with the Bonanno family leader. When Columbo alerted The Commission, Magliocco was forced into retirement, leaving Colombo the head of the family. When Gallo was released from prison in 1971, his determination to head up the family resulted in the shooting of Colombo, but his mentee Carmine Persico led a gang to push back against Gallo, who was exiled to the Genovese family in 1975. With Colombo out of action after his attempted execution, Thomas DiBella was named boss. Poor health forced DiBella to retire in 1977. Colombo died in 1978, leaving Persico the rightful and undisputed leader of the family for two decades.

Arrested in 1986 on massive Racketeer Influenced and Corrupt Organizations Act (RICO) charges as part of what was the Mafia Commission Trial, Persico was sentenced to 100 years in prison. Persico's loyalty to his superior was not mirrored in acting boss Victor Orena, who tried to take over the family, which was in complete disarray after his incarceration.

Persico's loyalists and Orena's men fought for two years, leaving 80 associates and made members imprisoned, including Orena, 12 members dead, and Persico the winner. Persico continued to lead the family as boss up until his death in 2019. Despite its active status, many believe the Colombo crime family is the weakest of the Five Families today.

Giuseppe "Joe" Profaci was the longest serving boss in mafia history, ruling the youngest of the Five Families for over three decades until he died in 1962

GAMBINO

TERRITORY: Brooklyn, Queens, Manhattan, Staten Island, Long Island, The Bronx, New Jersey, Westchester County, Connecticut, Grand Rapids, Michigan, Florida, and Los Angeles

As part of his victory, Moranzano appointed Frank Scalise head of the old D'Aquila/Mineo gang, one of New York's new Five Families. But after Moranzano's assassination, Lucciano overruled his decision and replaced him with Vincent Mangano, who renamed the gang.

Mangano made his brother Philip as his consigliere and dangerous mobster Albert Anastasia, otherwise known as "Lord High Executioner," his underboss. Mobster Carlo Gambino was also brought into the fold.

In April 1951, Mangano disappeared without a trace, never to be found again. Philip was found dead, and while no one was ever charged with the brothers' deaths, suspicion immediately fell on Anastasia, a much-feared personality within the mob – even The Commission were intimidated by him and named him as the next leader.

On October 25, 1957, Anastasia was murdered, leaving Gambino as the boss of the now newly named Gambino family, which he quickly built into the most powerful crime family in the United States. On October 15, 1976, Gambino died of a heart attack, passing the role of leader onto Paul Castellano. Queens-based capo John Gotti vocally critiqued Castellano as their leader. A protege of Aniello Dellacroce, Castellano's underboss, Gotti found his life on the line when potentially damning evidence almost fell into Castellano's hands, which would have exposed Gotti as a traitor.

Dellacroce protected Gotti, but after he died in December 1985, Gotti realized he had to act quickly and kill Castellano before he had the chance to question Gotti's loyalty. On December 16, 1985, as Castellano and his underboss Thomas Bilotti left for a Manhattan dinner meeting, four unidentified men shot them to death, leaving Gotti as the new boss come the New Year. The FBI were hot on Gotti's trail, but he escaped prosecution every time.

Eventually, the authorities snared him when they bugged an apartment above his Little Italy headquarters. In 1992, Gotti was convicted of five murders, conspiracy to commit murder, racketeering, obstruction of justice, tax evasion, illegal gambling, extortion, and loan sharking, and was sentenced to life in prison without parole. He died in 2002. Following Gotti's incarceration, his son John "Junior" Gotti took over as head of the family up until his incarceration in 1999 when Gotti Sr.'s brother took over the family reins. Imprisoned in 2003, he continued to run the family from behind bars for many years. The current family is believed to be under the control of Lorenzo Mannino, after Francesco "Frank" Cali was assassinated in 2019.

Albert Anastasia, known as "Lord High Executioner" and founder of crime syndicate Murder Inc., was a ruthless force in the Gambino family until he was executed during an infamous showdown at a Manhattan barber in 1957

DAILY NEWS

Gotti and pals acquitted

HE'S HOME FREE!

GENOVESE

TERRITORY: Manhattan, The Bronx, Brooklyn, New Jersey, Queens, Staten Island, Long Island, Westchester County, Rockland County, Connecticut, Massachusetts, and Florida

Known as the Luciano crime family from 1931 to 1957, its leader was sentenced to thirty to fifty years in prison in 1936, accused of being the ringleader of a major prostitution ring. From behind bars, Luciano continued to run the family, with his underboss Vito Genovese supervising the family. In 1937, Genovese was indicted on murder charges and fled the country to Italy, leaving Frank Costello as the new acting boss of the family, eventually becoming the leader in 1938 when Luciano stepped down.

When Genovese returned to New York, having been acquitted of the 1936 murder charge that saw him exiled, he was determined to regain control of the family. Costello suffered from depression and anxiety attacks, and after he was almost executed by Luciano mobster Vincent "Chin" Gigante and his powerful associate Albert Anastasia was gunned down in early 1957, he demurely retired, handing over the reins to Genovese. He was tricked into a narcotics scheme that resulted in a lengthy prison sentence in 1959. The Genovese family suffered further embarrassment when Genovese soldier Joseph "Joe Cargo" Valachi revealed the inner workings of La Cosa Nostra during a 1963 trial, helping authorities identify the Five Families and their inner workings.

After Genovese's death in 1969, Philip "Benny Squint" Lombardo was officially named family boss. With law enforcement watching the families closely, Lombardo's leadership status was protected by a series of "front bosses" to throw the FBI off his scent. When Genovese's acting boss was killed by the Gambino boss, a reshuffle meant drafting in Gambino ally Frank "Funzi" Tieri as the new front boss and Michele "Big Mike" Miranda as advisor. After Tieri's shocking imprisonment in 1981 under the new RICO Act, the family reshuffled its leadership again making Anthony "Fat Tony" Salerno, capo of the Manhattan faction, the new front boss. Lombardo, the de facto boss of the family, retired and Chin Gigante, the triggerman on the failed Frank Costello hit, took control of the family.

Following the Mafia Commission Trial, which saw front boss Salerno sentenced to 100 years in federal prison under the belief he was leading the Genovese family, his right-hand man Vincent "The Fish" Cafaro revealed to the FBI that Salerno had never really been the boss, but was merely a ruse for "The Oddfather" Gigante. Gigante died in 2005, passing the leadership onto Genovese capo Daniel "Danny the Lion" Leo who allegedly remains acting boss to this day.

Charles "Lucky" Luciano headed up The Commission, made up of the major crime bosses in the US

In a bid to convince court-assigned psychiatrists that he was mentally unfit and therefore avoid conviction for criminal charges, Chin Gigante, The Oddfather, would wonder through New York in his dressing gown

After crime boss Tommy Lucchese died, he had wanted his underboss Anthony Carello (pictured) to take over as family leader, but Carello was already in prison serving a sentence for the Marcus bribery case and so the role was passed on until his release

LUCCHESE

TERRITORY: The Bronx, Manhattan, Brooklyn, New Jersey, Queens, Long Island, Staten Island, Westchester County, and Florida

Established in the early 1920s, the Lucchese family was long celebrated as one of the most peaceful crime families in the nation. Following the Castellammarese War, Sicilian-born mobster Tommy Gagliano continued to rule the family, as he had done before the war broke out, until the early 1950s when he stepped down. Taking over from Gagliano was his underboss Tommy Lucchese, who carried on Gagliano's policies and ensured the family was one of the most profitable and well looked after in New York. The family made much of its profits by establishing control over Teamsters union locals, workers' co-operatives and trade associations, as well as rackets at the new Idlewild Airport, further expanding the family business around New York.

In 1962, an alliance between the Gambino and Lucchese clan was formed as a result of a marriage between the two families

– Gambino's oldest son and Lucchese's daughter. Lucchese died from a brain tumor on July 13, 1967.

He had intended for long-serving capo Anthony Carello to take over from him, but as he was in prison at the time, he named Carmine Tramunti as his successor pending Carello's release. On to of his ailing health, Tramunti was convicted of financing a large heroin-smuggling operation in 1974.

Luckily, Carello's release meant he could finally take over from the temporary boss – until the FBI bugged him, giving details of the syndicate's involvement in illegal gambling, labor racketeering, drug trafficking, and murder, giving way to the Mafia Commission Trial in the late 80s.

Carello was sentenced to 100 years, naming Victor Amuso the "Deadly Don" as his successor. Amuso and his underboss Anthony

Casso began one of the bloodiest reigns in Mafia history: over 100 murders were ordered by Casso, at least eight of which were carried out by NYPD detectives Louis Eppolito and Stephen Caracappa, and approximately 40 of those murders were committed by his own hand.

Arrested in 1991, Casso was sentenced to 455 years in prison, but with several men fearing for their life, they turned informant against the crime boss. Lucchese's acting boss Alphonse D'Arco became the first boss, acting or otherwise, of a New York crime family to testify against the mob, leading to the arrest of the entire Lucchese family.

Eventually, Casso became an informant too. Collectively, the testimony of several family members all-but destroyed the unit. Amuso has continued to rule the family from the Maryland institution where he is housed.

CONMEN & COMMON CRIMINALS

140

110

122

118

132

999

CHARLES PONZI

The fall of an infamous pyramid scheme and the man who came crumbling down with it.

Stepping off the gangplank of the SS Vancouver, the brisk winds of a Bostonian winter met an ambitious five-foot-two Italian immigrant named Charles Ponzi. Born in 1882 in Parma Italy, Ponzi made the grueling journey across the Atlantic in pursuit of his fortune. Arriving in Boston, Massachusetts, in 1903, armed with only a handful of cash, Ponzi hoped the streets of Boston would be paved in gold, and paved in gold they were, with each footstep belonging to a potential goldmine.

During the early twentieth century, international postal reply coupons became a regular occurrence when writing to people in other countries. This scrap of paper would accompany an international letter, allowing its receiver to send a reply at no expense. As one of these vouchers fell to his feet from an opened letter in 1919, so did the inspiration for Ponzi's iconic moneymaking idea. But how could a mailing coupon bring about a scheme that by the following year would make Ponzi $15 million richer? As a form of prepaid postage, these coupons held monetary value subject to exchange rates in different countries. Should a person from Spain, for example, send a coupon to the US, it could be exchanged at a US post office for its monetary value – much higher than that of its purchase in Spain.

This postal profit formed the basis for Ponzi's promising investment opportunity. Investors could hand over their hard-earned cash in his "Securities Exchange Company" under the impression that Ponzi would exchange these coupons en masse and then reap the benefits of America's higher exchange rate. With a Ponzi promise of a fifty percent return on investments in forty-five days or doubled in six months, it was an offer too good to refuse, and as word spread, both rich and poor began to line up outside the company's School Street office

It was reported that Ponzi was receiving around $250,000 a day. The scheme, based on math, was rather a game of the mind over money. In his 1936 self-gratifying autobiography, *The Rise of Mr Ponzi*, he writes, "People gambled with me as I thought they would. They gave me ten dollars as a lark. When they received fifteen at the end of forty-five days, all sense of caution left them. They plunged in for all they were worth."

As the money continued to pour in, his new-found fortune placed Ponzi firmly in high society, and with that came all its expectations of materialistic gluttony. At the height of his multi-million-dollar empire, Ponzi purchased a twelve-room mansion in Lexington, Massachusetts, stocked with the fixtures and fineries you would expect of an authentic gentleman of roaring 20s. However, one of his more lavish purchases came in the form of a bank, the Hanover Trust, which had previously denied him a loan of $2,000. Ponzi is said to have purchased 1,500 shares, making him the major stockholder in the trust, and in his eyes making him an owner.

His extravagant and scandalous dealings could only be described as true showmanship.

Ponzi managed to scam almost $7 million out of investors in the early 1900s

Ponzi's scheme was so successful that it still bears his name today

Ponzi was convicted as a conman and served time in and out of state prison from 1920-34

5247

To the rest of the world, Ponzi was a financial wizard; a revolutionary of his time, people were buying into his facade just as much as his schemes. In an interview with the *New York Times*, Ponzi said, "I landed in this country with $2.50 in cash and $1 million in hopes, and those hopes never left me." Posing as a self-made financial hero, Ponzi had made his dreams of incredible wealth a reality, void of any conscious or consequence – until the media caught wind.

Ponzi could not claim full responsibility for creating his rise to financial fortune. His dealings with the media helped skyrocket his scheme, but would ultimately be the cause of its catastrophic crumble. A gentleman in both style and demeanor, Ponzi wooed not only his investors, but also newspaper reporters, with his charm and charisma – including that of Mr. William McMasters, a former newspaper reporter, who by the recommendation of the Hanover Trust became Ponzi's publicist. As such, McMasters organized an interview with *The Boston Post*, a prestigious paper that had the power to drive Ponzi's business through the roof.

The Post featured Ponzi and his remarkable promises of high-return investments in their Saturday edition on July 24, 1920, and so began a media frenzy. Spread across the front cover of the prestigious paper reads the headline, "Doubles the Money Within Three Months; Fifty Percent Interest Paid in Forty-Five Days by Ponzi–Has Thousands of Investors." As a result, people flocked to the School Street office, giving Ponzi his biggest payday to date – around $3 million. News of Ponzi's investment opportunity spread across nearly every paper in America, causing him to become one of the most talked about businessmen of the time.

On paper, Ponzi was the perfect success story; he was a young immigrant with only a handful of cash, but a head full of dreams, who then made those dreams a reality. Ponzi's story, however, was not one of rags to riches, but an elaborate deception of the American dream. Suspicions began to grow around the validity of Ponzi's fantastical scheme and the bold claims he had made.

For the Love of Money. . .and Rose

Money wasn't the only love of Ponzi's life – an all-American girl named Rose Gnecco became the focus of his attention and stole his heart. In his autobiography, Ponzi wrote, "Rose is the most precious gift America could have tendered me."

Captivated by his charisma, Rose married Ponzi in 1918, a year after they had met. It's clear from his reflective writing that his love for Rose was as heartfelt as his love of money. It is reported that Rose wanted to settle down, but Ponzi's continued hunger for riches kept them from the simple life. Rose rode the roller coaster alongside her husband's fraudulent career and became a victim along with eight of her relatives. Ponzi had reportedly loaned around $16,000 from the family with no return.

Upon his release from jail and following his deportation to Italy, she is said to have waited a further two years for Ponzi to find employment before filing for a trans-Atlantic divorce. She went on to remarry and lived life by pinched purse strings.

Ponzi's wife Rose witnessed the highs and lows of his conman career

"The once sharply styled man of the roaring 20s had become unrecognizable"

Unknown to Ponzi, his publicist, Mr. McMasters, had become aware of the truth and, returning to his reporting roots, he wrote an exposé for the very newspaper that had put Ponzi on the map. Sprawled across the cover of *The Boston Post* read the headline, "Declares Ponzi is now Hopelessly Insolvent." The next morning, a line of people as long, if not longer, than the one that had gifted him millions stood outside his office. However, this time they wanted their money back. After official investigations into its legitimacy, it soon became clear that behind the scenes, this ingenious investment opportunity was no more than a scheme. Ponzi was using the money from one investor to pay another, with the purchase of postal coupons nowhere to be seen.

Ponzi continued to dominate the headlines of newspapers across America. However, a once-sensational story of a financial genius quickly became the tale of a scandalous swindler.

But his exposed pyramid scheme was not the only indiscretion the press uncovered during their crusade. Before arriving in Boston, it came to light that Ponzi had begun his swindling ways on a previous stop in Canada. There, he was convicted of forging a check in Montreal and sentenced to twenty months in jail.

In August 1920, Ponzi was convicted for fraud by Massachusetts state and sentenced to five years imprisonment, of which he served three and a half before being paroled. This provided Ponzi with another golden opportunity and he traveled to Florida in an attempt to sell swampland to raise outstanding debts. The

scheme broke apart as the previous one had, and he was arrested again for fraud. He wasted no time and skipped bail, heading to Texas.

During his state-crossing spree, the Supreme Judicial Court of Massachusetts had upheld his conviction, and Ponzi was soon picked up by officials in Texas. After bringing him back to Massachusetts, Ponzi served his final sentence for fraud in state prison until 1934. It's believed that on release, the once sharply styled man of the roaring 20s had become an unrecognizable, overweight, and balding version of his once-successful self.

Ponzi was deported back to Italy, where he went on to work for an Italian airline in Brazil, which faced hardship due to World War II and subsequently folded. Ponzi continued to work as an English teacher and interpreter until his death in 1949 at the age of sixty-six, a poor man in a hospital charity ward in Rio de Janeiro.

During his life, Ponzi reached the highest of highs and fell to the lowest of lows. His story is one of scandal, scheme, and showmanship, and in true Ponzi fashion he explains it best, writing: "A new rainbow had come within my range of vision. The most spectacular I ever saw. With renewed energy and enthusiasm, I chased after it. I caught up with it. When I did, I found fifteen million dollars at the end of it. I should have called it a day. And quitted while the quitting was good. I didn't. Hence, this story."

The Con Continues

The story of Ponzi is a tale of such monumental success and equally devastating downfall that it's hard to imagine that anyone could find inspiration from it. However, in the years to come, many did, and just as Ponzi had done, each inspiration came crumbling beneath them.

Although it appears no one has duplicated Ponzi's coupon scheme, many have used his concept of borrowing from one investor to pay another while pocketing money along the way. Conmen like Tom Petters, who swindled $3.65 billion through investments in nonexistent products, and Scientologist minister Reed Slatkin, who stole $600 million from his followers, are just some of the Ponzi enthusiasts that carried on his legacy.

Bernie Madoff, however, took Ponzi's scheme and truly ran with it, operating a "wealth management company" until 2008. Stealing $65 billion from the scheme's investors, Madoff had committed the largest fraud in US history, and as a result, he found himself sentenced to 150 years in prison.

Taking inspiration from one of the original conmen Ponzi, Bernie Madoff faced a similar fate

© Getty

SOAPY SMITH

From Texas to Alaska, one man conned his way around turn-of-the-century America, leaving fear and chaos in his wake.

In the 1890s, a gold rush drew all sorts of characters to northwest Canada and Alaska in search of their fortune. These included outcasts and criminals, who flocked to the gold rush towns in search of miners and prospectors – dupes they could steal from. One man the authorities had been keen to keep out of the goldfields was a particularly slippery individual – Soapy Smith, so-called "king of the frontier confidence men." The Canadian Mounties were responsible for policing the gold rush and had made a concerted effort to keep the mining fields around Dawson City in the Yukon "clean," so workers could safely carry their gold about without fear of attack. As a result, Soapy, described as "the blackest character who ever disgraced a mining camp with his presence," was kept beyond the city limits.

This dark character lived a relatively short life, but he certainly packed a lot into it. Born in Georgia on November 2, 1860 as Jefferson Randolph Smith II, he was not from a criminal family. In fact, he came from an educated, middle-class background, with his father being an attorney, and his grandfather a senator. However, their status changed with the Civil War. It ruined the family financially, so they decided to start again in an area where they and their problems were not known. Therefore, when he was sixteen, Soapy's family moved to Texas, settling in the town of Round Rock. For Soapy, the move also gave him the chance to start a career – as a conman.

Round Rock was part of the American West, straddling a fault line between the Blackland Prairie and the more undulating Texas Hill Country. Until 1854, it had been known as Brushy Creek, but it had been renamed by the town's postmaster after the rock that stood in the middle of the creek, which provided a crossing for the local wagons as well as cattle and horses. Cotton was grown here along with grapes, and many locals raized livestock – not only cows and sheep, but also goats. It was a small but growing place: in 1860, it was home to some 450 residents, but within the next decade, that number would rise to 800.

This was the rural, small-town environment that a young, excitable man looked for entertainment in. He waited for some time, but in the summer of 1878, it happened. There had been a robbery on the Fort Worth to Cleburne train, and one of the suspects, Sam Bass, had fled to the Round Rock area. He was found, but tried to run away. A gunfight ensued between Bass and local rangers George Herold and Richard Ware. Soapy and his cousin Edwin were standing near Ranger Ware, and on Bass being shot and killed, Soapy shouted, "I think you got him!"

Despite this excitement, however, Soapy realized he had outgrown Round Rock. His mother had died the year before and there was little keeping him in this small agricultural community, so he decided to move to Fort Worth, just under 200 miles north. Although today Fort Worth is a major city, in the 1860s,

Soapy Smith went from confidence tricking to politics where his criminal streak continued

A2 — Soapy

Soapy Smith, Wild West gangster, conman and swindler – never more at home than in a saloon, he started his cons on street corners

Fame or Infamy?

For those he conned, he was a figure to be feared or avoided. Yet to the uninitiated who read about his deeds from a distance, he was also something of a folk hero. His affairs were covered by newspapers across America and beyond – from the *Rocky Mountain News* to the *Skagway News*, and even to the English and Irish provincial newspapers. Although he was recognized as a "cool, heartless" swindler whose reputation prevented his victims from trying to seek retribution, stories of his more audacious cons were eagerly repeated by the press, even as they noted that his death "rid the Klondike of its terror."

Just a month after his death, the press reported plans to embalm Soapy's body and exhibit it publicly "in all the chief cities and towns of the West." The appeal of Soapy Smith's life has continued ever since. The first book about him was published in 1907, and he quickly became seen as a sympathetic figure, one who challenged authority and helped the poor. Today, there is even an annual celebration of the con.

A recent musical theater show in Skagway, based on Soapy Smith's life and crimes

the Civil War had devastated it, decimating its population. Soapy arrived as the city was in the midst of reconstruction; its population was again growing, and stores and businesses were opening. It was home to numerous saloons and taverns, and its residents were seen as prime targets to be conned.

It was in Fort Worth that Soapy started to develop a network of other conmen who he could work with on confidence tricks. They became known as the Soap Gang, and their numbers later included significant swindlers such as Texas Jack Vermillion and "Big Ed" Burns. Soapy would organize speedy swindles known as "short cons" that could be done quickly and easily, without the need for elaborate set-ups. They included poker games, which were, of course, rigged. Over the next two decades, Soapy and his gang traveled from town to town to con the residents with such skill that he became known as "king of the frontier conmen."

By 1879, he had developed the con that gave him his name – the prize soap racket. By this time, he was working in Colorado, and in Denver he started to place a display case, mounted on a tripod, on a street corner that saw significant

The final, deceptively peaceful, resting place of Soapy Smith, in Skagway, Alaska. He died in a gunfight here in 1898

In Skagway, Alaska, Soapy set up his headquarters at Jeff Smith's Parlor, the place proudly displaying his real name

"Nobody won anything – apart from Soapy and his gang members"

footfall. He would open the case and display bars of soap on it, "selling" their benefits to the curious onlookers who would soon gather in front of him. He would then wrap a few of the bars in dollar bills – anything from one to 100 dollars – and then wrap plain paper over them, so that all the bars looked identical. The bars would be mixed up, and then the crowd would be invited to buy a bar for a dollar each. A planted gang member would wave a bar around, claiming to have found a dollar bill in it. Convinced the salesman was genuine, onlookers would queue to buy their own bar – or even several. After a while, Soapy would tell the crowd the $100 bill still remained to be found and auction off the unsold soap to the highest bidders. Of course, Soapy had actually first replaced the soap bars containing money with ordinary ones, thanks to a skill with sleight of hand. Nobody won anything – apart from Soapy and his gang members.

Although Soapy had moved from town to town in order to avoid suspicion or capture, in Denver he found that his reputation actually protected him. He had money and power, and was able to bribe corrupt politicians and policemen. Those he hadn't bribed were often too scared of Soapy's infamous temper to arrest him, even when they suspected him of a crime, and he

> The name "Soapy Smith" came about when he refused to give police officers his name during his slippery swindle

had a network of "friendly" lawyers and contacts who could get him out of jail quickly if he was arrested. Even when there were allegations of corruption and fraud following local elections in 1889, focusing on Soapy, the Denver mayor, and the chief of police, Soapy was never charged – even though the mayor lost his job. Instead, he was able to open an office as a front for his more ambitious swindles, having already opened the Tivoli Club, a saloon and gambling house.

This is not to say there was nobody out to get Soapy. Indeed, he faced several assassination attempts and not only survived, but managed to shoot some of his assailants. His network of contacts and his loyal gang also ensured he could keep conning. He grew dissatisfied, though, and in 1892, in search of new communities to control, he moved to a Colorado mining town, Creede. Here, he bought up property along the main street, and opened another gambling hall and saloon, the Orleans Club, while developing contacts in the town council and growing richer and richer. However, seeing signs that the Creede boom was about to burst, he soon fled back to Denver.

More cons followed and Soapy even became deputy sheriff. When the closure of the city's saloons was ordered, he used his power to make fake arrests, letting individuals walk free if they

didn't try to recoup the losses they had made in his poker games. When Soapy was charged with beating up a saloon manager, however, he realized he had gone too far, and fled to Alaska. In Skagway, he started to build a new empire. He opened a fake telegraph office and a new saloon, which served as his "base." Finally, though, came retribution.

On July 7, 1898, Soapy's gang engaged in a rigged game with Klondike miner John Douglas Stewart. Stewart lost but refused to give up his money, so Soapy's men grabbed the gold and fled. The vigilance committee arranged a meeting at the Juneau wharf to discuss matters the following evening. Soapy tried to join them but his way was blocked by city surveyor Frank Reid. The men, joined by three other guards, started fighting. "My God, don't shoot!" shouted Soapy, but it was too late. Frank shot Soapy straight in the heart, killing him instantly. An eventful life had ended with death on an Alaskan wharf at the age of thirty-eight, marking the end of Soapy's swindles.

Gold Rush Greed

The Klondike Gold Rush saw around 100,000 gold prospectors rush to the Klondike region of northwest Canada, following the discovery of gold there in August 1896. A key route for prospectors was to start in Skagway, Alaska, and then sail down the Yukon River to the Klondike itself. Although Soapy seems to have avoided going to Klondike, he relied on the money the miners earned, and the gold they found, to make his own money in Alaska.

Skagway was a center for commerce based on the nearby gold rush, but had fewer controls than some other places – for example, Soapy had a short stay in Juneau, but was soon arrested for trying his swindles there. He fled to Hope, which was predicted to be the next goldfield to be discovered but the place was too small for Soapy to make a "living," and so he made his way to Skagway, which had rapidly become home to around 30,000 people, mainly gold prospectors. It was described at the time as "hell on earth," a place where there was a "lawlessness which was picturesque," It was this lawlessness that enabled Soapy to gain power quickly in the town.

The Klondike gold rush saw prospectors flood into Alaska and northwestern Canada: pictured is Dawson City, which managed to keep Soapy out

Soapy Smith is still remembered in an Alaskan museum today

GEORGE C. PARKER

Meet the conman who used his slick charm to sell newly arrived immigrants New York landmarks that he had no claim to.

By the end of the nineteenth century, the United States of America was truly hitting its stride. Following the tumult of the American Civil War, the US had once again built a reputation as a land of opportunity and possibilities. When the Brooklyn Bridge was opened in May 1883, it seemed to encapsulate everything the new, energetic United States wanted to be. As President Chester A. Arthur unveiled what was the world's largest suspension bridge at the time, the world stood and watched the achievements of the young nation, and as the world's press and the odd curious visitor ambled across the 531-yard span, their effusive praise spread across the globe.

Bjørnstjerne Martinius Bjørnson, future Nobel Prize winner, wrote home to describe the bridge as "the bold spirit, the tremendous abilities, the grand vision of the future of the nation". *The Brooklyn Daily Eagle* was if anything even more enthusiastic, announcing with just a hint of bombast: "May the sight of it inspire the emigrant who seeks a home here with new hopes and energy, telling him as he gazes at it in silent wonder that in America industry rises upward to the clear blue sky and spans with enterprise and ambition the river of life."

And for the 12 million immigrants who arrived on the nearby Ellis Island, the bridge, itself designed by a German immigrant, really did symbolize the possibilities that awaited the huddled masses in the nation they wished to call home. Immigrants would disembark at Ellis Island, the country's largest immigration station, having sailed past the Statue of Liberty, and would glance over at the nearby buildings glinting in the hazy light, staring towards the distant Brooklyn Bridge sprawling across the East River to join the cities of Brooklyn and New York together. Its noble towers reaching into the sky drew their attention like nothing else.

Another who saw the bridge as the symbol of opportunity was one George C. Parker. And, just like the *Brooklyn Daily Eagle's* euphoric reporter, it was to those wishing to start a new life in the US that he turned his attention. Playing on the US's reputation as a nation where anything can be achieved, Parker (and others who played the same trick) would bribe ship stewards to point out any notable travelers with an interest in buying property and the means to make it a reality. Parker, "a slick talker and snappy," according to the *Olean Times Herald*, would pose as the bridge's overwhelmed owner who was looking to rid himself of the stressful, burdensome landmark.

With oozing unctuosity, he would ingratiate himself with his prey, legitimizing his claims by producing carefully forged documents of ownership and whipping out a plausible backstory. Sucked in, the "mark" – meaning target – would most likely be whisked around the bridge, which was sufficiently large that Parker could skilfully dodge any police, where they

Parker managed to sell the Brooklyn Bridge multiple times by convincing people that he was the owner

As Parker conducted his walking tours across the bridge to prospective buyers, he would point out hastily erected "for sale" signs along its expanse

On the Promenade, Brooklyn Bridge, New York,
Copyright 1800 by Strohmeyer & Wyman.

would perhaps see some "for sale" signs that were erected as part of the fiendish scheme.

By this point, the mark would be almost completely convinced of the legitimacy of the deal. As one further play in this vignette of deceit, they would turn up to Parker's "office" in the city–and nothing symbolizes legitimacy more than an office. Thus convinced, the mark would part with his or her money, convinced they had handled this wonderful piece of business with great skill and guile, and were now ready to make their mark on the city. Parker's deals have been reported from $200 to $50,000, although it is hard to be sure as the crimes were rarely, if ever, reported due to a mixture of embarrassment and a forlorn clinging to the belief that it was a genuine misunderstanding in some way.

People weren't simply trying to buy the bridge because of its iconic status, even if the pride one would feel in owning such a landmark having only just arrived in the US would be a real draw. Instead, the marks were sold the dream of establishing tollbooths on either end of the bridge, charging people for the pleasure of crossing the river without the need to swim or build a boat. Strange as it may sound now, the Brooklyn Bridge did in fact charge a toll until 1911, so this was one of the more realistic aspects of the con. It has been often reported that the duped buyers had to be hauled away by police as they set up their tollbooths, oblivious to the fact they had no claim to the bridge until this rude awakening.

Parker, a New York native born to Northern Irish parents in 1860, is reported to have repeated this swindle multiple times on those new to the area, though of course an exact figure is impossible. Nor was he the only conman to have worked this racket: other notable swindlers supposedly doing the same were William McCloundy, pleasingly nicknamed "I.O.U. O'Brien," who in 1901 was sentenced to two and a half years in jail according to a 1928

article in the New York Times. Others were Charles and Fred Gondorf and a man named Reed C. Waddell, who performed many swindles until he was shot and killed by a crime partner in Paris.

This wave of tricksters was no aberration or something unique to New York and its neighboring cities. The US was awash with conmen and criminals. Writing in 1940, author David Maurer described the scene: "[At the end of the nineteenth century] the country was overrun with what was then called "confidence games'... They were played on the street, on passenger trains, in saloons and gambling houses, on passenger ships, with fairs and circuses – in short, any place where short-con workers could find people with a little money. During the last quarter there were thousands upon thousands of these short-con workers plying the country." These confidence men, having followed the money west, soon turned their attention to the increasingly wealthy and diverse east coast.

Parker, also going by names such as James J. O'Brien, Warden Kennedy, Mr Roberts, and Mr Taylor, did not limit himself to selling the big bridge, it has been mooted. Other property sales included the Statue of Liberty – another iconic landmark that immigrants would pass on their way to Ellis Island – presumably on the basis that visitors could be sold tickets to look around it (and, at $31 a ticket today, who could blame them for being tempted?). The original Madison Square Garden and also the Metropolitan Museum of Art are also mentioned. The tomb of Ulysses S. Grant, the legendary Union general and US president, was another of Parker's property sales, and the conman played the role of the great man's grandson in order to shift the tomb he had no claim to.

Despite being "endowed with "notoriously ingratiating" charms, according to the *Olean Times Herald*, Parker was no stranger to prison.

> Parker tried to sell many New York landmarks, including the Metropolitan Museum of Art and even the Statue of Liberty

Immigrants awaiting inspection on Ellis Island. With 12 million people passing through the inspection station, Parker had plenty of opportunity to select a target

When the Brooklyn Bridge was opened in 1883, it became a symbol of the United States as a nation in which one could prosper. Conmen like Parker took this message to heart

The Landmark Swindlers
New York wasn't the only city to have its landmarks "sold" by tricksters

While Parker went to work on immigrants in New York, other audacious conmen were working similar schemes elsewhere. The most famous of these is "Count" Victor Lustig, who sold Paris' Eiffel Tower in 1889 to a scrap metal dealer eager to tear the unpopular "eyesore" down and use the 7,000 tons of metal for profit. Lustig's mark, André Poisson, was apparently suspicious, but Lustig, playing the downtrodden bureaucrat who was open to a bit of corruption, proved a deal clincher. As author Gilbert King pointed out of the situation, "The bureaucrat must be legitimate; who else would dare seek a bribe?"

$70,000 richer, Lustig was so thrilled by the outcome of his daring sale that he decided to repeat

it. This time, however, he was rumbled, and was forced to flee. Almost inevitably, he headed off to the US to continue his swindling.

More recently, in 2006, the Ritz hotel in London was put up for sale by an impoverished lorry driver by the name of Anthony Lee. Claiming to represent the Barclay brothers who really do own the hotel, Lee set in motion a £twenty-five0 million sale that progressed far enough that a £1 million deposit was made before the web of lies and investors came crashing down on the "elaborate and outrageous scam" (in the words of the judge at Lee's trial). Lee was sentenced to five years in prison and proved that there are still people willing to risk their money for the chance to own an icon.

The Eiffel Tower, pictured in 1889, was successfully sold for "scrap" by Victor Lustig for a total of $70,000

The Statue of Liberty, a gift from the people of France, was another iconic landmark that was instantly recognized by immigrants, making it easier for Parker to sell

"Parker displayed the audacious confidence any conman thrives on"

The same newspaper reported that "thrice he was arrested for larceny and twice for forgery. He was in and out of jail so often that whenever he left it was taken for granted that he would come back." In one memorable episode, Parker displayed the audacious confidence any conman thrives on and simply walked out of prison. According to the *Brooklyn Daily Eagle*, while he was detained in Raymond Street jail on New Year's Day 1908, Parker spotted a chance and quickly donned a hat and overcoat that had just been laid down by the hapless Sheriff Flaherty before calmly strolling out of the jail, being wished a Happy New Year by a guard as he left.

But the law finally got a hold on the smooth and aging Parker, and in December 1928 he was sentenced to life in Sing Sing prison, having been caught and received his third conviction. The sixty-eight-year-old Parker, by then a

"pudgy little man," was caught on May 18, 1928 cashing a check "that had bounced with startling elasticity," the *Olean Times Herald* reported. Tired and world-weary, Parker pleaded guilty to grand larceny and, the *Brooklyn Daily Eagle* reported, was "a meek lamb as he faced Judge MacLaughlin."

Parker spent the rest of his life in Sing Sing prison, no doubt using his prodigious story-telling abilities to regale the other prisoners and guards with wondrous tales. He in many ways embodied the ideals of the American Dream, being a self-made man who used nothing but his wits to get ahead. He traded in nothing but promises and an idea – something legitimate businessmen and prospectors have always done and continue to do. Parker died in 1938 and has gone down in history as one of the greatest American conmen of all time.

Forging Myths

These roguish criminals thrived on spinning tall tales – so how much can we believe?

It is difficult to separate the fact from the myth. The very nature of the con "artist" role is to be no slave to the truth, so working out what they really achieved and what they would like the world to believe is a challenge.

Any self-professed stories are unreliable sources of information. Conmen also work under many names, further distorting the facts of who did what. Many confidence tricks, meanwhile, go unreported, and embarrassment plays a big role in these crimes staying hidden. For example, when Victor Lustig sold the Eiffel Tower to scrap metal businessman André Poisson in 1889, Poisson stayed silent, not wanting the negative attention that would come with the story breaking.

Most of the newspapers reporting on Parker's final arrest cast a slither of doubt about the sale of the Brooklyn Bridge and the true extent of his criminal exploits. The *New York Times*, for example, reported in December 1928 that Parker's "early exploits are said to have included the "sale" of the Brooklyn Bridge" and all refer to it simply as an event that happened many years ago.

Nonetheless, Parker had a long life as a forger and conman in the New York area, and if anyone was capable of selling the Brooklyn Bridge, it was him. And being so widely reported even before his last jail term, the story clearly had traction among the press and wider New York population. As a myth and a criminal, he has gone down in American history as an extraordinary conman, so one way or another his ability to spin a web of lies and deceit has ensured him lasting infamy.

BROOKLYN BRIDGE'S "SELLER" SENT TO SING SING FOR LIFE

Parker, 68 Now, Resigned to

The New York Times reports on a "resigned" Parker being sentenced to life in prison in 1928, one of several contemporary newspapers to cast some doubt on the true extent of Parker's swindles

THE GREAT DIAMOND HOAX

Uncover the elaborate plot that managed to fool
the great and good of American society.

The Wild West was packed with prospectors looking
for the next unearthing of gold, silver, or diamonds

The area where Arnold and Slack planted the soil is still known as Diamond Mountain, now in Colorado

L ate in the afternoon of June 4, 1872, six men gathered on a rocky plot of land near the border of Wyoming and Colorado Territories. They systematically scoured the soil with a rising sense of excitement and anticipation, hoping to make a discovery that would make them rich. "After a few minutes," one of them later wrote, "Rubery gave a yell. He held up something glittering in his hand. It was a diamond, fast enough. Any fool could see that much. Then we began to have all kinds of luck. For over an hour, diamonds of various sizes were being found in profusion, together with occasional rubies, emeralds, and sapphires."

Yet all that glistens is not always gold – or diamonds. Four of the six eager men who pulled the treasure from the soil that day were actually the unwitting victims of an elaborate hoax.

The so-called diamond field followed on the back of a number of discoveries over the past few decades. In 1848, gold was found at Sutter's Mill in California and, over the next few years, more than 300,000 prospectors flocked to the west coast. A lucky few made it rich. Ten years later, a second gold strike led to the Pike's Peak Rush in Kansas and Nebraska; the year after that, silver was discovered in Nevada. Further afield, diamond deposits had been uncovered

in Brazil, India, and South Africa. Thousands of prospectors were constantly looking out for a natural bonanza, aiming to strike it rich.

Also looking out for an opportunity to make a fortune were two Kentucky men, but they were willing to dabble in underhand methods to achieve it. One of them, Philip Arnold, was a forty-niner who moved to San Francisco in the original gold rush. After his original dream of digging up gold came to nothing, he settled down to a more mundane life as a bookkeeper for the Diamond Drill Company, a company that bored holes using diamond-headed drill bits. From there, he obtained a bag of uncut diamonds

A few lucky forty-niners struck it rich in the gold rush, but Philip Arnold and John Slack were among the majority who failed

When Caleb Lyon was appointed Governor of Idaho Territory by Abraham Lincoln in 1864, it was not a popular move. Regarded as an outsider by the tough miners who lived there, Lyon immediately provoked their ire by trying to move the state capital to Boise, a move so unpopular that it led to battles in court.

Hoping to stimulate Idaho's economy, Lyon claimed that a prospector had found a diamond near Ruby City. Hundreds of men rushed to the area and staked a claim to land there, but no more diamonds were ever found. Perhaps Lyon was gullible and fell for a fake find, or perhaps he was the hoaxer himself who invented the story to get more settlers in his territory. Whatever the truth, it did nothing to help his popularity and the local newspaper stated that only a "military escort could prevent him from violence or death."

Lyon's short tenure was racked with allegations of embezzlement by government officials, and Lyon himself came under suspicion when more than $40,000 of state funds disappeared as he left office. He claimed that he was carrying the money to give to the federal commissioner of Indian affairs, but it was stolen as he slept in a railroad bunk.

Caleb Lyon died in 1875, possibly just before an investigation recommended he be charged with theft

(whether legally or not is unclear) and put a daring and audacious plan into practice.

In November 1870, Arnold roped in his older cousin, John Slack, to accompany him to the office of George Roberts, a local banker who was always interested in the next get-rich-quick scheme. Arnold explained that the leather bag he carried held something of great value, but they could not deposit it in the bank because it had closed for the night. Roberts tried to get more information, but the visitors seemed wary and unwilling to give much away, until Arnold let slip that the bag contained rough diamonds. Now excited, Roberts pressed to know more, but neither Arnold nor Slack would reveal where they had found their bounty.

Roberts was hooked. Within minutes of the prospectors leaving, he broke his promise of confidentiality and was lining up potential investors to plunge money into a company that would mine the as-yet-unrevealed diamond field.

Arnold and Slack returned to Roberts a few weeks later with a second sack of diamonds and rubies they claimed to have found at the same site. Roberts had even more evidence that he had found the next

Crater of Diamonds State Park in Arkansas is the only location in the United States where diamonds are still being found

big thing and persuaded even more backers to come on board. Arnold initially asked for a down payment of $100,000 to give the rights to mine the land to Roberts and his company and took half of the money up front, asking to have the rest when they returned from a third trip to their mystery location.

Little did Roberts know that Arnold had no intention of traveling to the nonexistent diamond field. Instead, he and Slack purchased a ticket on the next transatlantic steamer to Britain. They found a London diamond merchant and, using false names, spent $20,000 on uncut diamonds and rubies. Upon their return to the United States, Arnold and Slack traveled to Wyoming Territory and planted half of the diamonds and rubies on the land they had singled out for their clever ruse. Then they returned to San Francisco with the other half of their precious cargo, declaring they had found another lode.

The investors eagerly awaited the package. Several gathered in a house, spread a sheet over a billiards table, and dumped the contents of the bag on it. The sight was amazing – a collection of twinkling gemstones that promized to make them all rich.

Some of the diamonds were sent to New York City, where jeweler Charles Lewis Tiffany promized to value them. Asbury Harpending, the investor sent to accompany the precious cargo, wrote that Tiffany proclaimed: "Gentlemen, these are beyond question precious stones of enormous value." Two days later, Tiffany declared excitedly that the sample he had been given – only a fraction of those bought by Arnold and Slack in London for $20,000 – were worth $150,000.

With the devious ploy having fooled the nation's foremost jeweler and with the potential yields higher than anybody dared to hope, Arnold secured a further $100,000 from Roberts and his investors and returned to London to buy

Clarence King, the surveyor who uncovered the hoax, was feted for his actions and later became the first head of the United States Geological Survey

Diamonds had been mined in Brazil for nearly a century and many prospectors hoped they would be found in North America too

"The surveyors worried that they had missed something of national importance"

more precious stones. The investors had engaged a mining engineer to survey the supposed diamond fields, and Arnold wanted to plant a few more jewels before he started his on-site work.

The engineer, Henry Janin, finally met with Arnold and Slack in May 1872. With three other men – Harpending, Alfred Rubery, and George Dodge – the prospectors traveled by train to Rawlins in Wyoming Territory. From there, Arnold led them on a four-day trek by horse, taking them on a deliberately circuitous and confusing route. Eventually, Arnold revealed his much-vaunted diamond field. The six men immediately set to hunting for diamonds

Charles Lewis Tiffany (left) made a fortune as a jeweler despite incorrectly valuing the hoax diamonds

and uncovered the precious gems almost instantaneously. Curiously enough, Arnold seemed to be particularly good at directing the others where to dig.

Janin, his professional judgement perhaps clouded by the offer of shares in the new venture, enthusiastically declared the diamond field to be the real thing. Once he was satisfied, it was decided to leave two men to guard the site: hoax conspirator Slack and fooled investor Rubery. However, the two men did not get along, and decided to abandon their posts after a couple of days.

Arnold returned to San Francisco with Janin, Harpending, and Dodge, collecting another $150,000 from the grateful investors. He also sold $300,000 of his stock in the new mining company to Harpending. In total, Arnold cleared $550,000 from the hoax, equivalent to around $8 million in today's currency.

Only now did the intricate deception begin to unravel. On their return journey from the planted diamond field, Arnold and his three companions bumped into a federal survey team led by Clarence King. Upon hearing that diamonds had been discovered in Wyoming Territory, an area King and his team had previously mapped, the surveyors worried that they had missed something of national importance. They determined to return and look again.

King and his colleagues braced themselves against the bitter October cold and traveled north. Although they did not know exactly where Arnold's fake diamond fields were, they examined their own maps and pieced together the few hints dropped by the prospectors. Before long they saw a claim notice that had been posted by Janin. Scouring the ground nearby, they stumbled across a small ruby on the floor. A few minutes later, one member of the survey team found a diamond.

The gems were so easy to find that it was not long before King began to have doubts. The diamonds and rubies were only ever found in disturbed ground or pressed into cracks in rocks. Anthills proved to be a good place to look, but only anthills surrounded by footprints ever produced a previous stone – those without footprints never did. One stone even looked like it had cut marks made by a jeweler. King quickly deduced that the so-called diamond field was a fake.

King revealed to the authorities that Arnold and Slack's find was too good to be true and the hoodwinked investors suddenly discovered their company was worthless. Share trading was immediately stopped and, faced with King's undisputed scientific knowledge, the investors

voted to dissolve the company. Unsurprisingly, the media had a field day with this news, joyfully reporting that the wealthy shareholders had been duped by two brazen con artists.

Arnold, the brains behind the operation, swiftly returned to Kentucky. Despite pocketing a vast amount of cash, he did not face criminal charges for his part in the fraud, possibly due to the swindled investors quashing the case to prevent embarrassment. He continued to live life on the edge, having a quarrel with a banker that ended up with him being shot in the shoulder by a shotgun in 1878. Although he survived the wound, Arnold died six months later of pneumonia.

What became of Arnold's cousin and accomplice, nobody knew. Slack disappeared after leaving his guard duties at the diamond field and nobody was able to trace him. Did he die, flee the country or, as one historian has suggested, live out his days making coffins in St. Louis? If so, it would have been a suitable trade – he was, after all, experienced at planting objects in the ground.

The Diamond Duped

Charles Lewis Tiffany
Tiffany inadvertently aided the hoaxers when he vastly overestimated the value of the diamonds that were brought to him. In his defense, he didn't have much experience with uncut gemstones, and the incorrect valuation didn't do him much harm – the jewelery business he founded is now a huge multinational company.

George McClellan
A former commander of Union forces in the Civil War and Abraham Lincoln's opponent in the 1864 presidential election, McClellan was appointed a director of the diamond mining company in the hope that having a name of his stature would encourage other investors to come on board.

Benjamin Butler
Nicknamed "the Beast" for his draconian rule of the occupied South during the Civil War, Butler subsequently embarked on a career in politics and was serving in the House of Representatives when he fell for the diamond hoax. He was considered an important ally who could wield political influence if the diamond field was on federal land.

Horace Greeley
Greeley, an influential newspaper magnate, began 1872 by investing in the diamond hoax. He was then selected to stand against the incumbent Ulysses S. Grant in the presidential election. His wife died five days before the vote took place, while Greeley himself died three weeks after losing the election. 1872 was not Greeley's finest year.

JOSEPH WEIL

The man who swindled millions from Mussolini believed all his victims deserved their fates.

For a man who spent much of his life in disguise, Joseph Weil ended up very well known indeed. The conman, nicknamed "the Yellow Kid," was notorious for much of his career, while his decision to tell all in an autobiography following his last release from prison made him into a cult figure. His conning career was so famous it became an inspiration for Paul Newman's character in *The Sting* and yet, despite bringing him fortune and fame, Weil was nonchalant about his crimes. Always convinced he was no worse than those he scammed, he remained one step ahead of everyone around him until the end of his very long life.

It's easy to see why Weil so captured the public imagination. Dapper, charming, well spoken, and cool to the point of detached, his conman career took him from the romance of the traveling trickster to the world of big-time hustles. Along the way he took on Mussolini, made around $8 million dollars, and was arrested more than 1,000 times. He served just six years in prison and boasted in his autobiography that crime had paid him very well.

That same book revealed a love of money that began at an early age. Weil was born on July 1, 1875, in Chicago, Illinois. His parents, who he rather formally called Mr. and Mrs. Otto Weil, ran a store, and the young Joseph would help them out until the lure of the horse racing track became too much and he began to spend more and more time among the gamblers and bookmakers there, even if he had no cash of his own to stake.

At the age of seventeen, he got a job as a collector in the local loan trade, but he soon realized that some of his fellow workers weren't as honest as they made out. Seeing them skim off money for themselves, Joseph promized to keep quiet if they gave him a cut. It was a short step to more organized protection rackets. Around the same time, he met Doc Meriwether and a life of outright hustling began.

Doc Meriwether was the last of a dying breed; an old-fashioned hustler who made his living touring and selling fake cures. Weil became part of his act, which also included dancing girls, standing in the crowd where he would pretend to be a patient cured by "Meriwether's Elixir." The magic medicine, a supposed cure for tapeworm, was in fact rain water and a few harmless extras. The experience gave Weil a taste of the big time, and soon he was branching out on his own.

Perhaps it was his time with Meriwether, who dressed the part in frocktail coat and boots, but Weil soon became known as a master of disguise. He took on all kinds of pseudonyms, including Count Ivan Ovarnoff, Dr. Henri Rueul, and Sir John Ruskin Wellington, as well as passing himself off as a banker, stockbroker, or chemist, creating characters to suit the sting he was attempting to pull off. As his hustles made him money, he invested some of his cash in clothes, and he was known as one of the most dapper men in Chicago, developing a style that remained all his own.

His crimes were many and varied. He made tens of thousands of dollars working with a sidekick named Fred Buckminster, who helped

Many of Weil's scams involved animals, often passing off stray dogs as pedigrees to his marks

Joseph Weil was known around the world for his swindles

Benito Mussolini was Weil's most famous victim, but the conman regarded all those he duped as equals

The Yellow Kid, seen here in his 80s, continued to cut a dashing figure around Chicago

him pass off stray dogs as pedigrees. Another scam saw him sell talking dogs who mysteriously fell ill as soon as money had changed hands. Animals were a recurring theme in Weil's cons, and so legendary was his ability to hustle that a story emerged of an early trick that was said to have given rise to the name of one of America's favorite foods. In 1889, a young Weil allegedly persuaded a visitor to Illinois to buy a chicken from him. The price was a nugget of gold. The term "chicken nugget" is said to come from that trick.

Joseph Weil worked hard at conning people, rarely stopping even as his riches began to build up. He had a ready supply of deeds for land

he claimed was rich in oil, but which its new owners discovered didn't actually exist once they had handed their payments over. One of his favorite tricks was to pretend to be a chemist who could make perfect counterfeit money, and he also loved to stage fake fights. One con involved wealthy men stumping up large stakes for illegal boxing matches only to see their fighter apparently drop down dead mid-tussle. While they fled the scene of the crime, the boxer would get up again while Joseph Weil, in disguise, counted the cash the investor had stumped up thinking he had backed a sure winner.

Much of Weil's wealth came from selling fake stocks, and before the Wall Street Crash of 1929,

he made a lot of money selling fake shares. But as he got more experienced, his hustles became more ambitious. Weil tried to sell the Cook County Bank for $150,000, and at one time ran a string of fake brokering offices.

He saw everything as an opportunity, including war. At the height of the First World War, he pretended to be the representative of German businessmen who wanted to see their stakes in a steel mine in Indiana. He told a wealthy banker his clients wanted to get rid of their holdings, as German ownership of American assets was a problem. His victim that time around parted with over $100,000.

The Conman-Turned-Author Tells his Own Story

Joseph Weil famously said he never swindled an honest man, and he found another way to justify the many crimes he committed. In 1948, he published his own account of his cons and tricks.

His book, *The Autobiography of America's Master Swindler*, tells first-hand how he pulled off many of his most famous jobs, with Weil claiming at the end that his words might well save others from falling for similar cons. In chapters with colorful headings like "From Nags to Riches," "Millionaires and Murder," and "Easy Money on Rainy Days." Weil brings to life a career that fascinated thousands.

The work also gave an insight into his criminal mind – and he shows little remorse. He always returned to the idea that those he conned were usually rich and greedy, and even boasted that crime had paid him handsomely. But, like many things in Weil's life, the book wasn't all it seemed. He had help writing it, telling his story to author W.T. Brannon who helped shape it into its final form.

The book is finally now back in print and seventy years later, the Yellow Kid's own version of how he got rich at others' expense is still fascinating readers around the world.

In his later years, Weil enjoyed talking about his life of crime, claiming that his victims had larceny in their hearts

Joseph Weil's last arrest on mail fraud charges was big news with journalists, who scrambled for photos of the conman, then in his 60s

"He was known as one of the most dapper men in Chicago"

Perhaps his most audacious con, however, came in the run up to World War II. He duped Italian dictator Benito Mussolini into handing over $2 million for land that didn't exist. It was a clever and risky move, but Weil had such faith in his understanding of human nature that he didn't baulk at the chance to try.

What really set Weil apart from his fellow conmen was his understanding of how people think. W.T. Bannon, who worked on his autobiography with him, said he knew more about people than some of the most experienced psychologists of the time, able to size someone up and work out how they would react in an instant. Weil used his knowledge of what makes people tick to turn himself into a very rich man and, as far as he was concerned, those he conned were no better than he was.

The man they called the Yellow Kid remarked more than once that he only scammed "rascals," claiming that everyone who ended up on the receiving end of one of his tricks was trying to make something from nothing, so he gave them "nothing for something." He admitted to walking away from just one hustle, involving a restaurant owner called John R. Thompson who he described as "the only man I have ever met who was 100 percent honest." Most other people were written off by Weil, who said that "the average person is ninety-nine percent animal and one percent human. . .the one percent that is human causes all our woes."

He even used his understanding of psychology to get himself out of jail. When faced with the prospect of a long prison term in 1925, he submitted to tests by a leading doctor who decided he had the intelligence of a sixteen-year-old. Weil agreed wholeheartedly with the psychiatrist and ended up serving just thirty days.

But pleading innocence didn't always work. In 1926 he was sentenced to five years at Leavenworth Prison in Kansas after being found guilty of owning bonds stolen in an armed robbery on a train at Roundout, Illinois. Weil said he had no knowledge of where the bonds had come from but was given a harsh sentence nonetheless. He would later describe prison as a "chance to catch up on my reading."

He got one final opportunity to do just that in the early 1940s when he returned to prison for mail fraud. After his release that time, he declared he was a reformed character and then he set about writing his autobiography. He also became increasingly judgemental of others who followed his life of crime and conning, stating "there are no good confidence men anymore."

In his 80s he took out a libel suit against a magazine that claimed he had actually died in 1934. He may well have needed the money. In his later years, spent in a retirement home, he had few assets, saying he had spent all he had conned. In his final years he was often visited by reporters, fascinated by the story of the Yellow

The Yellow Kid was a ground-breaking cartoon character with hard-hitting social commentary often printed on his famous nightshirt

Kid. One journalist arrived for a birthday celebration, bringing some cigarettes and lemonade for Weil. His nurses told him it was champagne. As the reporter left, Weil asked him to come again but told him next time not to bother with the drink, as he knew just what was in his glass. He died on February 26, 1976. To the end, he was the ultimate charmer, still one step ahead of those who thought they could get the better of him.

GASTON MEANS

From the death of a president to a kidnapping that shocked the world, there was a man who tried to make money from everything.

Gaston Means loved to boast that he had been accused of every felony in the law books, and for once in his life he wasn't exaggerating. A conman who managed to escape a murder charge, he attempted to make money whenever he could, and even started scams in prison. But not even a jail term could stop Gaston Means' life of crime, and as he got older, his schemes got bigger and more dangerous. No matter the consequences, Gaston Means just couldn't help but hustle.

The man who would try to make money out of the most famous kidnapping case in the world and who claimed a US president had been murdered in another get-rich-quick scheme began life in much more respectable surroundings. Gaston Bullock Means, born on July 11, 1879, in Concord, North Carolina, was the son of a small-town lawyer, William Means, and his wife, Coralie Bullock. However, behind the ordinary facade of an education at the local high school and time at North Carolina University was a gnawing resentment, for the family had once been wealthy but lost much of its cash in the Civil War. In 1902, after a brief stint working at local elementary schools, Means became a salesman. His job with cotton firm Cannon Mills led to him traveling between New York and Chicago, and in 1911, he fell from a Pullman carriage during his commute. He sued but suspicions arose, he had engineered the accident himself. Means lost this lawsuit but it wouldn't be the last time he would try to charm his way through a court case.

A classmate claimed the accident had affected his personality – certainly, from the early 1910s onwards it was never clear whether Means was telling the truth. By 1914 the fast-talking and charming Means was working for the detective agency run by William J. Burns, who was still being feted for his role in bringing those responsible for a bomb attack in Los Angeles to justice. It was well paid, but it also opened the door to a world of scams that proved addictive to the man his friends called "Bud."

As war loomed in Europe, Means found yet more opportunity to make money. He was approached by the Germans to provide information on possible war preparations and soon began spinning all kinds of tall tales, which he promized to investigate for them at a very steep rate. In 1914 his job at the detective agency also led him into the ambit of wealthy widow Maude King, who soon made him her business manager, providing access to a fortune that ran into hundreds of thousands of dollars.

After siphoning off all her money, he ended up implicated in her death, but after being acquitted of her murder he was soon back on trial for forging a will he claimed was written by her late husband. As the case went against him, Means tried to wriggle out of trouble by striking a deal to hand over a trunk of documents for German spies. The box was, of course, empty, but Means was somehow off the hook, just in time for a scamming opportunity almost too good to be true.

Prior to World War I, Means had been feeding intelligence on shipbuilding to Germany

Gaston Means described himself as a private detective but was one of the most prolific conmen of the early 20th century

In 1921, the new administration of Warren G. Harding made sweeping changes in Washington, with the president surrounding himself with old colleagues from his native state of Ohio. Harding's campaign manager, Harry M. Daugherty, was rewarded with the prime job of attorney general and set his sights on William J Burns to head up the FBI. Once installed, Burns brought Means in as a special investigator. It was a move that many would live to regret.

Means quickly set about making as much money as he could from his new position. He promized all kinds of criminals protection from prosecution in return for large sums of cash and also began hiring staff who didn't really exist, their salaries making their way to his bank account instead. He quickly made a small

fortune, and his wife Julie and their young son Billy found themselves living in a nice house in Washington with chauffeur-driven cars at their disposal. Senior officials, including Daugherty, became suspicious of Means and he was briefly suspended from his job, but Burns liked him, protecting him with a placement in New York, and Means continued to flourish.

While America was outwardly living under Prohibition, which had come into force in 1920, the illegal alcohol trade boomed, and among those that Means took bribes from were bootleggers. But the Harding administration was beginning to wobble as rumors of scandals began to do the rounds. Harding died in August 1923 and within a year his successor, Calvin Coolidge, began a series of official inquiries, including one into how Prohibition had been upheld. Means found himself under investigation for violating the Prohibition Act, as well as for conspiracy.

Means tried to talk his way out of trouble, turning up at a Senate committee to point the finger at a range of senior officials, including Daugherty. While he was forced to quit as attorney general, he was put on trial for perjury and tax fraud. In 1924 he went to prison in Atlanta where he would serve four years. His wife found a job nearby as a schoolteacher as the family's life of luxury disappeared. But while Julie worked, Gaston was up to his old tricks again.

He became a spy for the prison wardens, which helped him get by day to day, but he soon spotted another money-making opportunity. While in jail he got to know Mae Dixon Thacker, a freelance writer who soon became one of many to be fascinated by his claims to know all the background goings on of President Harding and his Ohio gang. Soon after his release from prison in 1928,

Gaston Means smiling for the cameras as he arrived at prison in Atlanta to serve a jail term linked to bootlegging

he worked with her on a book, which caused a sensation when it was published two years later.

The Strange Death of President Harding tapped into the huge appetite for details on a man who had been hailed a hero on his election in 1921 and whose reputation was being pulled apart by scandal in the years after his death. Warren Harding had been accused, posthumously, of knowing of wrongdoings by his Ohio set, and Means capitalized on that. In his book, he told a public hungry for gossip that he had been an investigator for former First Lady, Florence Harding, and that she, worried about her husband's reputation should the scandals become public knowledge, had killed the president with poison. Mrs Harding had died not long after her husband so couldn't defend herself, but her own reputation was permanently scarred. Means admitted several years later that the book was lies, but it made him a lot of money while he

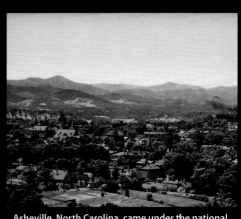

Socialite Evalyn Walsh McLean was duped by Gaston Means, but would ultimately bring about his downfall

The Millionairess Party Girl

Maude King's life was a fairytale in the making that went very wrong indeed. The daughter of Samuel and Anne Robinson, Maude had been married young to Chicago millionaire James C. King, who had made a fortune in the lumber trade. Their big age gap meant that Maude was soon a very wealthy widow who liked to party so much she was once found dropping bottles from the top of the Eiffel Tower. Her reputation soon made her an easy target for conmen.

In 1914, she was rescued from tricksters by Gaston Means, who was then working for the Burns Detective Agency. Within weeks he was her business manager. While Maude partied, Means worked his way through her vast fortune, but by 1917 even she was beginning to question

what had happened to her cash. Means then produced a forged will giving Maude the millions her husband had left for an old people's home.

Lonely Maude then accepted an invitation to holiday with Means and his family in his home state of North Carolina. On August 29, 1917, she went rabbit hunting with her business manager at Asheville. Hours later, Means carried her body out of the forest, claiming she had accidentally shot herself. Her death was soon national news as a coroner found no powder marks on her head. However, the local Means was soon acquitted by a hometown jury. Maude kept gossip columns going for a few more months but was soon forgotten, as lonely in death as she had been in life.

Asheville, North Carolina, came under the national spotlight when Maude King died in mysterious circumstances in its forests

Gaston Means was no stranger to a courtroom, always playing to the crowd as he stood trial for serious crimes

Gaston Means made such a mark on American culture that the producers of hit HBO series *Boardwalk Empire* based a character in the award-winning show on him. Means appeared in series three and four of the show, first broadcast in 2012 and then in 2013.

Many of Means' actions in *Boardwalk Empire* were based on his real-life exploits. His first appearance came in an episode called "Spaghetti and Coffee" as a "special investigator" with ties to Harry Daugherty. He would go on to feature in eight more episodes, shown as a larger-than-life character with an array of quips and one-liners that masked his confidence tricks, bribery, and attempts to sell information. The character was finally arrested for perjury, just as Means was in real life, and makes his final appearance in an episode called "Havre de Grace."

He was played on screen by actor and comedian Stephen Root, also known for playing Jimmy James in the sitcom *NewsRadio*, and for his voicework in the cartoon *King of the Hill*. He'd been a TV and film star for twenty-five years by the time he took on the part of Gaston Means, often seen in the movies of Oscar winners Ethan and Joel Cohen.

Stephen Root played Gaston Means in two series of hit HBO drama Boardwalk Empire

also pocketed a large chunk of cash that should have gone to Mae Dixon Thacker.

Even that wasn't enough to stop him hustling. In the early 1930s, he made money by convincing wealthy New Yorkers worried about the rise of communism that he knew the whereabouts of two Soviet agents who he could spy on and track for them. At a rate of $100 a day, he made a good living for several years while allegedly following his imaginary spies who mysteriously disappeared when his benefactors became suspicious. By then, Means had found an opportunity for scamming on a giant scale. It was a hustle that would lead to his ultimate downfall.

On March 1, 1932, the infant son of hero aviator Charles Lindbergh was kidnapped from his family home in New Jersey. The little boy, also called Charles, was just twenty months old, while his father was one of the most famous men in the world, having become the first person to make a solo transatlantic flight in 1927. The kidnappers demanded a huge ransom, but no news of the baby emerged.

Gaston Means made contact with the wealthy socialite Evalyn Walsh McLean, who was soon convinced that he could help find the baby. Means convinced her he knew who had taken the child and where he was being kept, and said he could pass on the $100,000 ransom if she could stump up the cash. Once he had the money, along with $4,000 for expenses, he disappeared, only to re-emerge a little while later demanding more cash. In the end the police were called and Means was arrested for grand larceny in May 1932. The money was never recovered. Sadly, Charles Lindbergh Junior's body was found on May 12 that year in a grove of trees a few miles south of the Lindbergh home.

Means was jailed for fifteen years not long afterwards and sent to Leavenworth Prison in Kansas. It would be his final home as he died there on December 12, 1938. He took many secrets with him to his grave but it was clear for many years before he died that there really was no crime on the books that he hadn't been linked to at least once in his colorful life.

> **Means spent his final years behind bars after being found guilty of grand larceny**

Harry Daugherty, former attorney general, arrives for his trial. Gaston Means worked for the FBI during Daugherty's tenure and would testify against him

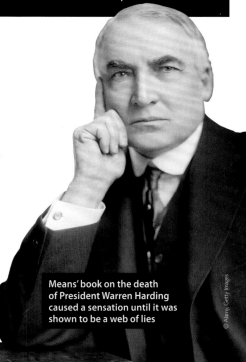

Means' book on the death of President Warren Harding caused a sensation until it was shown to be a web of lies

© Alamy, Getty Images

BONNIE AND CLYDE

America's favorite outlaw couple has been glorified beyond belief, but their grisly reality was very different indeed.

In a hail of bullets, Bonnie and Clyde – America's most wanted outlaw couple – went down together. The pair had wrought havoc on the Deep South for almost two years, stealing, kidnapping, and sometimes even murdering. But when the law finally caught up with them, their bloody demise was inevitable. Their reputation as a couple of romantic robbers endures, as does their movie-star popularity – but was this the whole story?

Far from the swashbuckling gangsters of film legend, the real Bonnie and Clyde were working-class, backcountry folk. Bonnie Parker was born to dirt-poor Texan parents on October 1, 1910. Her father died when she was four, leaving her mother to raise three children by herself. At school Bonnie was a bright kid with high hopes for the future, but just before she turned sixteen she married class heartthrob Roy Thornton and dropped out of school.

Her marital bliss was abruptly cut short. Thornton quickly became abusive towards Bonnie, and he had affairs with other women frequently. Plus, he started doing time in prison for theft. Without wasting any more time on her deadbeat husband, Bonnie moved in with her grandmother in 1929 and refused to see him ever again. However, she never formally divorced him.

Bonnie's future partner, Clyde Barrow, was a year older than Bonnie, born in a different part of Texas on March 24, 1909. His family were farmers whose fortunes tanked when a drought wrecked their farmland. Not wanting to be defeated, Clyde was introduced to a life of crime by his older brother, and he dabbled in grand theft auto – and sometimes even in armed robbery.

The ill-fated duo finally crossed paths in January 1930. Bonnie was staying with a friend in Dallas, and when Clyde came to visit the same mutual friend they quickly fell head over heels for each other. Their romance lasted only a matter of weeks before Clyde was thrown into jail for car theft. Not to be taken away from his new love that quickly, Clyde wanted to escape, and Bonnie was only too happy to act as an accessory. She smuggled a gun to him, and before long he had broken out of his cell.

Sadly, his escape plan was foiled, and Clyde was recaptured. Sentenced to fourteen years of hard labor in a higher security prison, it seemed that this was the end of the road for the two young Texans. Clyde suffered terribly at the hands of another inmate while on the inside, and he was repeatedly raped and abused.

Once again, the young man started dreaming of getting out of jail and back to Bonnie. There was very little he wouldn't do, and he even cut off his big toe in an "accident" to gain leniency. A few weeks later, though, his despairing mother secured his parole, and he walked (or rather, hobbled) free. He had only served twenty months of his sentence.

Bonnie and Clyde were reunited and for a while they laid low, committing only minor crimes and trying to stay under the radar of the

The photographs of the pair and Bonnie's poems that were found at their safe house are partly what made them famous

Bonnie points her shotgun at Clyde in this playful scene, one of the images found in the safe house

police. It's in this happy period when the famous, carefree photographs of the two bandits were captured, playing with firearms and chomping on cigars.

But trouble was never far behind. The pair had started working with other criminals, and their robberies progressed from gas stations and small businesses to actual banks. Interestingly, they never quite made the big bucks – their maximum take was about $1,500 – but their crimes were enough to get their name on a wanted poster. Slowly, their gang began to grow.

Even though they attacked businesses across Texas, Oklahoma, Missouri, and New Mexico, the group still managed to elude the police. But in late 1932, a key piece of evidence led to their identification. Clyde, usually meticulous, had abandoned a stolen Ford filled with evidence of his existence, including a prescription bottle for his aunt. Police traced this bottle back to a pharmacy in Texas, and extracted information from the locals to find who their targets were – Bonnie and Clyde.

A full-blown manhunt began. A warrant for their arrest went out in May 1933, by which time the criminal gang numbered five people. A hastily deserted safe house had also been discovered with a roll of undeveloped film, which police developed. It revealed the faces of the wanted couple, showing a young, petite woman and a man of dishevelled – but handsome – appearance. They played with guns, pretending to shoot each other, and they looked remarkably happy doing so. A local newspaper saw these images as an unmissable opportunity, publishing them for all to see.

At the height of the Great Depression, these star-crossed outlaws seemed like the perfect antidote to the impoverished, unfortunate Dustbowl victims they shared their region with. The pair seemed to ooze glamour, and as they had not yet acquired a violent reputation, the public actually began to warm to the irreverent couple. Their crimes took on a "Robin Hood" dimension – Bonnie and Clyde seemingly stole from the wealthy only to help their poor Texan families. Readers clamored for more – so much so that the newspapers sensationalized

This 1934 wanted poster for Bonnie and Clyde was personally issued by the first director of the FBI, J. Edgar Hoover

their crimes, and a few of the papers even took to making some up.

But fame is fickle. They had evaded police for too long. In January 1934, Bonnie and Clyde orchestrated a prison break, helping their friend Henry Methvin to get out – as well as four other unruly prisoners. But two police officers were killed in the ensuing chaos, which made the law even more determined to catch up with the gang.

Things went from bad to worse. When their car was approached by two police officers,

Methvin shot and killed one of them in a panic. Clyde, though he had always been a reluctant killer, shot the other. He wanted to make sure he'd never end up behind bars again. However, the officer was one H.D. Murphy, a young man on his first day on the job. He was well-known in his community, and soon to be married. Murphy's wife-to-be came to his funeral in her wedding dress, sobbing for the husband she would never marry. That same week, the group killed another police officer and wounded a police chief.

Dreams of Stardom
Despite their criminal status, the two never gave up their dreams of being superstars

Like many young people growing up in 1920s America, Bonnie and Clyde both harbored dreams of fame and fortune. Clyde was a lover of music. He joyfully sang as a child, and learned to play the guitar and saxophone. He carried musical instruments wherever he went for entertainment, and a guitar was found among their possessions in the abandoned safe house.

Young Bonnie, meanwhile, dreamed of the movies. At school she was said to be rather pretty, with the correct poise to become a star. She wanted to become an actress, dabbling in school productions and talent shows.

She also showed a great talent for literature and art, especially poetry, which she continued

to write even as she was fleeing from the police. One of her poems, "The Story of Bonnie and Clyde," gives us a unique, inside view of the couple. Bonnie viewed herself and her partner as anti-heroes as they raced around America, and her poem begins to construct the image of them as legends, even long before they died:

Some day they'll go down together;
And they'll bury them side by side;
To few it'll be grief
To the law a relief
But it's death for Bonnie and Clyde.

Bonnie was never known for her poetry, but it may have helped her achieve her lifelong dreams of fame in the end.

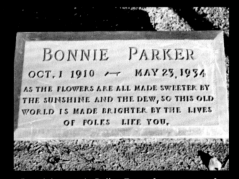

Bonnie's grave in Dallas, Texas, features one of her short poems

Bonnie and Clyde's bullet-ridden car is now on display in a Casino in Nevada

"The newspapers sensationalized their crimes"

Now the public wanted blood. The FBI plastered "wanted" posters with their fingerprints, photographs, and other vital information in police stations across the region. It was only a matter of time before they would be caught.

Bonnie, Clyde, and their crew were traced to a specific part of Louisiana in 1934. They were close to where Henry Methvin's family lived, at the end of an isolated dirt track. An FBI agent in the area made inquiries and deduced that the gang made frequent visits there, as Methvin was particularly close to his family and couldn't go too long without seeing them. The gang respected this, as both Bonnie and Clyde loved their own families dearly.

However, these close family ties meant that Methvin's family would pay any cost to protect their son. Knowing that he was with a bunch of high-profile fugitives, Methvin's father made a deal with the police, betraying Bonnie and Clyde's whereabouts in exchange for clemency for Henry.

The police now knew that Bonnie and Clyde would be returning to Methvin's family home on May 23, 1934, so law enforcement set a trap, planning to ambush the couple as they journeyed along the only road leading to the house. They hid in the bushes, lying in wait for their targets to appear. Methvin's father then pretended to break down in order to attract the pair's attention and slow their escape.

Sure enough, they came. The car whizzed down the road and slowed down before the notorious passengers realized it was a trap. They tried to turn around but it was too late – 150 bullets ripped through their car, killing them in the blink of an eye.

Though by the time of their deaths they had killed approximately thirteen people, they were still so prolific that fame-hungry people swarmed the scene, trying to steal locks of hair, blood-stained clothing and apparently even body parts. Bonnie's mother estimated that 20,000 people flocked to the funeral home where Bonnie was laying to get a glimpse of the "gun moll" who had captivated them.

Cementing their legacy, in 1967 a Hollywood film was made about the outlaw duo starring Warren Beatty and Faye Dunaway. Far from their inelegant existence of constant driving and bathing in dirty rivers, the movie romanticizes their exciting life of crime, instilling the image of the couple we are familiar with today.

Their impact on American popular culture is arguably far greater than any other outlaw – perhaps even more than the cowboys of the Wild West. When the majority of people in the Deep South and the Midwest lived in Depression-era poverty, this young man and woman seemed to defy the capitalist system, hitting the wealthy precisely where it hurt most. However, the historical evidence shows they were fairly small-time robbers whose time was mostly spent on the run. They died just as ingloriously as they had lived – in a beat-up old car, running from police along dusty, deserted roads.

Although smiling here, the criminal couple had their fair share of pain.

Wounded in Action
Far from the young, healthy couple of movie legend, Bonnie and Clyde suffered debilitating injuries during their career

Clyde's first brush with pain was during his time in prison, where he chopped off his big toe in an attempt to get out of hard labor due to his "accident." As well as ultimately failing to secure his release, it meant he walked with a limp for the rest of his life. Humiliatingly for him, it also impacted his driving, as he could not drive properly with shoes on – so he had to drive in his socks when he was trying to make a quick escape.

Bonnie, although she kept all her toes, suffered a far more catastrophic injury in 1933 – and this time, it was genuinely an accident. As they were zooming along, Clyde missed a detour for a road that was still under construction, and the car plunged into a dry riverbed. The battery shattered, spraying acid all over Bonnie's right leg.

Naturally, as a wanted woman, they could not risk taking her to hospital. She was carried to a nearby barn and treated with baking soda and salve to stop the acid from burning away her skin. Thanks to their experience nursing gunshot wounds, it worked, but Bonnie's leg never healed properly. Her strident walk became a painful hop.

A crowd gathered at Chicago's Biograph Theater after John Dillinger's death

The Dalton Gang after their disaster of a robbery (left to right) Bill Power, Bob Dalton, Grat Dalton, Dick Broadwell

10 INFAMOUS BANK HEISTS

Some of the most notorious bank robberies of the American Outlaw era still live on in infamy today.

As the American West was gradually tamed – with mixed results – through the nineteenth century and into the twentieth, a system of infrastructure had to be built up. Of course, that included banks to safely store the wealth being created in this fast-evolving society, often locked inside reinforced safes and even vaults as the banks grew. How safe everyone's money actually was, however, may be a matter of interpretation, as the latter half of the nineteenth century saw an unprecedented rise in bank heists and gangs of outlaws relentlessly preying on these nascent institutions, which at first bore very little resemblance to the extreme safety measures we see in every bank today.

Dozens of bank heists would occur every year and even as the banks stepped up their security methods and bolstered their infrastructure, the robbers quickly followed suit with more elaborate weapons, tools, and methods to get at the treasures within. Making a "top ten" list of bank heists from this era would be an exercise in futility, so instead, here are a selection of some of the more famous ones, including some that went catastrophically wrong but still live in infamy even today.

Manhattan Savings Institution

New York | 1878

The crowning glory of the architect-turned-King of Bank Robbers

George Leonidas Leslie was born to a rich family. His father founded a successful brewery in Ohio, and Leslie became an architect with his own firm after graduating. However, when his parents died in 1867, he sold the firm and all his family assets and turned to an extraordinary life of crime.

Establishing a gang of expert robbers, Leslie orchestrated a sensational run of bank robberies over the next decade. Aided by his architectural expertise, he routinely obtained blueprints of his targets to plan them meticulously ahead of striking. He quickly became known as the King of Bank Robbers, such was his notoriety, and his success even outlived Leslie himself.

He was murdered in late May 1878, but his gang still successfully robbed the Manhattan Savings Institution in October that year, based on his plan. This robbery marked the highest amount of money ever stolen to that date, about $2.5 million (about $63.4 million in today's money), but it also marked the end of the Leslie Gang, almost all of whom were captured or killed soon after this daring raid on one of the most secure bank vaults of that time.

In the 1870s, Leslie made Philadelphia, Pennsylvania, his base of operations

Emmett Dalton was the only Dalton brother to survive the disastrous double robbery in Coffeyville

Two banks

Coffeyville, Kansas | 1892

The Dalton Gang's disastrous double-bank heist

Ironically, the Dalton Gang was formed by three brothers, Gratton, Bob, and Emmett after they had enough of not being paid for their work as lawmen. The gang quickly acquired notoriety for their daring bank and train heists, although they didn't always come up with a lot of money for their efforts. In an attempt to turn their fortunes, Bob Dalton concocted a plot to rob two banks at once, "in broad daylight." In Coffeyville, Kansas, two banks, C.M. Condon & Company's Bank and the First National Bank stood on opposite sides of the main street, so the Daltons put on disguises and split up.

However, it all went catastrophically wrong. One of the townspeople recognized them right away, and an employee in one of the banks managed to falsely convince them the safe was on a time lock, so couldn't be opened for 45 minutes. Word got out and residents quickly mobilized and armed themselves. When the gang eventually exited the banks, a deadly shootout ensued. Four members of the gang were killed, and Emmett Dalton was shot twenty-three times but survived. He ended up serving fourteen years in prison for his crimes.

San Miguel Valley Bank
Telluride, Colorado | 1889

The heist that put Butch Cassidy on the map

The white building on the right of the picture was the scene of Butch Cassidy's first bank heist

Butch Cassidy is today known as one of the most famous American outlaws of all time, what with his time in the "Wild Bunch" and his famous escape to and last stand in South America. His beginnings were relatively humble, though.

After a short series of misdemeanors, Cassidy's first bank heist took place in Telluride, Colorado in June 1889. He teamed up with partner-in-crime Matt Warner and two others to rob San Miguel Valley Bank. They stole about $21,000 – equivalent to about $636,000 today – in the heist, and evaded capture using a method that would quickly become a staple of Cassidy's heists; immediately split up and fled in all directions, only to gather again later in a predetermined location.

In this case it was the now-famous Robbers Roost, a remote hideout across the state lines in Utah. This robbery made Cassidy famous among other outlaws, and ultimately led to the formation of the legendary Wild Bunch, one of the United States' most notorious outlaw gangs in history.

"This robbery made Cassidy famous among other outlaws"

Dillinger was named Public Enemy Number One by the FBI in 1934

First National Bank
East Chicago, Indiana | 1934

The most daring stop on John Dillinger's wild ride

Of all the Depression-era gangsters, few are as fascinating as John Dillinger, declared Public Enemy Number One in 1934. The reason? His gang's hard-to-believe string of high-profile bank heists that year. One of the most outlandish was the First National Bank robbery in East Chicago, Indiana on January 15, in which Dillinger would commit his first and only murder, killing a police officer.

Just before closing time, the gang's car pulled up in front of the bank, and Dillinger and his partner John Hamilton, wearing bulletproof vests, went in. With an incredibly laid-back demeanor, Dillinger pulled a Thompson submachine gun out of a bag and started rounding up the people present in the bank, before finding Hamilton and starting to scoop cash into a leather bag. The alarm was raized and police surrounded the bank, but astonishingly no one noticed the running getaway car double-parked in front, with the driver relaxing in the front seat.

Dillinger and Hamilton rounded up a number of hostages to use as human shields on their way out. After a shootout in which Dillinger shot dead police officer William Patrick O'Malley, the gang successfully managed to escape and lived to rob another day.

Jesse James has become perhaps the most famous American outlaw of all time

Clay County Savings

| Liberty, Missouri | 1866 |

The first daylight bank robbery during peacetime in the US

Jesse James and his brother Frank were Confederate soldiers in the US Civil War but although the war came to an end, their violent streak did not. Unhappy with the South's defeat, they set about harassing Union forces after the war's end. They are widely considered the culprits in the first daylight armed bank robbery in US history during peacetime. This took place at the Clay County Savings Association in Liberty, Missouri on February 13, 1866. Chosen as it was owned by Republican former militia officers, the robbers made off with a considerable amount of money, but in the shootout during their escape an innocent bystander was tragically shot dead.

This, along with a series of other heists shortly after, made James and his gang notorious across the country, leading to authorities placing a bounty on their heads, which was rare at the time (despite what the movies would have you believe). The James-Younger Gang, where the James brothers teamed up with Cole Younger and his brothers, would go on to become the most wanted group of criminals in the US in the 1860s and 1870s. Jesse was eventually shot dead in 1882 by Robert Ford, a member of his own gang who wanted to collect the bounty.

"This made James and his gang notorious across the country"

Lincoln National Bank

| Lincoln, Nebraska | 1930 |

A mastermind robbery that is still a partial mystery today

On the morning of September 17, 1930, five unmasked men stormed Lincoln National Bank in Nebraska as it opened in one of the most notorious high-value bank robberies in US history. Not content with emptying out the teller drawers, two of the robbers took the assistant trust officer down into the vault for the real treasure. The loot the mysterious gang ended up hauling was almost $3 million, or about $40 million in today's currency. The bank only had $60,000 in insurance, so was forced into liquidation by the robbery.

What made this robbery even more unique is that unlike the often-unsophisticated smash-and-grabs of the past, this heist was conducted with military precision, where each member had a clear sense of their role throughout, everything was timed for maximum efficiency, and the identity of the robbers remained a mystery for years.

The real mastermind was only unveiled much later – it was Edward Wilhelm "Eddie" Bentz. He would plan everything meticulously ahead of time, carefully staking out the target and dictating everything, down to getaway car's precise route. He later went on to work with many infamous Depression-era gangsters, but was ultimately caught in 1936, and spent twelve years in Alcatraz, America's most notorious prison.

Bentz worked with and even mentored some of the Depression era's most notorious bank robbers

U. S. PENITENTIARY
ALCATRAZ
307

United States Trust Company
New York | 1934

A mysterious disappearance with international repercussions

On December 14, 1934, a total of fourteen securities totalling $590,000 – over $10 million today – simply vanished from a securities cage at the offices of the United States Trust Company in New York City. Due to the extensive safety measures at the company all of the employees were interrogated, but as they all had alibis, it was simply thought that the securities had been misplaced. That is until two of the securities, worth $10,000 apiece, were redeemed for cash at the Federal Reserve Bank the very next day.

An FBI investigation was immediately launched, but a whole year passed before the first arrest was made. Eight more men were arrested in 1936, including the alleged mastermind Charles Hartman – after which an additional $1.456 million had been stolen from the Bank of the Manhattan Company in 1935 in a near-identical scenario. Eventually, the investigation reached all the way to southern France and even Greece, where the rest of the gang was found and apprehended. The majority of the securities were never found.

J. Edgar Hoover, the head of the FBI, was heavily involved in the investigation of the USTC and Manhattan Company securities thefts

FABIAN FORTE & KAREN BLACK as "LITTLE LAURA & BIG JOHN"

...THEY'LL STEAL INTO YOUR HEART-- THEN SHOOT THEIR WAY OUT!!

Ashley's life and romance with Laura Upthegrove were made into a film in 1973

Pompano
Florida | 1923

The exuberant reign of the King of the Everglades

John Ashley was one of nine children to a poor family in Florida. His father was a fisherman and hunter, but was also briefly a county sheriff in West Palm Beach. The son would never follow down that same law-abiding path. Suspected of murder at only twenty-three, John's life was littered with criminal activity from his teenage years to his death in 1924.

What's more, he never made much of an effort to hide that part of his character from society either. The most famous example of that is when his gang robbed a bank in Pompano in November 1923, making away with $23,000 in cash and securities. Instead of fleeing, the gang celebrated exuberantly in the streets, stealing a taxi and boasting of their success to anyone who happened to come across their path.

Of course, this reckless behavior quickly caught up with Ashley as he was killed on a bridge near Jacksonville, in a confrontation with Sheriff Baker, with whom he'd had a personal feud with for years.

"The gang celebrated exuberantly in the streets, stealing a taxi and boasting of their success to anyone who came across their path"

The story of the Newton Gang was adapted into a 1998 Hollywood film starring Matthew McConaughey

Hondo

| Texas | 1921 |

A two-for-one robbery under cover of night

The Newton Gang, led by Willis Newton, was more prolific than any other known gang of robbers in the entire "Outlaw Era." Operating from 1919 to 1924, it boasted of robbing up to eighty-seven banks and six trains. Even more impressively for such a busy bunch of criminals, their heists never led to a single death. One major factor in that is that most of their bank jobs were conducted at night. Whenever they did encounter resistance, they had a reputation for being extremely polite, even going out of their way to ensure their hostages were comfortable and safe during the robberies. One of their most famous heists took place in Hondo, Texas, when they found the vault door of their target bank unlocked and open, so they used the opportunity to rob a neighboring bank at the same time. The hauls from most of their heists were not very large and as a life of crime can be very expensive, this "stroke of luck" sustained the gang for quite some time. They were eventually apprehended, but as irony would have it, they were sentenced to ten years in prison for a bank robbery they didn't commit.

Laketon State Bank

| Laketon, Indiana | 1925 |

The final stop on a busy month of robbing for Earl "The Kid" Northern

George Earl "The Kid" Northern was one of the most prolific and successful bank robbers of the Prohibition era, highlighted by two series of bank heists in 1924 and 1925. A famous collaborator of Harry Pierpont, the two ran a large gang of criminals who terrorized the state of Indiana. After a part of the gang was apprehended following a string of bank heists in December 1924, Northern lay low for a while before recommencing his tour de crime in March 1925. However, due in part to sloppy methods of evasion, the police were quickly on their tail.

While the Laketon State Bank robbery was a success in that they got away with over $1,000 in cash, Northern and his cohorts were quickly identified as they didn't vary their methods and hadn't even changed number plates on their getaway car. In April 1925, Northern was arrested and he was sentenced later that year. True to form, shortly after release in 1932 he robbed another bank in Amo, Indiana, and was put in prison, where he died in 1936.

Earl was a known associate of the infamous Harry Pierpont

©Getty, Alamy

PRETTY BOY FLOYD

He was a murderer, gangster, bank robber, and trigger-happy criminal – yet the Phantom Bandit's death was mourned by thousands.

It was a crisp autumn morning in Oklahoma City. There was something of a carnival atmosphere that Monday, with thousands of people flocking the streets, drawn to the city from fifteen different US states. "It's a Roman holiday!" one remarked to a press reporter as he, and the rest of the crowd, blocked the roads. The cortege was stopped in its tracks by the crowds for over an hour as police tried to clear a path for it through the city streets and out to the rural cemetery near the Arkansas border. Behind the hearse were five other cars, full of wild flowers and carnations – but by the time they reached their destination, barely anything remained, so successful had the onlookers been in grabbing their own floral memento of the day.

The funeral itself saw a respectful group of pallbearers carry the coffin to the graveside; but a mob had gathered here, too, forming a crush around the grave so great that women and children present were said to have fainted. The excitement was palpable – many had traveled some distance and had been camped in the hills around the cemetery for three whole days, so keen were they to attend. They brought their lunches with them, and pistols, and kept hydrated with homemade whiskey. It was October 29, 1934 – a date the ghoulish onlookers would remember for a long time.

Who was the individual being so mourned by people in Oklahoma City? Was he a film star or politician, someone who had made the world a better place during his lifetime? That last point was debatable, for the dead man was one Pretty Boy Floyd, described in his obituaries as "the phantom

bandit of Oklahoma." His death, perhaps inevitably, had been violent: the result of being shot by federal agents near East Liverpool, Ohio, the previous week. The events that led to his killing, however, were the stuff of legend.

Although he became notorious as Pretty Boy Floyd, a moniker said to have been given to him by a prostitute, it was a name he loathed. It was, however, apt – for he was a young, somewhat chubby, and cherubic-looking Southern man. His innocent looks belied his origins: as Charles Arthur Floyd, he was from a large, poverty-stricken family. Born in Adairsville, Georgia, in 1904, he was brought up on a farm in rural Oklahoma. Even before the Great Depression hit in 1929, closely followed by the economic trauma of the Dust Bowl, a period of dust storms that destroyed farming in several counties in the 1930s, the sign of what was to come was clear.

The Floyd family was struggling economically. Young Charles had to help with farm labor for his family from a young age, and as a child, he not only helped his family with their farm, but also picked cotton for neighboring farm workers. Pretty Boy Floyd's childhood, then, was a rather short one, and by the time he got out of his teens, he was a married man – and a criminal. He had actually started his criminal career in a smaller-scale way, making liquor illicitly – for this was the time of Prohibition, a nationwide ban on producing alcohol that had been in place in Oklahoma since 1919.

On June 28, 1924, in the small settlement of Akins, Oklahoma, twenty-year-old Floyd married Ruby Hardgraves, aged just eighteen. He now

In Oklahoma, Pretty Boy Floyd was known as the Robin Hood of the Cookson Hills

3999

Pretty Boy Floyd's mugshot images from around 1933 show the nattily dressed bank robber looking defiantly into the camera

The Dusty South

The early 1930s were the "Dirty Thirties," also known as the Dust Bowl, a time of great economic hardship in the United States. From the summer of 1930, and reaching a peak in 1934, areas of the American Southern Plains suffered from severe dust storms and a subsequent drought and farming disaster.

Oklahoma was at the heart of this disaster, which saw thousands of destitute families leave their farms as they were unable to grow any crops. Many migrants made their way west to California, only to find conditions little better than home; many migrants ended up living hand-to-mouth in temporary camps, trying to get work. They were resented by longer-term residents, and the Oklahoma refugees became known as "Okies," the word then becoming a derogatory term for any poor migrant of the time.

In 1936, photographer Dorothea Lange was sent to California to photograph some of these Dust Bowl migrants for the government. She photographed Florence Owens Thompson in her famous image, *Migrant Mother*, and described how she had sold her car tyres for food. Although Pretty Boy's family stayed in Oklahoma, they found the Great Depression and the Dust Bowl a huge strain on their resources and ability to maintain themselves – as did so many others.

Migrant Mother, an iconic image of a Dust Bowl migrant living a hand-to-mouth existence

needed to support himself and his wife, and did so in an unconventional way: through theft. His initial haul was $350, stolen in coins from a post office. In 1924, he robbed a grocery store's payroll delivery while in St. Louis, Missouri, and spent the money on clothes and a car. Unsurprisingly, he was caught, convicted, and sentenced to five years in prison. His wife was pregnant at the time, and gave birth to the couple's son, Charles Dempsey Floyd, known as Jack, while her husband was incarcerated. By the time he was released, Ruby had divorced him.

On leaving prison, Floyd initially went back home and, to his horror, found that his father, Walter Lee Floyd, had been murdered shortly before, on November 14, 1929. A man, Jim Mills, was charged with the crime but when it came to trial, he was acquitted. Pretty Boy Floyd was heard saying that he would kill Mills and soon after, the acquitted individual disappeared. Although Floyd never admitted it, many believed

thus freeing many mortgage-holders from their commitments. The money he stole was often shared with others, and resulted in him being shielded by many Oklahoma residents, who saw him as something of a Robin Hood figure. Whether or not Pretty Boy had set out to help the poor initially, he liked this image of himself as a beneficent character, coining himself a catchphrase to go with it: "If you ain't gonna do nothing to help the little guy, Pretty Boy Floyd will!"

In June 1933, Floyd took part in a particularly infamous plot, which left him a wanted man. Escaped convict Frank Nash was being returned to a penitentiary in Leavenworth, Kansas, and Floyd, together with Vernon Miller and Adam Richetti, was hired to free him. On the morning of June 17, they made their way to Union Station in Kansas City, Missouri. As Nash, in handcuffs, was being taken from the station to the FBI's car, the three armed men ran up from

"He had committed this, his first murder, in order to avenge his father's death"

he had committed this, his first murder, in order to avenge his father's death.

Floyd didn't stay long in Oklahoma. Instead, he moved to East Liverpool, an Ohio town notorious as a hiding place for gangsters and bootleggers. He became a "hired gun," a hitman and enforcer, working for the bootleggers who worked along the Ohio River. He also started robbing Ohio banks, together with a group of accomplices, carrying out so many robberies that bank insurance rates rocketed.

Although he was feared by the banks, he became a folk hero to many ordinary people who were suffering the effects of the Great Depression, as he was said to have destroyed the mortgage papers held by the banks he targeted,

a neighboring vehicle. A voice shouted, "Let 'em have it!" The three men opened fire, but as well as killing four officials – Kansas City police officers Frank Hermanson and W.J. Grooms, FBI agent R.J. Caffrey, and Oklahoma police chief Otto Reed – they accidentally killed Frank Nash as well.

This was the era of John Dillinger, a gangster who had twice escaped from prison and was, like Floyd, a bank robber and scourge of local law enforcers. He was killed by FBI agents in Chicago in July 1934, leaving a vacancy for the dubious title of America's most wanted. That vacancy would soon be filled by Pretty Boy Floyd, whose record made him the FBI's number one target. By the end of his life, he was said to have murdered

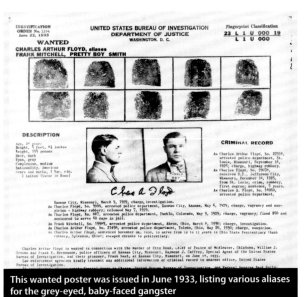

This wanted poster was issued in June 1933, listing various aliases for the grey-eyed, baby-faced gangster

His status as America's most wanted meant that by October 1934, FBI agents and local officers alike were hunting for Pretty Boy Floyd

The Life of Frank Nash

Frank "Jelly" Nash was a native of Indiana, a former army soldier who carried out numerous bank robberies. It was back in 1913 that the twenty-six-year-old Nash shot a friend who he had just carried out a store robbery with. He was convicted of murder and ordered to serve a life sentence at the Oklahoma state penitentiary – but he was pardoned five years later, after stating that he wanted to fight in the Great War.

Two years later, he carried out another burglary, this time involving explosives, and was sentenced to twenty-five years in prison, but only two years later he was released. He then assaulted a postal worker, and in 1924 was sent to the penitentiary at Leavensworth, Kansas. Faced with serving twenty-five years, on October 19, 1930, Nash escaped and went on the run. He kept in touch with other prisoners, and on December 11, 1931, seven more escaped from Leavenworth, apparently with the help of the fugitive.

Two years later, after receiving a tip-off, two FBI officers tracked Nash down to a store in Hot Springs, Arkansas. They captured him and arranged for him to be taken back to Leavenworth via Kansas City. He never reached his destination.

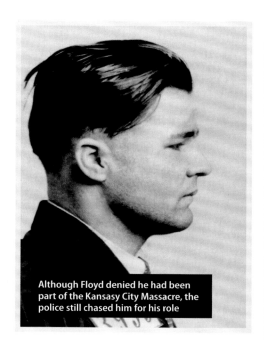

Although Floyd denied he had been part of the Kansasy City Massacre, the police still chased him for his role

Union Station in Kansas City today. It was near here that Frank Nash was shot dead during the Kansas City Massacre

at least ten men during his "career" – many of them law enforcement officials – and to have robbed many banks, as well as stores and gas stations. He was increasingly flamboyant, robbing banks and then throwing money out of the window of his car as he fled. Money was, in turn, offered for his capture – a reward of $twenty-five,000 – but nobody seemed to want to venture information that would get them the cash.

Yet Floyd's time as America's most wanted was about to end. He was in hiding in New York, but then made the decision to head back to Ohio with Adam Richetti and two women they had picked up. It was foggy as they approached East Liverpool, and the car crashed off the road into a pole. The men sent the two women to fetch help, but suspicion was aroused, and soon news reached the FBI of the two men in the damaged car. Police Chief Fultz managed to capture Richetti – he would be executed four years later for his part in the Kansas City Massacre – but in the resulting chaos, Floyd escaped into the nearby woods, and vanished for two days.

It was autumn, the trees and land burning with color. The rural Ohio landscape was at its best, shimmering with the rich reds and oranges that set the world alight before winter's colder colors and harsher weather. For Floyd, though, it was hard to see the beauty in his hiding place. He was starving and exhausted. Eventually, he approached a local farm, persuading the farmer to give him some food. Then the FBI caught up with them. Floyd tried again to flee, but was shot in the shoulder. He fell, but as Agent Melvin Purvis approached him, Floyd managed to reach for his gun. Reacting quickly, Purvis shot him again. Floyd's last words were said to have been, "I won't tell you nothing." He died, aged just thirty-four, a criminal so infamous that crowds would soon be stealing the flowers from his cortege.

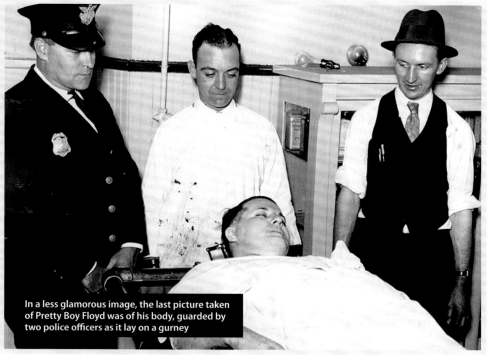

In a less glamorous image, the last picture taken of Pretty Boy Floyd was of his body, guarded by two police officers as it lay on a gurney

DEAFY FARMER

Though only a mediocre criminal himself, Deafy Farmer played a starring role in protecting some of the most notorious figures of the late 1920s and early 1930s.

If you were a career criminal during the 1930s, it paid well to be organized. The members of the infamous Karpis-Barker Gang were particularly skilled at arranging their nefarious itineraries. When they were on the run from the authorities, or simply in need of rest and relaxation, they headed to relatively isolated spots such as Reno or Lake Tahoe. If plans for future capers had to be hatched, they preferred the bustling surroundings of St. Paul, Minnesota, and when a prolonged break from their criminal antics was required, Hot Springs, Arkansas, was their destination of choice. Here, under aliases, they would spend lengthy periods posing as ordinary, law-abiding citizens: it helped that the local chief of detectives, Herbert "Dutch" Akers, was always willing to turn a blind eye in exchange for a generous cash donation.

The leaders of the gang, Alvin Karpis and Fred Barker, also knew the value of a safe house, and none was more reliable in this part of the world than the one run between 1927 and 1933 by Deafy Farmer and his wife Esther. Six miles outside the town of Joplin, Missouri, the couple's twenty-three-acre farmstead served, by turns, as a meeting place, a hideout, and a makeshift underworld post office. Criminals, including an alarming number of bank robbers, could have their wounds treated by an obliging local doctor, stash their getaway cars in barns and outbuildings, or simply hide out from the law.

Karpis and Barker (a friend of Farmer since childhood) more than once availed themselves of Deafy's services, most notably in December 1931. They had been cornered by a suspicious sheriff in West Plains, Missouri, opened fire, killed the overly inquisitive officer, and fled the scene. They headed, without delay, for the safe haven of Deafy's farm. During their stay, one local tipped off the police about their presence, but of course the officer was on Deafy's payroll. A raid on the farm was obligingly delayed for several hours, by which time the two gangsters had set off for the anonymity of the big city in St. Paul. Here, following Deafy's instructions, they made contact with Harry Sawyer, patron of the Green Lantern speakeasy and an expert in arranging mutually beneficial deals between corrupt law enforcement officers and fugitives such as Barker and Karpis.

Herbert Allen Farmer was not a particularly successful criminal. Born in 1891, he and his family moved to Webb City, Missouri, in 1910. Youthful indiscretions gave way to a life of gambling, grifting, and pickpocketing and then, in 1916, Farmer found himself incarcerated at the Ohio State Penitentiary after being convicted of assault with the intent to kill. While inside, he first met Frank Nash, a figure who would play a fateful role in Deafy's future, and after two years it was back to the nomadic life of a petty criminal in places as far-flung as Texas, Oklahoma, Colorado, and California.

But if Deafy Farmer had not set the underworld ablaze with his own exploits, his safe house would become one of the lynchpins of organized crime. It lent succour and safety to

Adam Richetti, who would be executed in October 1938 for his role in the Kansas City Massacre

The Sanctuary Seekers

Many notorious criminals made use of Deafy Farmer's Missouri safe house, including members of the notorious Bailey-Underhill Gang. In 1933, Wilbur "Mad Dog" Underhill, also known as the "Tri-State Terror," famously presented his wife, Hazel Hudson, with an unconventional wedding present: the proceeds of a bank raid undertaken especially for the occasion in Frankfort, Kentucky.

While the couple were honeymooning in Shawnee, Oklahoma, a twenty-four-man team surrounded the newlyweds' cottage. It was the early hours of the morning and Underhill, wearing just his long-johns and armed with only a Luger pistol, attempted to shoot his way out of an unwelcome situation, Underhill died from the wounds he had sustained.

Underhill's partner, Harvey Bailey, was one of the era's most adventurous but also most careful bank robbers. He was arrested in March 1920 but then avoided capture all the way until March 1932. He is said to have stolen more money than John Dillinger and included major heists like the raid on the Lincoln National Bank in Lincoln, Nebraska on his unsavoury resumé. Another associate of the Bailey-Underhill gang, Robert "Big Boy" Brady (who embarked on an epic five-month crime spree across five states in 1932) also spent time at the safe house.

Harvey Bailey, one of America's most successful bank robbers. Late in life, he married Deafy Farmer's widow, Esther

some of the most notorious figures of the age, and these commodities were in high demand at the time. Levels of crime had rocketed in the wake of the stock market crash in 1929. It was a nationwide epidemic and the statistics were quite astonishing. At the beginning of the 1920s, Dallas had endured only seventeen bank and drugstore robberies per year. By 1930, this had risen to 965. In Saginaw, Michigan, the leap was from nine such crimes to 836. Economic decline provided a motive, faster cars and more efficient guns streamlined the process, and increasingly determined law enforcement agencies made the need for safe houses ever more urgent.

Safe houses did not always live up to their name. One of the regular visitors to Deafy's farm, Harvey Bailey, would suffer a rather rude awakening at another establishment – Ora Shannon's farm outside Oklahoma City – in 1933. Federal agents, at the farm on other business, spied Bailey, who had recently escaped from the Kansas State Penitentiary, snoozing in the yard. An officer crept up to Bailey, pointed a gun at the gangster's head, and gave him no opportunity to make use of the Winchester rifle and Colt '45 pistol by his side. $1,200 of illicit money was found in Bailey's shirt and trousers and he was carted off to jail. This sort of thing didn't happen at Deafy's farm.

As of 1933, everything was ticking along nicely for Farmer. His reputation was soaring and he even found time to indulge his gambling habits in places like Kansas City and Hot Springs. Then, however, Deafy and his safe house secured their place in the annals of criminal history, largely thanks to the man Deafy had met back in the Ohio State Penitentiary, Frank "Jelly" Nash.

Nash had been a prolific offender. He managed to gain early release from the Ohio jail after promising to serve in the First World War and he saw some action in France. Upon his return, he embarked upon an impressive spree, graduating from burglary to bank robbery and raiding as many as 200 institutions over the course of his career. He also had a knack for escaping justice. This had been demonstrated once more in 1930, when Nash broke out of Leavenworth. A manhunt was launched and federal agents finally caught up with Nash in June 1933 in Hot Springs while he was enjoying a beer at a local cigar store. The two agents, Joe Lackey and Frank Smith, planned to return their captive to Leavenworth, but Nash had many resourceful allies.

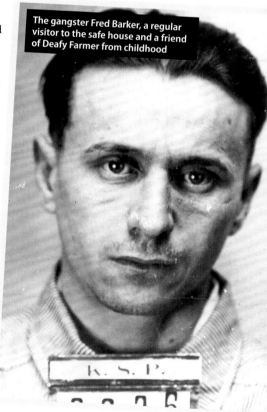

The gangster Fred Barker, a regular visitor to the safe house and a friend of Deafy Farmer from childhood

Deafy Farmer was imprisoned in Alcatraz for two years

"At the beginning of the 1920s, Dallas had endured only seventeen robberies per year. By 1930, this had risen to 965."

One of them, Dick Galatas, the owner of the cigar store and a key figure in the local underworld, paid a visit to Dutch Akers, the town's chief of detectives. He mentioned nothing about Nash's arrest, instead spinning a tale about a local businessman being kidnapped and driven off by two ne'er-do-wells. The goal was to send police in search of the agents transporting Nash to slow down their journey. It worked, at least for a while, and the agents had to explain themselves at roadblocks but, soon enough, the deception was revealed. A new plan was required, and this was where Deafy Farmer came in.

Nash would travel through Joplin, close to Deafy's farm, so Galatas and Nash's wife Frances flew to Joplin in the hope of arranging the interception of the federal agents. Unfortunately, suspicion was in the air and when the agents arrived at Conway, close to Little Rock, Arkansas, they contacted their boss. He advized them to avoid Joplin and head for Fort Smith instead and from there take an evening train to Kansas City. News of this reached Nash's wife and she made use of Deafy Farmer's phone to contact a friend, Verne Miller, in Kansas City. Snatching Nash when his train reached its destination now seemed like the best strategy.

At At 7:30 the next morning, June 17, the train pulled into Union Station. Agents were transferring Nash to a car in the nearby plaza when the bullets began to fly. Charles "Pretty Boy" Floyd and Adam Richetti had come to Nash's rescue. Alas, they managed to kill the man they hoped to save, as well as four lawmen, though some have suggested that Miller had employed Floyd and Richetti not to rescue Nash, but to murder him in a gangland hit. In any event, the carnage, which came to be known as the Kansas City Massacre, created uproar.

Just a month later, J. Edgar Hoover delivered a thunderous speech to the International Association of Chiefs of Police. "The problems of organized gang warfare," he barked, "and the defiance by desperate armed criminals of the forces of society and civilization may no longer be ignored." A "recent illustration of this armed defiance occurred on June 17 last at the Union Station Plaza at Kansas City, Missouri." It was "a challenge to law and order and civilization itself" and Hoover and his agency had "accepted the challenge."

Long before this, Deafy Farmer's role in the incident had been uncovered. Phone records proved that the crucial calls to Kansas City had been made from his farm and he was duly arrested. He was charged with obstruction of justice and received the maximum sentence of two years' imprisonment, which he served at Leavenworth and Alcatraz, and a $10,000 fine, while Esther was fined $5,000 and placed on probation.

Upon Deafy's release, the couple sold up the farm and moved to Joplin. Their eventful days of harboring felonious characters had finally come to an end. Deafy Farmer ultimately died in January 1948. Esther, who seems not to have learned her lesson about consorting with delinquents, went on to marry that infamous former visitor to the farm, the bank robber (though by then retired) Harvey Bailey.

> Deafy's farm was known to be a hideout, medical center and communications hub for criminals

A postcard from c.1910 depicts Joplin, Missouri, the closest town to the safe house

Going to extreme lengths to evade the law: Alvin Karpis shows his hands with fingerprints removed

A photograph of the aftermath of the infamous Kansas City Massacre

Alvin Karpis

Alvin Karpis was the leader of a gang described by J. Edgar Hoover as "the brainiest and most desperate of all." Of all the gangsters who made use of Deafy Farmer's safe house, none was more fearsome than Alvin Karpis. His gang, founded jointly with Fred Barker, terrorized the nation between 1931 and 1935. The outfit, sometimes twenty-five men strong, was unusually prolific. In 1932 alone they robbed eleven banks.

Karpis, though lacking any significant education, was reputed to be fiercely intelligent and possessed a photographic memory. He was also utterly ruthless, once declaring that he didn't "see anything wrong about robbing a bank, or kidnapping a person, or killing anybody who interferes during the performance of the crime." J. Edgar Hoover commented on Karpis' boundless greed: he "wanted everything in the world without working for it."

In 1933, Karpis and his associates began to focus on the lucrative business of kidnapping. They secured two handsome paydays. A $100,000 ransom was received for the beer magnate William Hamm Jr. and $200,000 reached the gang's coffers following the abduction of the banker Edward Brenner. Such antics only served to make federal agents redouble their efforts and Karpis was the last member of the gang to be arrested, at New Orleans, in May 1936. He was incarcerated at Alcatraz until 1962 and, after seeing out the remainder of his sentence elsewhere, finally regained his freedom in 1969.

Alvin Karpis outshone most of his contemporaries when it came to daring and thuggery

Outlaws and criminals have inspired Hollywood for decades thanks to their misdeeds and escapades

Mobsters have been remembered in 1932's *Scarface*

FROM VILLAINS TO HEROES

How books and films have turned some of America's most notorious criminals into celebrated heroes.

Billy the Kid. Butch Cassidy. Jesse James. Machine Gun Kelly. Al Capone. John Dillinger. All of these names – and many more – are etched into the human consciousness due to their notoriety. They have become iconic, repeatedly portrayed on film, TV, and in literature throughout the decades, watched and read about by millions, over and over again.

The legacy of the outlaws of that era in literature is almost as old as the outlaws themselves. The post-Civil War era saw the rise of so-called "dime novels," short stories sold as cheap, easily digestible reading material for the public, whose literacy levels were also rising rapidly at the time. Those stories spanned a

multitude of narrative genres, one of which was the Western. Pretty soon, real-life legends made their way on to the pages of the dime novels, turning some of the most violent and ruthless criminals of that time into lovable heroes in the eyes of the public, thanks to the highly fictionalized accounts published in these books. Written literature wouldn't have a monopoly on this very profitable drinking pool for very long, though, as the dawn of a new century spawned an entirely new media of entertainment: cinema.

These turbulent, often dangerous, and violent eras in American history spawned two of the largest and most enduring film genres of the last century: the "Western" and the "gangster" genres. The earliest Westerns date back to the first decade

Butch Cassidy and the Sundance Kid **saw Paul Newman and Robert Redford in the titular roles**

James Cagney defined the stereotype of the Hollywood gangster

"Real stories and real-life personas from the era would dominate the genre"

of narrative cinema, making them almost as old as cinema itself. The Great Train Robbery from 1903 is widely considered the first Western, but it came in at only twelve minutes long and was entirely fictional. Soon though, real stories and real-life personas from the era would come to dominate the genre, the infamous outlaws making for rich pickings for filmmakers.

The same applied to gangster cinema, which had its beginnings in generic, fictional films of the late 1920s, but would blossom in the Depression Era before World War II, quickly transplanting real-life events and protagonists to the silver screen.

Through these portrayals, archetypes have been formed and reinforced. Billy the Kid? A reckless, charming anti-hero who went out in a glorious blaze of gunfire. Jesse James? A self-made legend who sought revenge against a society that had abandoned him and his troubles after the Civil War. John Dillinger? A methodical, principled, well-mannered, modern-day Robin Hood fighting the unfair FBI and the system that had failed so many Americans with the Great Depression.

However, what these romantic portrayals often tended to leave out is that these people were hardened criminals, many of them ruthless murderers who devastated families and communities and left death in their wake. These stereotypes persisted throughout much of the twentieth century and although the portrayals did become more varied, often revising previous perceptions of their subjects, it's often the romanticized versions that have endured the most.

The case of Butch Cassidy is perhaps the clearest example of this tendency of Westerns to portray villains as more heroic than they may really have been. Cassidy, a violent criminal

who couldn't even stay away from Union Pacific Railway long enough for them to consider dropping their many ongoing charges against him before robbing yet another of their trains, has been immortalized in George Roy Hill's *Butch Cassidy and the Sundance Kid* from 1969. The film turns Cassidy and Harry Longabaugh, nicknamed the Sundance Kid, into empathetic heroes of their own tale in a film that's been celebrated as one of the greatest films ever made.

Similarly, Jesse James has often been described as a cowboy Robin Hood, despite there being no evidence of him and his gang ever sharing their loot with the poor. He was a celebrity even before his death, thanks to massively successful dime novels in which Jesse James was turned into a charming rogue, helping the little man get back at the heartless authorities. His death, which came at the hand of one of his own gang members who wanted to collect the large bounty that had been placed on James' head, only served to elevate his celebrity. Only in the late twentieth century did that perception of James start to crack. Even in recent adaptations the "charming rogue" still prevails. In *The Assassination of Jesse James by the Coward Robert Ford* from 2007, we do get a glimpse of James' precarious mental state, the severity of his violence, and the fractious relationship he had with the people around him, but even then James is the most empathetic character among the film's gallery of villains.

The lawmen of the era got their due too, of course, especially those who didn't exactly stick to the letter of the law when it came to upholding order in the Wild West. Wyatt Earp, Pat Garrett, John Hughes, Bat Masterson, and John Hicks Adams all achieved notoriety for their hard-nosed approach to law and order, and all would find their legacy solidified through

The Hollywood Face of Gangland America

In the 1930s, James Cagney became synonymous with gangster cinema

Few actors impacted gangster cinema as heavily as James Cagney did. After making his debut as a vaudeville actor in 1919, Cagney finally broke through as a star in the early 1930s, thanks to his performances in the gangster films that were causing so much sensation across the US.

At first, Cagney was cast as a tough-guy antagonist, garnering near-universal praise for his convincing performances in *Little Caesar*, *The Public Enemy*, and *Taxi!*, which came out between 1931 and 1932. In particular, his intense presence, paired with his handsome but rugged appearance helped him carve out a monopoly on charming gangsters in Hollywood. Later that decade, his fame afforded him the opportunity to switch to more sympathetic roles, such as playing an FBI lawyer in 1935's *G Men*, and even more notably as Rocky Sullivan in *Angels with Dirty Faces*, a gangster intent on turning his life around after getting out of prison, which earned him his first Academy Award nomination.

Until his retirement in 1961, Cagney would remain synonymous with gangster cinema. Even though he never played a real gangster or outlaw, the mention of his name today conjures a vision not dissimilar to that of John Dillinger, Baby Face Nelson, or Machine Gun Kelly.

literature and cinema. Garrett was a personal acquaintance of Billy the Kid, a fact that has made the real-life story of him being tasked with arresting him, which ended with Garrett shooting Billy to death, such a popular one to adapt to cinema. Between 1911 and today, over twenty feature films center on Billy the Kid and his complex relationship with Pat Garrett, where Pat has more often than not been portrayed as the real antagonist of the story. Other films have successfully focused on the lawmen of the era, such as 1993's Tombstone, which tells the story of Wyatt Earp and the posse of gunfighters he assembled to take down a ruthless gang of cowboys terrorizing the area, often by bringing out the nefariousness in their nature.

This blurring of good and evil, where the line between villainy and heroism is nearly wiped out altogether, is also found throughout the genre of gangster cinema.

Gangster movies came to the fore during the 1930s, when the US was struggling in the aftermath of the Great Depression, and bank robbers and criminals were updating their methods as the country became more metropolitan and its technology advanced. The birth of the FBI provided additional fuel for filmmakers, especially where the biggest criminals of the era, such as Machine Gun Kelly and John Dillinger, clashed with this nascent force, which was still feeling out the limits of its powers. Add to that the invention of the Thompson submachine gun, or the "Tommy gun," and you have an explosive, morally complex, movie-ready environment ripe for the picking.

From early entries such as 1931's *The Public Enemy* and 1932's *Scarface*, we were treated to anti-heroes who could transgress societal norms and rules, and even though they almost always paid the price of their criminal ways by the end, the image of the criminal-as-hero would persist through the genre's golden age, which stretched into the 1960s.

Al Capone was a popular subject of these films right from the start, although most films settled for thinly veiled "versions" of him until the late 1950s, over a decade after his death. The first high-profile portrayal of him was when Rod Steiger played Capone in the biographical *Al Capone* in 1959. After that, Capone provided no shortage of inspiration, even reaching into the realm of science-fiction, where a reincarnated Capone wreaks havoc in the twenty-seventh century in Peter F. Hamilton's *Night Dawn* trilogy of novels.

Westerns and gangster films largely ruled Hollywood cinema until the 1960s when they took a back seat to more modern concerns such as the Civil Rights Movement, as well as Vietnam, which saw a meteoric rise in the number and popularity of war films. However, both Westerns and gangster films made a notable comeback in the 1990s and onward, and even though modern gangsters provided plenty of new inspiration for filmmakers, the "old guard" is still a popular subject matter.

Butch Cassidy and the Sundance Kid was selected for the United States Film Registry due to its cultural significance

Some very popular recent examples of gangster films include 2009's *Public Enemies*, which details John Dillinger's sensational run of heists around 1934, and 2012's *Lawless*, which tells the (largely) true story of the Bondurant brothers' bootlegging business in 1931 Prohibition America. The Western has made an even bigger comeback, with major historical hits such as a remake of the aforementioned *Tombstone* from 1993; 1995's *Wild Bill*, which centers on the story of Wild Bill Hickok, an infamous lawman who embellished large parts of his achievements in the Old West and 2012's TV series *Hatfields & McCoys*, which dramatizes a bitter blood feud between two large families in the years after the Civil War, leading to a violent showdown.

Furthermore, novels, biographies, documentaries, and TV shows continue to come out at a steady rate as the world remains fascinated by this tumultuous time in American history, where even the most hardened criminals still have an aura of romanticized rebellion around them.

The era of the American outlaw may be in the distant past, but it still lives on in our popular culture, and likely will for the foreseeable future.

PUBLIC ENEMIES

A promotional poster for Michael Mann's 2009 film Public Enemies, in which Johnny Depp portrayed notorious gangster John Dillinger

The celebrity of Jesse James was amplified through mostly fabricated accounts of his life in nineteenth-century dime novels

Child-Friendly Outlaws?
How one comic kept the Old West alive in children's imagination

The criminals of the Old West were undeniably violent and their crimes often truly reprehensible, unlike the romanticized accounts of some of them in the nineteenth century's famous dime novels. However, in the twentieth century one Franco-Belgian comic book managed to balance the violent reality with the bright colors of fantasy.

The *Lucky Luke* comics, centerd around a fictional traveling lawman of the same name, take inspiration from several real-life stories and characters from the Old West. Most prominent among those stories are the Daltons, two of whom famously met their end in a double bank heist attempt in Coffeyville, Kansas. In fact, that story is at the center of one of the earliest *Lucky Luke* stories, except in Morris' version all four of the brothers met their end in that robbery. The authors, then introduced the Daltons, the "real" gang's fictional cousins.

Although mostly comical bumbling fools for Luke's heroics, there is a lot of real-life inspiration within their stories too, all taken from across the Old West, such as the appearance of Ma Dalton, a thinly veiled parody of Ma Barker, the infamous mother of the Barker Gang, who was ultimately shot dead in 1935.

Morris and Goscinny's fictional Dalton cousins incorporated features and stories from a multitude of real-life Old West villains and events